Living Sustainably

Living Sustainably

What Intentional Communities Can Teach Us about Democracy, Simplicity, and Nonviolence

A. WHITNEY SANFORD

Copyright © 2017 by The University Press of Kentucky
Paperback edition 2019

Scholarly publisher for the Commonwealth,
serving Bellarmine University, Berea College, Centre
College of Kentucky, Eastern Kentucky University,
The Filson Historical Society, Georgetown College,
Kentucky Historical Society, Kentucky State University,
Morehead State University, Murray State University,
Northern Kentucky University, Transylvania University,
University of Kentucky, University of Louisville,
and Western Kentucky University.
All rights reserved.

Editorial and Sales Offices: The University Press of Kentucky
663 South Limestone Street, Lexington, Kentucky 40508-4008
www.kentuckypress.com

Library of Congress Cataloging-in-Publication Data

Names: Sanford, A. Whitney, 1961– author.
Title: Living sustainably : what intentional communities can teach us about
  democracy, simplicity, and nonviolence / A. Whitney Sanford.
Description: Lexington, Kentucky : University Press of Kentucky, 2017. |
  Includes bibliographical references and index.
Identifiers: LCCN 2016058959| ISBN 9780813168630 (hardcover : alk. paper) |
  ISBN 9780813168647 (pdf) | ISBN 9780813168654 (epub)
Subjects: LCSH: Sustainable living—United States. | Communal living—United
  States. | Community life—Environmental aspects—United States. |
  Democracy. | Simplicity. | Nonviolence.
Classification: LCC GE196 .S26 2017 | DDC 304.20973—dc23
LC record available at https://lccn.loc.gov/2016058959

ISBN 978-0-8131-7752-6 (pbk. : alk. paper)

This book is printed on acid-free paper meeting
the requirements of the American National Standard
for Permanence in Paper for Printed Library Materials.

Manufactured in the United States of America.

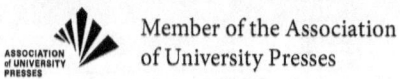

Member of the Association
of University Presses

*This book is dedicated to my father,
Charles Steadman Sanford Jr.,
who always encouraged my crazy ideas.*

Contents

List of Illustrations   viii

Introduction   1
1. Examining Change   21
2. Standing on the Shoulders of Giants   44
3. Choosing a Life   58
4. Creating Cultures   91
5. Asking What's for Dinner   107
6. Sustainability in Community   131
7. Rethinking Abundance   161
8. Extreme DIY for Interdependence   185
9. Bringing It Home   224

Acknowledgments   243
Appendix A: Communities Discussed in This Book   245
Appendix B: Resources   251
Appendix C: How to . . .   255
Notes   257
Bibliography   265
Index   281

Illustrations

Decorated streets in front of LA Eco-village   13
New construction at Belfast Cohousing and Ecovillage   17
Solar cooker on display at Dancing Rabbit's open house   55
Path and houses at Cobb Hill   75
Balcony at Daybreak Cohousing designed for social interaction   76
Pavilion at Twin Oaks Communities Conference   79
Possibility Alliance daily schedule, including bread labor   95
Baltimore Free Farm/Horizontal Housing   101
Outdoor kitchen at the Possibility Alliance   110
Wheel of nonviolence   111
Mural at Cherith Brook Catholic Worker House   115
Selection of toiletries at Cherith Brook Catholic Worker House   117
Milkweed Mercantile welcome sign   127
Pyramid of integral nonviolence   140
Community meeting agenda at LA Eco-village   157
Bicycle-powered washing machine at Lost Valley
    Educational Center   168
Mixing plaster   193
Award-winning maple syrup at Cobb Hill   200
Garden pond in Sirius ecovillage community building   208
Dancing Rabbit's electricity color chart   210
Sirius community building   213
Dining room at Pioneer Valley Cohousing   231

Introduction

When you get connected to creation and you get connected to real heart connections with people, you see that the world is beautiful, and it's full of unimaginable potential.
—Mark Becker, Possibility Alliance

HOW CAN WE LIVE together in ways that are healthy and sustainable for people and the planet? This book tells the story of people attempting to live intentionally and sustainably by practicing ideals of nonviolence, participatory democracy, and voluntary simplicity. Between 2011 and 2015, I visited intentional communities, which can be broadly defined as residential communities organized around shared values, to see how they incorporated these abstract values into their lives. These communities understood themselves as demonstration communities; that is, they were willing to share their successes and failures with others. More important, they saw themselves as experimental, as communities developing and testing, but not imposing, new patterns of living, eating, and communicating.

I wanted to learn about these communities and their experiments because their values of nonviolence, participatory democracy, and voluntary simplicity are important to me; they are also my values. Each of these values is important individually, but they become even more potent as a cluster. Nonviolence and voluntary simplicity appeal to many people, but how to go about living these values—at the personal, community, and, perhaps, global scale—is not always clear. *Living Sustainably* discusses intentional communities that are trying to do just that.

Residents of intentional communities come together purposefully to test out ways of living, and in so doing illustrate ways in which we might live more intentionally and sustainably. The communities in this book illustrate multiple ways of coming together—ecovillages, Catholic worker communities, and cohousing communities—but the important point is that they came together as communities to demonstrate living shared values. As Americans, we tend to focus on the future, but these communities demonstrate that we can learn from the past. In reviving agrarian skills, for example, to work toward self-sufficiency, they are questioning which almost-forgotten skills and values might be worth revisiting and adapting to present needs.

The language of intention is significant because it offers people many different ways to engage. Everyone already participates in multiple communities—residential, social, and virtual—and we can be intentional about nonviolence, participatory democracy, and voluntary simplicity in those communities. Most people do not live in intentional communities, but we can all be more deliberate about how we live our lives, as individuals and as neighbors. Although most of our neighborhoods do not form around shared values, neighborhood associations could coalesce around voluntary simplicity and sustainability by sharing tools, for example, or, in my neighborhood's case, shared concerns for the health of our lake.

Some people can do more, and some less—it would be wrong to ask those with little access to resources to embrace voluntary simplicity. Living intentionally is one way to *be the change you wish to see in the world*. This phrase communicates a critical idea: it is not enough to simply condemn or criticize the world we live in. Instead, we must create and inhabit the world we desire. This book explains my experiences with intentional communities and what I have learned about bringing these lessons home.

Seeking Communities

In the spring of 2011, I started to look for communities in the United States that were trying to be the change by living out values of nonviolence, voluntary simplicity, and interdependence. I sat down with my laptop one afternoon and started with Google. Since "be the change" has been extraordinarily influential, this phrase became a starting point in my search. I paired it with a variety of search terms (such as "community," "nonviolence," and "simplicity") to see what types of communities might pop up. I tried a variety of permutations and found a range of communities that appeared innovative and exciting. I quickly amassed a collection of blogs and magazine articles as well as promotional literature produced by the communities themselves. Moreover, I found that the Federation of Intentional Community (FIC) maintains an extensive database of intentional communities, from established ones to those in the process of creation. The FIC website states that *intentional community* is an inclusive term for ecovillages, cohousing communities, residential land trusts, communes, student co-ops, urban housing cooperatives, intentional living arrangements, alternative communities, cooperative living schemes, and other projects where people strive together with a common vision.[1]

Simply put, intentional communities are residential communities with a shared vision. Religious studies scholar Timothy Miller proposes four criteria to help distinguish intentional communities from shared living arrangements: shared purpose, some kind of common living space, some shared resources, and critical mass.[2] The FIC definition of intentional community is extraordinarily broad and includes a range of institutions, from monasteries to housing co-ops, that might be located in almost any neighborhood. In some communities, such as communities that share income or have a "common purse," the residents' lives are tightly integrated, while at the other end of the spectrum, cohousing groups are more loosely affiliated and mainly share physical resources, such as common space.

For many people, intentional community conjures up images of drugged-out hippies and the Haight-Ashbury ethos of the late 1960s and early 1970s. In the 1970s, idealistic youth established communal societies such as the Farm in Summertown, Tennessee, to experiment with alternative economies, child-rearing philosophies, and social relations. Most of these communities developed organically and haphazardly, without prior planning, and their physical, governance, and social structures demonstrated more youthful enthusiasm than skill. Movies such as the 2005 documentary *Commune* and the more popular 2012 *Wanderlust* reinforce entrenched stereotypes of 1970s-style communes and make it difficult to imagine the competence and forethought evinced in contemporary intentional communities, many of which are populated by residents highly skilled in areas such as building, governances, and agriculture. Today, while residents of intentional communities tend to be idealistic people searching for alternatives like their predecessors, they have absorbed the lessons learned by previous generations and have stabilized in terms of residency, governance, and infrastructure. The Farm, for example, still exists and now boasts an Ecovillage Training Center that conducts classes and workshops for residents and guests in areas such as agroforestry and midwifery.

My guiding frame of nonviolence, demonstration or education communities, voluntary simplicity, and interdependence or regional self-sufficiency helped narrow my choices of communities to investigate. There are an enormous number of intentional communities in the United States, but I was especially interested in those that are responding to contemporary concerns, particularly concerns around sustainability. Further, I did not seek out insular communities that remove themselves physically or psychologically from the rest of society. Instead, I sought communities that stressed their roles as demonstration sites and viewed outreach and service to neighbors and broader society as vital. These communities aim to live within their bioregions and to create strong ties with neighbors. I originally searched for intentional communities that emphasized self-sufficiency, but I quickly realized that interdependence, or perhaps self-reliance at the village or regional level, was a more appropriate criterion. Being completely self-sufficient is virtually impossible, and ultimately not desirable. For example, if I get sick, I want ready access to good medical care, and most community residents maintain contact with friends and family through social media. So in reality, most communities want to meet their food, clothing, and shelter needs in ways that are the least disruptive to the environment and the most beneficial to their friends and neighbors, but still remain connected to larger health and communication systems. In other words, these communities are striving to create interdependent self-sufficiencies.

My four parameters also closed off a broad range of intentional communities such as gay and lesbian separatist communities, communities that require strict religious or belief ideologies, and white separatist communities. It is difficult to know how many communities I excluded; the FIC website lists thousands, and many others choose not to be listed with the FIC. My demographic, then, reflects a subset, albeit large, of self-selected communities that advertise their existence on the FIC website and/or attend events such as the annual Communities Conference at Twin Oaks in Louisa, Virginia, both of which tend to attract an educated, middle-class population.

My online search immediately pulled up the Possibility Alliance, a small community in rural northeast Missouri that abstains from using electricity, among other things. (It seemed ironic to me that I found numerous blogs and articles discussing a community that forswears electricity and thus computers.) A short article on *Sustainablog* described the completely electricity-free and petroleum-free Possibility Alliance as a "radically daring example of simple living."[3] If those words weren't enough to draw me in, the picture that accompanied them proved irresistible: a bicycle pulling a trailer with a bale of hay. Ever since my graduate school days in Philadelphia, I've used my bicycle for transportation whenever I can. When I saw this picture, I wanted to ride that bike and I wanted to meet the residents of the Possibility Alliance.

I discovered that the Possibility Alliance was located in a cluster of intentional communities in northeast Missouri. Approximately forty miles away lay Dancing Rabbit and its partner communities: Sandhill, an income-sharing farm, and Red Earth, a community of approximately seven individual homesteads. I was immediately intrigued by Dancing Rabbit's plan to build a village of five hundred to a thousand people from the ground up, based on principles of regional self-sufficiency, gender equity, and sustainability. The location of these communities surprised me—I was not expecting Missouri. I had anticipated finding intentional communities in more usual-suspects locations, perhaps California or the Pacific Northwest, and after fifteen years of living in the flat terrain of Iowa and Florida, I had hoped for something in the mountains or perhaps the coast of Maine. However, I knew there had to be a creative synergy or generative buzz between these four communities and I was excited to learn more.

When I first visited Possibility Alliance and Dancing Rabbit in 2011, I was overwhelmed by their positive energy, can-do spirit, and creativity. I met people who were testing new ideas of governance, reviving older, low-energy technologies, and engaging with residents of nearby communities. They did not see themselves as *the answer*, but rather as incubators of ideas about how to approach specific problems. Dancing Rabbit's innovative approach to participatory governance intrigued me, in part, because it was crafted to avoid authoritarianism and rigid hierarchies. Further, I chose communities that consciously emphasized and addressed all three aspects of *sustainability*: equity, economy, and ecology.

Residents of the first communities I visited during my four years of research directed me to other communities, and I scoured the FIC website for examples of communities that differed in terms of geography, economy, and longevity. I hoped to see how values such as nonviolence were grounded in specific community geographies. I sought a mix of rural, urban, and suburban communities and communities that spanned a range of social and economic structures, from communes such as Twin Oaks and Sandhill to cohousing communities such as Two Echo in Brunswick, Maine, and Pioneer Valley in Amherst, Massachusetts, that closely replicate mainstream structures of individual family homes. I saw how residents, drawn together by common values of sustainability, social equity, and community, worked to enact these values in different geographic and social contexts. Catholic worker communities in Dubuque, Iowa, and Gainesville, Florida, share goals of sustainably feeding the hungry, yet the logistics of doing so differ greatly in each community.

Despite the different models of communities and the diversity of residents, common themes and challenges emerged. For example, values such as nonviolence, consensus-style governance, and interdependence provided a framework for decisions about virtually all aspects of life, including what food to eat and how to produce it, and I learned about some of the necessary trade-offs inherent in applying these values. For example, decisions about which vegetables should be grown and under what conditions might be made by consensus so that all residents had a voice in the process; however, the trade-off is that this process might diminish the influence of those who have the most agricultural experience. Competing values—consensus versus privileging agriculture skill—demonstrated the difficulties of actually living a set of values.

I made shorter visits to some communities to learn more about different kinds of ventures, but I spent extended periods in some so that I could understand them more deeply. For example, I returned several times to the Possibility Alliance and Dancing Rabbit in Missouri. Neither is a regional movement—each boasts a broad geographic distribution of residents from across the United States and abroad. In fact, Dancing Rabbit's founding residents came from California, and numerous prospective residents dropped out when the group chose Missouri as the site for their community. Missouri has relatively inexpensive arable land, and rural northeast Missouri has few, if any, building codes or other restrictions. This is important for groups that want to experiment with sustainable building techniques and water-reclamation systems, such as graywater, that violate existing building codes in most places. As a result, intentional communities often settle in states such as Tennessee, Oregon, Maine, and Missouri, where land is not suitable for large-scale agriculture. And in Missouri, the presence of Amish and Old Order Mennonites provides support and infrastructure for self-sufficient intentional communities. Amish and Mennonite communities have maintained traditional construction, animal husbandry, and agricultural skills that enable them to survive with little or no use of fossil fuel, an attraction for other sustainability-oriented communities.

I loved spending time in Missouri; the beautiful rolling hills and the rhythms of rural life drew me back repeatedly—to the point where it made me homesick for the rural Midwest and my previous life in Ames, Iowa. The spatial isolation of rural communities makes them a critical space for testing new ideas. For example, although communities like the Possibility Alliance interact extensively with the broader community through community service, trading, and education, their remote location insulates them from the rush and hubbub of urban and suburban life and is one of their great attractions. This relative isolation yields an inward and meditative focus because these comparatively small communities comprise the primary work, social, and leisure sites for residents. Aspects of their lives are less diffused into offsite jobs, social engagements, and recreation, even though, for many residents, one or more of these activities do occur elsewhere. Simply put, residents of rural communities tend to spend more time with each other in both community work and social interaction.

Of course, it is simply not realistic for everyone to move to rural ecovillages. Instead, change must occur within existing suburban and urban built environments where the energy and frisson of diverse populations render such regions crucibles for positive change. Thus I was also eager to visit urban communities because of this potential for grassroots social change and because, according to the 2010 Census, 80 percent of the US population lives in urban areas. Urban agriculture presents enormous possibilities and challenges.[4] Intentional communities such as LA Eco-village and the many urban Catholic worker communities demonstrate opportunities for bringing the cluster of sustainability values to others who seek change in those directions. LA Eco-village, one of the more established and recognized ecovillages in the world, blends its focus on sustainability with a focus on social justice in an urban context. Ethan Hughes of the Possibility Alliance directed me to several Catholic worker communities in both the rural and urban Midwest, and I have spent time at the Catholic worker house in Gainesville, Florida. I visited cohousing communities such as Belfast because although they are focused on sustainability, they best replicate mainstream US lifeways. As such, cohousing and similar structures and lifeways might be more readily integrated into existing urban and suburban communities.

Twin Oaks' annual Communities Conference in 2013 demonstrated both how communities represent themselves to potential residents and how they dialogue among themselves, brainstorming about issues such as consensus and labor that all face. In choosing communities, I experienced an embarrassment of riches—I could never visit all these examples of community living. And so, in seeking a broad range of community types, I inevitably missed some well-established and venerable communities, including Earthaven Ecovillage in western North Carolina and Ecovillage at Ithaca (EVI) in Ithaca, New York, which are both well documented in print and online. The communities that I visited, however, bore witness to the broad array of alternatives currently being tested and practiced across the United States.

What unites these diverse communities is a commitment to practice nonviolence in virtually all facets of life, from agriculture to infrastructure to interpersonal communication. Further, each group reflects historical understandings of violence: they understand that state and other forms of authority can be coercive and violent, so they are experimenting with forms of participatory decision making. The rural communities are especially attuned to the systemic violence imposed on human and nonhuman communities by industrial agriculture. These communities understand themselves as experimental responses to the violence of environmental and social crises and as demonstration sites and models for broader social change.

In writing this book, I focused my inquiry more on how the communities created governance systems for themselves and less on their political interactions in the broader social arena. Nonetheless, these are important questions—perhaps the seed of a future project. Most of the urban communities, such as LA Eco-village and Catholic worker communities, coordinated with local communities on food and transportation. LA Eco-village's in-house food business was racially diverse and brought in people from the neighborhood, which is mostly poor and African American as well as Korean. Of the urban groups I visited, LA Eco-village was probably the most politically engaged with local politics, and its members worked hard to maintain good relations with city commissioners and others. Since LA Eco-village, like most of these groups, was neighborhood focused, they built coalitions within their neighborhood and surrounding areas, not necessarily across Los Angeles.⁵ Similarly, the Cherith Brook community opposed a nuclear program because the proposed plan would have brought contaminants, but no economic benefits, to the neighborhood.

The rural or suburban communities I visited wanted more ethnic and racial diversity, but recognized the difficulty in attaining that. Like the urban groups, they focused on coalition building with neighbors who, in rural regions, tended to be either the poor or Old Order Mennonite and Amish farmers. Rural communities tended to be more successful reflecting diversity in LGBT matters than in race and ethnicity, and critiquing existing gender and sexuality norms formed an integral aspect of their rationale for existence. Dancing Rabbit and Twin Oaks both claim to "question everything" regarding sexuality and conventional arrangements. Cohousing communities, overall, tend to be more conventional, and although individuals might engage in broader political efforts, the communities as a whole are less likely to do so. In general, most communities built bridges with their neighbors—whoever they were.

In conducting the research for this book, I visited more than twenty communities and spoke with community representatives at two community-focused conferences: the 2013 Communities Conference organized by Twin Oaks in Louisa, Virginia, and the 2012 International Communal Studies Association held at Findhorn Foundation in Findhorn, Scotland. These conferences both enabled me to hear how community residents spoke with each other about mutual concerns and helped me put my fieldwork in the context of larger discussions about community and sustainability. I also gained perspective on communities from residents who had lived in or visited different communities.

During my visits, I interviewed a number of community residents, and many of them are quoted in the following pages. I shared drafts of the manuscript so that they could see how I represented them and their communities, and the final book benefited from their feedback. For those individuals who have moved on from the communities (interns, in particular), I used only their first names. Some individuals preferred not to be identified by name, and I honored their wishes. Some people have gone on to new communities or new endeavors, and some communities have closed. This book presents a slice of time, describing the goals and aspirations of a set of communities and individuals between 2011 and 2015.

Since the book describes my journey through these communities, I have included a list and brief descriptions of them in appendix A. Throughout the book, I will refer to communities by their full name at the first mention in each chapter; then, for simplicity's sake, I will use their shortened name: for example, Dancing Rabbit Ecovillage becomes Dancing Rabbit. Similarly, although the communities have multiple opportunities for engagement, including different levels of residence and membership, I use the term *resident* broadly to avoid confusion.

The vignettes that follow illustrate the types of intentional communities I visited, what they do, and what they might teach us. I outline briefly each community's vision, food practices, and relationships with the wider communities of which it is a part.

An Alternative Community: The Possibility Alliance

Ethan Hughes and Sarah Wilcox-Hughes founded the Possibility Alliance in 2007. They purchased an existing Amish homestead based on the criteria that it be located near a railway station, be proximate to Mennonite and Amish communities, and have arable land. Since their arrival, like-minded families and groups have purchased land and established homesteads nearby, and the number of residents in the affiliated communities has tripled. In 2012, the Possibility Alliance had about twelve full-time residents, but the population swells during the growing season, when about six interns arrive from across the United States to stay for a nine-month period. Several interns have become full-time permanent residents. During the growing season, the Possibility Alliance also hosts shorter-term volunteers and interested guest-volunteers like me. Cofounder Sarah Wilcox-Hughes and her parents, who are heavily involved with the community, bring a strong Quaker flavor to the otherwise nondenominational Possibility Alliance, and the group holds a Meeting on Sunday mornings. There is also a Friday evening Shabbat dinner to which residents, friends, and neighbors are invited to reflect on the joys and challenges of the week. The Possibility Alliance also collaborates with regional Catholic worker houses and farms in both rural and urban areas.

Hughes and Wilcox-Hughes specifically articulate their vision in terms of several Gandhian values, including nonviolence, self-sufficiency, equity, and voluntary simplicity. Hughes and his friend and colleague Chris Moore-Backman coined the term *integral nonviolence* to illustrate Gandhi's understanding that nonviolence must be practiced in all aspects of life, from the personal to the political.[6] As part of their practice, they abstain from fossil fuels and electricity, both for environmental reasons and because of the economic and political violence wrought by oil-production systems, especially in the developing world. Similarly, they abstain from foods that must travel long distances and that are typically produced through unfair labor practices, such as coffee and chocolate, and primarily eat foods produced in their bioregion. They initiated a Peace and Permaculture Center, a concept drawn from Catholic worker Peter Maurin's agronomic universities, which links farming skills and scholarship. The Peace and Permaculture Center reflects the outward focus of the Possibility Alliance and teaches skills to fulfill basic needs (food, shelter, and clothing) directly from the land. Though small, this energetic community hosts numerous workshops and events throughout the year. Summers culminate in a month-long Superhero Bike Ride in which residents and friends create superhero identities and ride to a town or city to offer assistance in whatever needs to be done. These superheroes, such as Love Ninja and CompashMan (as in compassionate man), serve anyone in need, from helping the homeless to digging a community garden, and have also responded to crises such as Hurricane Katrina.

Ecovillages: Dancing Rabbit and LA Eco-village

Dancing Rabbit and the LA Eco-village demonstrate the growth of the ecovillage, defined by the Global Ecovillage Network (GEN) as "an intentional or traditional community using local participatory processes to holistically integrate ecological, economic, social, and cultural dimensions of sustainability in order to regenerate social and natural environments."[7]

Dancing Rabbit and neighboring communities Sandhill and Red Earth are about forty miles northeast of Possibility Alliance. Although the groups communicate and cooperate, the distance between them is disproportionately large given the abstinence from fossil fuels at Possibility Alliance—it's a long bike ride, even in the relatively flat Midwest.

In 1993, a small group of Stanford students crafted a plan to build an ecovillage from the ground up. In 1996, six people broke ground in Missouri, so a great deal of Dancing Rabbit's energy has gone into developing alternative construction techniques and actually building the infrastructure that exists today. Dancing Rabbit's food and other practices reflect Gandhi's values of nonviolence, self-sufficiency, equity, and voluntary simplicity. Dancing Rabbit's mission statement and sustainability guidelines announce the community's intention to create a nonexploitive—what I understood to be essentially nonviolent—and ecologically sound society.[8] This statement explains that ecological degradation largely affects oppressed people, and that Rabbits (as members refer to themselves) therefore should consider how their purchases and practices exacerbate or alleviate environmental damage and oppressive conditions.

Prior to breaking ground, the founders created a consensus-based system of governance based on principles of nonviolent communication. All residents receive some training in nonviolent communication during three-week visitors' programs, but many seek much more rigorous training in group-facilitation techniques. Rabbits emphasized that building community is far more difficult than the physical labor of farming or construction, especially when you cannot escape into the anonymity of urban life. Rabbits are always in close proximity to each other, so it can be difficult to find a balance between group harmony and individual space. The intimate conditions and the small, sometimes shared, spaces in the community render meaningless the public/private dichotomy that structure and enable mainstream social interactions. The processes for nonviolent communication and conflict resolution fill a real need here, and Rabbits can ask one another to facilitate difficult discussions. Additionally, Dancing Rabbit established several mechanisms to resolve the conflicts that inevitably arise, including a conflict resolution committee and, more recently, restorative justice circles.

In 2012, Dancing Rabbit had approximately seventy long-term residents plus short-term residents, work exchange students, and summer interns. Like many intentional communities, Dancing Rabbit offers long-term residences for individuals who are considering membership or those in the process of becoming residents, which might take up to two years. Dancing Rabbit has six ecological covenants that govern all residents. For example, no one may own an individual vehicle, all building materials must be of local origin or repurposed, and all agriculture on Dancing Rabbit property must be organic.

The coming years will test Dancing Rabbit's forms of consensus-style governance and its use of resources. The original goal was to develop into a self-sufficient village of five hundred to a thousand people, but the community is already facing challenges as it scales up, and some residents are questioning this goal. To maintain participatory democracy with their growing numbers, residents have implemented a town hall–style of gover-

Decorated streets in front of LA Eco-village

nance that enables committees to make some decisions but maintains consensus for major decisions.

When I arrived at LA Eco-village, first by train and then on foot, I saw large, colorful murals painted on the pavement in front of the entry gate. Because one of LA Eco-village's primary initiatives revolves around public transit and safe bicycling, taking public transit from the airport seemed appropriate. Later, LA Eco-village's visionary founder, Lois Arkin, explained that these murals were traffic-calming devices and that on some Sunday afternoons residents set up a table and have tea in the middle of the street.

The LA Eco-village neighborhood is situated in the north end of the Wilshire Center/Koreatown area and at the time of my visit consisted of a two-block, eleven-acre community of approximately five hundred residents, forty of whom comprised the LA Eco-village intentional community, that is, those who moved there intentionally to demonstrate the processes of a neighborhood going sustainable. With a few dozen of her organization's constituents, Arkin had spent nearly a decade planning a new-construction state-of-the-art ecovillage on an eleven-acre city-owned site about seven miles from the current location. But the LA riots of 1992, which happened in

Koreatown, convinced members of the planning committee that they needed to work in and with this neighborhood, which had been substantially affected by the riots and several major fires, and where Arkin and her organization had lived for the previous thirteen years. So, in 1993, Arkin and the planning group started the LA Eco-village as a demonstration site for "intentional, 'whole-systems' sustainable living in the heart of the city."[9]

They developed the Cooperative Resources and Services Project (CRSP) to provide "educational resources for small cooperatives." According to the CRSP website, the whole-systems approach, similar to the permaculture approach, integrates the "social, economic and ecological or physical aspects of neighborhood life with the goal of raising the quality of life while radically reducing environmental impacts. CRSP intends for its efforts to reduce the burden of government, while increasing local self-reliance in the areas of housing, livelihood, food production, health, energy, water, transportation, recreation, waste processing and education."[10]

Arkin noted that it was a few years before intentional neighbors started moving into the neighborhood, but a dozen or so volunteers had substantially transformed the feeling of the neighborhood by that time.

Like the other communities I visited in 2011 and 2012, LA Eco-village applied concepts of nonviolence, voluntary simplicity, and participatory democracy according to its specific needs. Although the communities I visited are idiosyncratic and follow their own internal processes, they illustrated broader themes and perhaps trends of growing demands for more control over food and its production and the recognition that stronger social ties are more satisfying than atomized lives. As I considered what I might bring home to apply in my own life and community, I began to realize that many of us could incorporate these themes, trends, and practices at some level.

Catholic Worker Houses and Farms: Florida, Iowa, and Missouri

Dorothy Day and Peter Maurin started the Catholic Worker Movement in response to the crises of the Great Depression. Mohandas K. Gandhi influenced the movement as it developed, and the food practices of individual Catholic worker farms and houses and associated agronomic universities reflect Gandhi's emphasis on self-sufficiency, nonviolence, and self-discipline. The Catholic Worker Movement draws on Catholic social thought, a body of teachings that articulates the Roman Catholic Church's stance on social and economic justice, but it has no official connection to the Catholic Church. Catholic worker houses and farms instantiate the traditional Christian Works of Mercy (for example, feeding the hungry, clothing the naked, extending hospitality to the homeless). However, in contrast to the Catholic Church, the Catholic Worker Movement is anarchist, meaning that each house and farm is different, and each community chooses for itself how best to practice the Works of Mercy.[11] There is no central structure or hierarchy, and there are no official requirements on what it takes to be a Catholic worker house or farm.

Despite the variety of Catholic worker houses and farms, they all draw from Peter Maurin's three planks: roundtable discussions, houses of hospitality, and farming communes. Day and Maurin envisioned farm communes, or agronomic universities, populated by workers and scholars who could share ideas and skills. Maurin wanted to create a group of "Catholic Radicals" in order to get "back to the roots," to a society not structured by the wages, anomie, and stratification wrought by the Industrial Revolution. Instead, his farming communes would preserve the dignity of all individuals as they mastered skills and trades.[12] While many communards of the 1970s and today might not accept Day and Maurin's Catholic beliefs, their values of interdependence and community resonate with the population that is attracted to intentional community.

My visits to the Mustard Seed in Ames, Iowa; Cherith Brook Catholic Worker in Kansas City, Missouri; and the Catholic worker house—the little Green House—in Gainesville, Florida, helped me see how Catholic workers apply these principles in the context of their own—and their communities'—needs and geographies. For instance, the Gainesville Catholic Worker (which has since closed) served homemade organic meals to people in need, including many who were homeless or lived in Gainesville's now-disbanded tent city. Most of the food was locally sourced, much of it from the house's own garden.

Many Catholic worker communities bridge, and perhaps blend, the urban and rural in at least two ways. First, many urban houses partner with rural houses or farmers to circulate food, ideas, and people. White Rose Catholic Workers House in Chicago, for example, farms on land an hour outside the city, and the farm site offers a "non-violent living apprenticeship." Second, many Catholic workers bring the rural into the urban in the form of raised-bed gardens or backyard chickens, and their focus on food and hospitality combines with their agronomic universities to attune people to issues of food production as well as traditional skills such as canning. This urban/rural blend creates unique places to help reskill diverse urban populations and take new food movements (such as organic or slow food) beyond the white middle class.

Cohousing: Belfast Cohousing and Ecovillage

When I first visited Dancing Rabbit, the Possibility Alliance, and other communities, I thought I was off to new lands, exotic locales, even though some communities were in the US heartland. I assumed that communities experimenting with common property and shared governance had to be counterculture. My visits and discussions with residents quickly disabused me of any notions that these communities were radically out of step with the US mainstream, and I realized that they shared tensions about food, community, and authority that concern many North Americans. Residents of these communities had to find a balance between individual autonomy and group cohesion, or between adherence to values and strong personalities, for example, which are the same tensions that plague anyone who has ever sat on a committee.

As I mulled over the commonalities between intentional communities and the rest of us, I became interested in cohousing, a form of intentional community that closely replicates familiar living arrangements such as co-ops and condominium associations. Originating in Denmark in the 1960s, cohousing is defined as "a type of collaborative housing in which residents actively participate in the design and operation of their own neighborhoods."[13] Although most cohousing communities form around a desire for stronger community ties, many also incorporate sustainability and social equity goals.

When I visited Belfast in May 2013, I was eager to explore this new form of community. Belfast is located in rural coastal Maine, about three hours north of Portland and due east of the state capital, Augusta. This relatively new community begun organizing funding for development in 2007 and had sold all but two of its thirty-six available residences in 2013. Like many of the communities I visited, Belfast is a work in progress as residents continue to build homes and infrastructure.

Community and sustainability are two chief goals of Belfast, According to its website, "Simple and elegant, the homes combine eco-design principles with a sensible degree of convenience. They are situated to maximize casual social interaction, to create a safe environment for children, and to preserve open space for recreation and agriculture."[14]

Cohousing communities, like most intentional communities, try to attract families with children because these families foster stability, especially if the children later return with their own children. Many of the houses at Belfast are joined (duplexes), creating a proximity that promotes drop-in visits and easy socializing. The community encourages a culture of reciprocity;

New construction at Belfast Cohousing and Ecovillage

a young mother, for example, can easily run next door to arrange an hour of childcare while she runs errands. The helpful presence of neighbors also attracts older residents who foresee needing some assistance in the future. Cohousing and related intentional community arrangements, such as shared housing, provide palatable alternatives for baby boomers who cannot imagine themselves in traditional retirement communities.

Although the community was formed according to the shared goals of community, openness, and sustainability, Belfast is structured like a homeowners' association in that anyone may join simply by purchasing a unit—unlike at Dancing Rabbit—and agreeing to obey the bylaws. Although residence is a self-selection process, the sustainably designed homes and shared garages are likely to attract those with similar values.

Of the communities I visited, Belfast and other cohousing groups best replicate the suburban lifestyle of the United States in terms of both potential and challenges. Cohousing communities tend to be comparatively expensive and so necessarily exclude some potential residents, a common critique of ecovillages and cohousing communities. Cohousing communities typically have common spaces and residents may share meals, just as many gated communities and homeowners' associations share amenities such as a pool or a common house available for parties. Cohousing communities and homeowners' associations both often have strict covenants governing what you can and cannot do with your home and yard, although the focus tends to be different. Whereas many homeowners' associations regulate against front-yard gardens and clotheslines, sustainability-focused communities have ordinances banning toxic agricultural chemicals and limiting attached garages. However, cohousing communities—even if they are designated as ecovillages—seem less likely to create alternative energy structures or to promote the use of composting toilets, the dry toilets that process human waste with little or no water, than communities such as Dancing Rabbit. In short, aspects of cohousing might be the easiest to incorporate into the US mainstream without major structural changes, although the costs could be prohibitive for many.

Plan of the Book

The initial chapters of this book explore why people come to these communities, who comes, and what they do when they get there, including growing food, creating governance systems, and building community. Although I visited diverse communities in rural, suburban, and urban regions of the United States, each faced similar sets of challenges that are familiar: most of us are ambivalent in our attitudes toward authority, regulation, and community. We wrestle with questions such as: How much do I want to share with my neighbors? Am I working for a car to get to work to pay for my car? Many people want to understand how we can live out ideals of voluntary simplicity, for example, in the context of our own lives and regions.

The first chapter, "Examining Change," explores some of the social tensions around aging, food, and consumerism that these communities address. While independence is a central American value, many people crave stronger community ties, especially as they age. Similarly, a newly food-aware US public wants the freedom to experiment with foods such as raw milk, but demands the safety that accompanies regulated foods. This chapter outlines why some people want change and how intentional communities are testing solutions to social problems. Contemporary intentional communities have built on the successes and failures of those who have gone before, especially those of the 1960s and 1970s. Chapter 2, "Standing on the Shoulders of Giants," explores lessons learned from previous individuals and communities who have experimented with new forms of living.

Chapter 3, "Choosing a Life," illustrates the process of choosing a community and highlights questions that arise as potential residents consider new lifestyles. Intentional communities draw a broad range of individuals and families, from older individuals seeking stability to young families with children. Potential members must consider a host of questions, including how much they want to merge their lives with a community. Residents of intentional communities aim to develop new patterns of living and eating, and chapter 4, "Creating Cultures," describes how residents create new cultures through integrating abstract values such as voluntary simplicity into their daily practices. Communities like the Possibility Alliance draw upon the concept of "bread labor"—that all people should contribute physically to fulfilling their material needs—as an ethical framework to govern how they eat.

The final chapters suggest ways to apply what these communities have learned in the context of our own lives and regions. Food co-ops, pocket neighborhoods, and cohousing, for example, offer some benefits of intentional communities, such as control over food, but require fewer drastic lifestyle changes. Chapter 5, "Asking What's for Dinner," illustrates how communities enact values such as nonviolence into their food practices. For example, what would it mean to eat nonviolently? Communities such as the Possibility Alliance, Dancing Rabbit, and Cherith Brook Catholic Worker consider what and how to eat in the context of their specific cultures and geographies. Deciding "what to eat" as a community requires a robust and responsive governance system, and community members noted that creating a civil society was one of the most difficult community tasks. Chapter 6, "Sustainability in Community," demonstrates how communities create governance and conflict-resolution systems that enable them to live together.

Chapter 7, "Rethinking Abundance," explores how communities interpret voluntary simplicity and ask, "What do we need to be happy?" For example, residents of some communities have reframed abundance to include social connections and the excitement of seasonal tastes rather than the accumulation of goods. Chapter 8, "Extreme DIY for Interdependence," illustrates how intentional communities are reviving and adapting practices such as gardening and home building to meet contemporary needs. Communities are teaching basic skills to their own members and to the general public as the desire to learn such skills becomes increasingly mainstream. Chapter 9, "Bringing It Home," explores how the values and skills lived in these intentional communities are coming home to our own communities. Intentional communities experiment with alternative ways of living, eating, and governing, and others can learn from these demonstrations. I wrote *Living Sustainably* for readers who are excited about understanding what we can learn from intentional communities and eager to explore ideas for transforming their own communities.

1

Examining Change

> *Gandhi walked a fruitful path. We've been gifted with this amazing potential to work for the people that we love and the land that we love. I owe a lot of my thinking and who I am to Gandhi.*
> —Mark Becker, Possibility Alliance

ALMOST A CENTURY AGO, Mohandas K. Gandhi—commonly known by his honorific title Mahatma, the great-souled one—prescribed a paradigm for democracy that bundled concepts such as nonviolence, self-sufficiency, equity, and voluntary simplicity. Frustrated by the fetters of centralized corporate power, he argued that individuals and localities must retain control of their own ability to produce and receive basic human needs (food, clothing, and shelter) or they would become enslaved to the dictates of external forces such as governments and corporations.

I hear Gandhi's warnings about food and violence both at the professional and the personal level. I live and work in Gainesville, Florida, where I teach courses such as Religion and Food and Being Gandhi at the University of Florida, and both my classes and my research and writing projects are bound up with issues of food, democracy, and self-sufficiency. But my interest in these issues extends beyond the academic. I also care deeply about where my food comes from and the social consequences of my food choices.

Pondering these professional and personal dilemmas has led me to explore intentional communities in the United States within this framing question: Can a constellation of ideals such as nonviolence, radical democracy, voluntary simplicity, and self-sufficiency yield an innovative, sustainable, and equitable paradigm for how we might live *sustainably* upon the earth? Equally important, how do we enact these values? For example, what does voluntary simplicity mean in the context of my daily life? More broadly, how can we begin to address large-scale problems collaboratively, as communities? I knew that answers to these and related questions lay, if anywhere, in communities whose existence is bound up with enacting these values. These communities, I hoped, could model collaborative solutions to our large-scale problems because our individual efforts—whether recycling, shopping at farmers' markets, or cycling to work—though laudable, are simply inadequate for creating sustainable lifeways. I also wondered about the benefits of life in community: cooperative life and teamwork might be fun and nurture a richness that too often gets lost in our increasingly hectic and disconnected lives.

Between 2011 and 2015, as I visited intentional communities, I learned that a certain set of values—including nonviolent communication, radical democracy, voluntary simplicity, and self-sufficiency—has shaped how these communities eat, build, live, and govern. The bundling of these values is significant; while each carries merit in and of itself, when considered together, they facilitate the crafting of holistic paradigms that incorporate economy, governance, and equity. The residents of these communities are reviving and adapting traditional agrarian skills, testing alternative building materials, and developing community governance systems that balance needs for both community and individual autonomy. In response to concerns about food, fraying social ties, and consumerism, they are crafting communities and lifeways around sustainable food, building, and social systems. Intentional communities enjoy unique opportunities to experiment with alternative forms of governance, food, and shelter because their small size and intentionality provide the flexibility to continually test and assess new practices. We all benefit when these communities model new practices and generate new ideas because we can evaluate what alternatives might work for our own communities and decide which practices to bring home. In my travels, I became increasingly aware that these communities are negotiating concerns we all share and that their small-scale experiments addressing broad social anxieties hold important lessons for everyone.

Social Anxieties

We live in frightening times. The United States is crawling out of a recession, our government cannot pass a budget, and repeated extreme weather events have convinced even notable former deniers (such as New Jersey

Governor Chris Christie) of the perils of climate change. Prolonged drought and water shortages in California and elsewhere have forced farmers to idle land and raised concerns about rising food prices and even the very availability of food. Debates over food miles and whether corn should feed cars or people, coupled with rising needs for assistance at food pantries, illustrate social anxieties about food—not only what we will eat, but also how we will produce that food. Like many North Americans, I have taken individual action to exert some control, but I would never claim that I could grow enough in my garden to feed my husband and myself. However, growing at least some of my own food offers me some control over what I eat and some resilience to higher food prices. I live in Florida, a state prone to hurricanes, and we are advised to keep provisions on hand during hurricane season (June 1–December 1). Perhaps if supply chains were cut for a week or so, our garden might see us through, but I doubt our ability to sustain our food supply over a longer term.

I see my own food anxieties reflected in the popularity of food and gardening groups and workshops in Gainesville. For example, Grow Gainesville holds biannual seed swaps and offers workshops and tool-lending libraries, and each year more small farms and community-supported agriculture (CSAs) appear at farmers' markets in Alachua County. Websites such as LocalHarvest provide a database of small farms and CSAs across the United States, with information directed at consumers and producers.

My own steps toward self-sufficiency are echoed in larger social movements that advocate preparedness for any disruption in the supply chain, whether the cause is weather, a terrorist attack, or a broader state of collapse. What happens when your local supermarket closes? How will you take care of yourself and others? Both the older survivalist and the more recent *prepper* movements address self-reliance and preparedness in the context of disaster or social collapse. Preppers tend to hold a middle ground between those who do nothing and survivalists, who anticipate a collapse of all systems. Interestingly, Dancing Rabbit Ecovillage, one community I visited, was featured on the Green Survivalist blog *Preparing to Survive*: "No matter if you're *preparing* for the end of times due to religious beliefs, governmental and economic *failure*, or zombie attacks, it is better to be *prepared* than not to. My family knows that anything is possible and although unlikely, we will be capable of survival. Will you? My family will spend 1 year working towards self-reliance. This is our journey!"

The author of this blog refutes my stereotypes of survivalists when he states that he is not a hard-core survivalist, is not counting days until the end times, and is not a militarist. Instead, he simply wants to prepare himself and his family for the possibility of disruptions. He stresses that his preparations are reasonable—for example, given weather fluctuations, everybody should be more prepared for short-term disruptions.

A 2013 *New York Times Magazine* article documented the mainstreaming of the prepper movement in New York City—hardly, as author Alan Feuer notes, a typical site for it. Yet after 9/11 and Hurricane Sandy, perhaps such preparations make sense in New York City. Feuer interviewed Dr. Irwin Redlener, the director of the National Center for Disaster Preparedness at Columbia University, who stated, "Ordinary people have a central role in emergency preparedness. The government reacted decisively after 9/11, establishing the Department of Homeland Security, so why shouldn't everyday citizens react?" Why shouldn't all of us take some responsibility for ourselves in the event of disaster? As Dr. Redlener noted, "We are all first responders."[1] Before I read this article and subsequent literature, I had never heard the word *prepper*, but I realized that I had nevertheless been taking steps, especially regarding food, recommended by preppers.

One notable aspect of the prepper movement, and perhaps the survivalist movement as well, is its focus on the individual or family level, reflecting our extreme emphasis on the individual in the United States. And the prepper movement has a significant commercial aspect, in that individuals or families gather to purchase necessary food, medical, and other supplies. This emphasis ignores the importance of other people and communities, even if they are temporary communities.

By contrast, in *A Paradise Built in Hell: The Extraordinary Communities That Arise in Disaster,* Rebecca Solnit illustrates the grassroots response efforts—what she calls "disaster communities"—that arose during emergencies such as 9/11 and Hurricane Katrina. Solnit demonstrates that these small-scale efforts at rescue—enacted by communities that formed in response to the disaster—were more effective than large-scale government responses because they could react immediately, a feat not possible for bureaucratic entities that were bound by rules and regulations. After 9/11, New Yorkers spontaneously created structures to get supplies such as cough drops and boots to rescue workers. "For a short time, during the first few days after 9/11, I felt that 'beloved community' that we talked about in the Civil Rights Movement," said Temma Kaplan, a participant in the Freedom Summer of 1964, as she reflected upon the desire for connection and reassurance of human goodness in the face of disaster.[2] Solnit's discussion of the flexibility and resilience of grassroots communities reflects William Easterly's critiques that large-scale development organizations have often caused more harm than good to developing nations by squelching indigenous self-help efforts.[3] Solnit's and Easterly's works suggest that small-scale, self-organized communities could remedy social problems because they tend to be flexible and adaptable.

Security for the Old and the Young

The flexibility of small communities in dealing with disaster or social problems also has the potential to allay broad social anxieties around aging and disability. Even though I am fairly fit and independent, I'm not sure I could carry all of the materials in the recommended *bug-out bag* assembled by Aton Edwards, the founder of the International Preparedness Network.[4] Bug-out bags include equipment deemed necessary to survive the first seventy-two hours of disaster and include gear such as ropes, dried food, and occasionally weapons. In an extended disaster or social collapse, I, as a fifty-something woman, simply could not survive on my own without a community.

Small, flexible communities can help us address challenges with aging. A significant population in the United States—the baby boomers—are reaching their seventh decade and will require varying levels of assistance in the coming years. For those of us with no children, facing the challenges of aging is especially distressing. Although I envision and hope for many years of good health ahead for me and my husband, we, like many of our friends, have begun to think more about community and to consider the sorts of communities we could help create to support us as we age.

The *AARP Bulletin* writes that older women and baby boomers are increasingly seeking shared housing opportunities and have enrolled in programs to help them find housemates.[5] While these shared housing arrangements do not necessarily form according to shared values, as do many intentional communities, the article suggests that these houses form out of desire for community and security as much as from financial need.

Families with young children are on the opposite end of the spectrum. Coleen O'Connell, a founding resident of Belfast, an ecovillage and cohousing community in Maine, stated, "This is how humans could support each other. Working moms and dads could come home to cooked meals, shared with everyone. We raise kids in a nuclear family, and everybody's isolated. Here you come home at night, eat a meal in the Common House, talk to other parents, and give your children instant friends. We share the work of raising a family."

Parents of young children especially appreciate the support provided by intentional communities. A mother of an infant from this Maine community commented on her adjustment to life in community: "Coming from our individual cultures has been tough, but having a baby has made us focus on how this is an amazing place. So many people have helped us. I didn't cook for six weeks."

Seeking Alternatives

In 2013, radio personality Glenn Beck proposed a utopian community that, according to comedian Jon Stewart, was more centralized than even Marxists might imagine. Independence, USA, based on Ayn Rand's principles of a free market and limited government, followed Smart Growth Principles (smartgrowthamerica.org) that encourage walkable neighborhoods and local economies. Chains such as Ann Taylor and the Gap would be prohibited. Instead, Beck's community would foster freedom, creativity, and entrepreneurship through a marketplace that featured artisans, craftspeople, and small businesses.[6] To me, Beck's proposal suggests that many North Americans, from all walks of life and political persuasions, are questioning the consumerism and anonymity of contemporary society and seeking alternatives. In short, even as these communities seek alternatives to mainstream life, their searches reflect concerns that many share.

In 2007, I left Ames, Iowa, and moved to Gainesville, Florida, a city almost twice the size of Ames. I felt the difference as I moved to the larger city and a much larger university. When I lived in Ames, many of my friends lived within several blocks, and almost any destination I wanted to reach was within easy cycling or walking distance. If I needed a friend for some sort of help, someone was always nearby, and that presence gave me a sense of security that I only partially feel in Gainesville. Tellingly, one afternoon in Ames as I was discussing intentional communities with a friend who questioned the need for them, I looked around her yard and neighborhood and realized that she already had the community bonds that entice others to intentional community. Now, in retrospect, I wonder if losing these tight community bonds contributed to my interest in intentional communities.

Many people seek stronger social connections to replace support systems that were previously supplied by religious or cultural ties. With the rise of the middle class and concurrent focus on the nuclear family, more people are purchasing the help and security that familial, cultural, and religious bonds once provided. Oak Hammock, an upscale retirement community in Gainesville, exemplifies one model: it provides comprehensive services to its elderly residents, such as meals and yard care, work that families or neighbors might have done in previous times. However, communities like Oak Hammock are expensive and beyond the means of many, if not most, Americans. Less well-off or rural Americans cannot necessarily buy themselves security. Further, purchased services—ties forged solely by money—might offer a false sense of security. What happens when the money runs out? Communities bound by love or mutual affinities might prove more resilient, and I wonder how we can replace the benefits of community connections and obligations without oppressive hierarchies or rules. These questions direct us toward intentional communities.

Be the Change

Communities that practice values such as nonviolence, self-sufficiency, and voluntary simplicity exemplify the quotation popularly attributed to Gandhi: *Be the change you want to see in the world.* For some groups, this phrase means creating and inhabiting a world in which nonviolence, self-sufficiency, equity, and voluntary simplicity function as guiding paradigms. By living as if these values were the norm, community residents become the change they wish to see.

However, it is virtually certain that Gandhi never said those exact words, and no one really knows the exact source of this quotation. Some trace it to Gandhi's grandson, Arun Gandhi, as a distillation of his grandfather's thought, and, at the least, Arun Gandhi has popularized it. "Be the change you want to see in the world" figures prominently on his website, and Arun Gandhi describes his grandfather's advocacy of "being the change" in print and in radio interviews.[7] Over time, Gandhi's words and practices have been condensed into this pithy and engaging phrase that adorns mugs, T-shirts, and posters. For those who seek social change and different ways of living, Gandhi has become an iconic figurehead for nonviolent resistance to social, economic and, more recently, environmental injustices, and being the change has achieved mantra status.

I have found that Gandhi's bundling of values and his attitude of experimentation have deeply influenced residents of intentional communities, whether explicitly or implicitly. The mantra gains popularity, in part, from being linked to Gandhi's name. But Gandhi's social thought and values are reflected and echoed in many other thinkers and activists of the past century. Catholic workers, in particular, cite the influence of Dorothy Day and Peter Maurin, who founded the Catholic Worker Movement in response to the Depression. Peter Maurin's idea of the agronomic university parallels Gandhi's Constructive Program, and these small communities embodied critical linkages between social and ecological sustainability and between nonviolence, equity, and democracy. Henry David Thoreau's civil disobedience and rejection of the banality of suburban life inspire others, many residents have read all of Wendell Berry's works, and others heed calls for peace and nonviolence from Buddhist luminaries Thich Nhat Hanh and the Dalai Lama.

None of the communities I visited adhere to a specific religious tradition, although individuals or families might consider themselves Quaker, Jewish, or Buddhist, for example. Some communities, like Sirius in Shutesbury, Massachusetts, coalesce around personal development and spiritual practices, such as meditation, but have no formal doctrines or requirements regarding belief or participation. Even residents of the Catholic worker houses and farms are not necessarily Catholic—or even Christian, for that matter. Although these communities do not share a common religious or philosophical worldview, as a whole, the groups I visited do desire to create and practice lives that reflect nonviolence, voluntary simplicity, and self-sufficiency.

Many of the people I spoke with identified as either secular or in that nebulous "spiritual" category, and, if Christian, identified with groups such as Quakers, the Catholic Workers Movement, or the Jesus Radicals (http://www.jesusradicals.com/). For residents of these intentional communities in the United States, the bundled values of nonviolence, radical democracy, voluntary simplicity, and self-sufficiency provide a nonreligious—or at least ecumenical—discourse and a vocabulary they use to consider their food and other practices in a moral framework. In particular, their emphasis on nonviolence and service has given these communities a set of tools, practices, and processes to help them think through the balance between community service and the integrity of the individual and a vocabulary for examining the communities themselves.

Community, Regulation, and Autonomy

Although we can approach these communities by exploring their bundled values, we need to think carefully about the practical implications of translating abstract values into specific practices in the minutiae of our daily lives. As the popular saying goes, the devil is in the details, so we must ask what it would mean to eat nonviolently. What do you eat, and who decides what you eat? Further, equity and nonviolence, for example, are social values; that is, they are held by individuals but practiced in a community context. Individuals, for example, rely on larger social and economic systems for their food choices, while eating is generally a social activity. Although luminaries such as Gandhi and the Dalai Lama have inspired many individuals to rethink and change their lives, enacting values such as nonviolence requires more than individual effort. Ushering in a world that takes seriously these values requires community participation. Nonetheless, concepts of communal responsibility and social change often arouse deep suspicion in the United States.

Our highly individualistic US culture values individual initiative and many efforts toward social change, such as recycling, which occur at the individual or family level, are lauded as environmentally friendly behavior, especially when they are voluntary. However, achieving environmentally friendly practices on a broad social scale has proven much more difficult. For example, in some states, public resistance—often sponsored by industry—has derailed efforts to pass container laws or bottle bills that would require a deposit on each beverage container sold. The U.S. Public Interest Research Group (U.S. PIRG) found that "the beverage industry and its representatives spent about $14 million in campaign contributions aimed at defeating a national bottle bill between 1989 and 1994."[8] Interestingly, many people who resent government intrusion into their lives willingly submit to homeowners' associations that strictly regulate choices in house color and landscaping, and many places that resist container laws support government intrusion inside women's bodies. To me, discrepancies such as these reflect a deep ambivalence about community life and social obligations.

The tension between individualism and society has been an enduring factor in American religious and social history. Sociologist Robert Bellah traces this tension to frictions between the individualism of sectarian religion and the communalism of the church. The church demands a social or group orientation, and this orientation is reflected in early American concepts of the *covenant,* in which adherence to group norms allowed individuals to achieve a virtuous existence. *Sects* have emphasized individual freedoms and resistance to church authority, resulting in those who claim to be "spiritual, but not religious." Bellah argues that these historical and contemporary tensions have left us without a language to mediate between extremes of self and social controls, to find opportunities to retain autonomy and, at the same time, value community reciprocities and obligations.[9] The heightened individualism of the United States in religious and social contexts provoked Robert Putnam to write *Bowling Alone: The Collapse and Revival of American Community,* which laments our fraying social connections. The loss of social capital, he argues, threatens our democratic institutions as the ties that bind us become looser and more market driven.[10]

On the other hand, intentional communities illustrate how bundled ideas of nonviolence, radical democracy, voluntary simplicity, and regional self-sufficiency have taken root in the United States, and further that these spaces provide opportunities to create communities of practice around these values. Brian Morton criticizes how quotations from thinkers such as Henry David Thoreau, Nelson Mandela, and Gandhi are "tweaked" and stripped of nuance once they enter popular culture. Gandhi and Mandela both worked for deep social transformation and recognized that social change demands more than individual effort. Yet, Morton argues, as the "bogus quotations" are tweaked, they emerge in the realm of the personal rather than the social, locating responsibility for change in the individual.[11] Intentional communities—those that work for social change—must negotiate the difficult balance between community responsibility and personal autonomy, which is an enormous challenge for us in the United States.

I hoped to find new paradigms for living with each other and upon the earth. I share concerns about our food and how it is produced, finding a balance between personal autonomy and community ties, and our ability to sustain our current practices and lifestyles. These problems require action at the community *and* policy levels; we need to work together to solve these large-scale problems. Small communities occupy a middle space between individuals and the larger body politic, and I wondered what their collaborative experiments in sustainability might teach us.

When the Exotic Becomes Mainstream

When I discuss intentional communities and their goals of voluntary simplicity, radical democracy, and sustainable foods with others, some people immediately dismiss these communities as exotic or unrealistic, and they assume that communities such as Dancing Rabbit and LA Eco-village—with their goals of strong community bonds and sustainable transportation—are irrelevant for the mainstream. Instead, I have found that the goals and dialogues in these communities reflect broad social concerns and debates. The desire for walkable communities, for example, reflects the needs of multiple constituencies. An NPR blog notes that walking preserves mobility and thus prolonged independence for the aging, and journalist Christopher Leinberger writes that walkable and bikable communities have become the most valuable real estate, desired by a broad constituency of Americans.[12] Similarly, developers have responded to public demand for farm-to-table foods by creating "agrihoods," residential neighborhoods centered on working farms. Residents of Agritopia in suburban Phoenix enjoy traditional suburban life paired with the benefits of an on-site CSA and sixteen acres of organic farmland.[13] While Agritopia was the first, at least a dozen more developments like it are under way.

The necessity for strong communities appeared in unexpected places and reinforced my suspicions that intentional communities' experiments are responding to real although sometimes unarticulated needs. My husband Kevin and I anchored our sailboat *KneeDeep* at the Laishley Park Marina in Punta Gorda, Florida, in November 2014. As new sailors, we were eager to learn about marina life from veteran residents and sailors. The small community of "liveaboards" immediately welcomed us and helped us learn the ropes. One evening—without prompting—several residents launched into a discussion about community, and they agreed that tight social ties and community bonds drew them to marina life. One couple noted that they had land and a house nearby, but they felt that life there was isolating in comparison to the marina, where neighbors were only a few feet away. Like residents of communities such as Dancing Rabbit, marina residents must construct some boundaries for privacy because their activities are so transparent to fellow residents, but they crave the conviviality of these close quarters.

While the residents of the Laishley Park Marina are arguably not residents of an intentional community as defined by the FIC, their choices reflect similar choices and trade-offs. These marina residents have consciously traded suburban lifestyles—for many, the American dream—for community and life on the water. To live in this way demands voluntary simplicity—whether or not voluntary simplicity was a driving factor in the initial decision—because living on a boat requires fewer possessions and less consumption. For these residents, the benefits of community and waterfront living outweigh the hardships associated with a less consumerist lifestyle. Similarly, a friend who lives in a beach house on Tybee Island, Georgia, commented that you simply can't have too much stuff if you live at the beach—in his view, a worthy trade-off. Further, practices such as voluntary simplicity present their own rewards, such as a less complicated life, and those secondary rewards reinforce practices in a virtuous circle of sorts. In this sense, practices such as reduced consumption and sustainability emerge as by-products of other life choices.

While intentional communities such as Dancing Rabbit make values such as voluntary simplicity and sustainability central to their existence, these values play a much larger role in the US mainstream than we might suspect, whether they are goals in themselves, as in community for the marina residents, or acceptable trade-offs for benefits such as waterfront living. Intentional communities, though, help us by testing and demonstrating how these values can enrich our lives and communities.

What We Can Learn from Intentional Communities

These communities and their ways of being stress practice over theory or narrative, and this emphasis challenges the assumption that once we get our stories and values straight, people will change their behaviors. My previous book, *Growing Stories from India: Religion and the Fate of Agriculture,* explored stories and narratives about agriculture, asking what narratives have made industrial agriculture seem inevitable and how we can create new agricultural narratives and practices. The question of practice continued to nag me because I knew that translating stories and values into actual practice would be difficult and both geographically and historically contingent. In Florida, I participated in a series of Values to Practice discussions hosted by colleagues Anna Peterson and Les Thiele, who are both theoretically and practically engaged in sustainability, and the discussions made me question the processes and trade-offs inherent in translating values into practice.

Exploring questions of food and nonviolence helped me understand how these communities practice their values. Ethical food practices are central to all the intentional communities I have visited, and residents have made deliberate choices about their food and its sources. We all make food choices on a daily basis, and choosing organic or local food alternatives is easier than making changes in areas such as housing or transportation. Residents of the communities I visited question the dominant narrative of what constitutes good food and what our responsibilities are regarding food production. Their participatory decision-making models demonstrate reflexive processes in which residents continually consider and assess how values such as regional self-sufficiency, voluntary simplicity, and nonviolence apply to contemporary dilemmas and demonstrate alternatives to the individualism of US society. I saw experiments—and residents consciously articulate their work as experimental—in radical, values-based democracies that are testing different ways of relating to other people and the earth.

The emphasis on radical democracy helps to alleviate concerns raised by scholars such as sociologists Melanie DuPuis and David Goodman that a "romanticization of community" obscures existing oppressive hierarchies.[14] Many people have found small towns or traditional communities suffocating and have fled to perceived opportunities in urban regions. Further, community bonds can reinforce gender, race, or class hierarchies that newer intentional communities seek to erase or transcend. Most people also resent being told what to do, and imposing rules can incite rebellion—even when we agree with the principles. So, our attitudes toward community waver between romance and suspicion, yet the lack of community ties leaves many adrift and seeking connections.

Anthropologist Joshua Lockyer argues that contemporary intentional communities have learned important lessons from past communities that tended toward autocracy or chaos and have developed robust systems of shared governance.[15] These lessons rebut criticisms that these communities are simply recycling the ideologies and experience of the 1960s. While contemporary communards might appreciate the openness and revolutionary freedom associated with the 1960s, newer communities—and older communities such as the Farm and Twin Oaks, which have restructured in response to social and financial challenges—have drawn on their collective experience and demonstrate innovative solutions to contemporary challenges in areas such as food production and energy usage. In experimenting with innovative and integrated forms of governance, sustainable agriculture, and religious practice, residents are reenvisioning how we might relate to biotic and human communities and demonstrating how these relations within small communities contribute to broader social change.

Melanie DuPuis and David Goodman's concerns about romanticizing community echo those raised by geographer Emma Mawdsley and sociologist Meera Nanda that communities rethinking and reviving forms of agrarianism are "facing backwards" towards a romanticized past.[16] Nanda's *Prophets Facing Backward* reiterates criticisms of sustainability-focused intentional communities that I have heard many times. Invariably, when I give a talk or otherwise discuss my research, someone points out that "we can't—or shouldn't—live in the past," as if reviving and adapting seeds and skills is somehow taking us back to a dismal and bleak past. Envisioning a drudgery-filled life, devoid of comfort and technologies such as iPads and Twitter, they want no part of this life. Ironically, such critics point to a significant contribution of these communities—they focus on the world they desire instead of simply criticizing what exists. These communities are not nostalgic for a premodern utopia, nor do they seek to reclaim a romanticized past. Instead, they draw on historical strengths to negotiate innovative responses to contemporary crises.

Most important, these communities demonstrate that the seemingly impossible might indeed be possible—that is, it is realizable to be the change. One mother raising her children in a Catholic worker house commented that people have told her that her life is "utopian," suggesting that her lifestyle is idealistic and out of reach. Her response: "It is not utopian; it's my life." She is indeed being the change. This conversation reminded me of remarks people have made to me about activities such as commuting by bicycle: "You're so good" or "I wish I could do that," implying that such activities are unattainable or unrealistic for the average person. For many people, once they actually try bicycling to work or vegetable gardening, they realize that it is not only doable but also enjoyable. Intentional communities live these so-called utopian experiments and demonstrate practical and lived responses to current questions.

Reskilling, Regulation, and Risk

Most of the communities I visited are consciously reviving and teaching traditional practices, such as canning, grafting, animal husbandry, and construction, which contribute to self-sufficiency. However, they are rethinking and refining these skills in the context of contemporary needs and resources. Some construction skills, for example, have become the province of the working class, so this reskilling represents technology transfer from the working class to the middle class, since a significant portion of intentional community residents hail from the latter. Economists have deemed this class-segregated specialization of skills efficient, but I wonder whether everyone shouldn't possess basic survival skills in building and agriculture. To me, such skills represent an important measure of personal and regional security.

This reskilling fosters resiliency as more people both know and adapt basic skills. The revival of older skills is not a one-way ticket to a low-tech past, but a means to rethink how and why we need certain technologies. What does this revival do for us? Choosing low-input technologies echoes Gandhi and Wendell Berry's pleas for appropriate technologies.[17] At Dancing Rabbit, residents' lives and language critique the paradigms of modernity, such as reliance on the power grid, so their wind turbines power up their network and enable them to communicate and exchange ideas over the Internet. Both Dancing Rabbit and the Possibility Alliance struggle to determine what technologies are useful, appropriate, and equitable, and their experiments provide a public vocabulary with which to discuss and critique individualism, hidden forms of violence, and unbridled consumption.

Reskilling, in the context of the desire for self-sufficiency and personal autonomy, resonates deeply with North American values of independence and a bootstraps mentality, the idea that each one of us should be capable of taking care of our own material needs. Many people want to learn—or are learning—building, preserving, and farming skills that might provide even a small measure of self-sufficiency. I wonder, though, about the extent to which these activities impose risk on others and what reskilling says about attitudes toward regulation.

In addition to gardening, I have also learned to can jams and some vegetables. At this point, I feel confident canning high-acid and high-sugar foods, such as pickles and jams, because they are far less likely to become hosts for botulism. After I had been canning jams for several years, my friend Janet and I attended a public canning workshop in Gainesville presented by the

University of Florida/Alachua County Institute for Food and Agricultural Science (IFAS) extension office. To a crowd of approximately forty people, mostly women, the presenter illustrated the basics of canning as well as the associated risks when done improperly. To emphasize the importance of proper technique, our instructor led us through a call and response of what to do and what not to do. She reminded us—several times—that many people have died from poorly canned food, foods like green beans that we tend to consider safe and healthy. Although Janet and I both took canning seriously before this workshop, we left apprehensive (if not terror-stricken) about what could go wrong. Consequently, because low-acid and low-sugar foods such as green beans are more prone to botulism and require pressure-canning methods, I am not willing to take this risk.

Activities such as canning and construction carry a certain amount of risk to the actor and others who might not realize the risk they have assumed. Despite the emphasis on individualism in the United States, we are a risk-averse nation and have created pages upon pages of rules, codes, and regulations to control our food and our buildings. Current arguments about raw milk, for example, demonstrate both our ambivalence about regulations and that debates about issues such as food and building regulations cut across the political and ideological spectrums. In May 2013, raw milk producer Vernon Hershberger was acquitted of three of four charges of violating Wisconsin's food and dairy codes, an acquittal that Farm-to-Consumer Legal Defense Fund vice president Elizabeth Rich called a victory for the food rights movement.[18] Fundamentally, the raw milk issue centers on rights to privately sell and distribute food without government interference.

When I go to the Gainesville Farmers Market, I buy acorn-finished hog sausage from Live Oak, Florida, well aware that "acorn-finished" is a fancy code for the (tasty) feral hogs that plague north Florida. I also thoroughly enjoy the goat cheese that is designated for pet consumption only, and I do not share it with my cats. Most consumers seem to agree—in practice, anyway—on the importance of small-scale business and local markets and the freedom to eat and produce foods. In 2011, Florida passed the Cottage Food Act, which allows small businesses to sell low-risk foods (such as jams, pastas, and cookies) with fewer licensing requirements that those required for higher-risk foods (for example, meats and dairy products).

While we want the freedom to eat, produce, and sell local foods such as jams, cheeses, and sausage, we also want to be safe from contaminated food. So how do we balance between freedom and safety, and who decides? Some of our decisions must come down to our trust in and knowledge about the producers, a feat that is far easier in smaller communities and localized economies. While I know and trust Stephanie Hamblen, who owns the (now legal) Illegal Jam Company, I am less familiar with food entrepreneurs from farther away and am not in a position to assess their work. Several years ago, a locally sourced meal that several of us ate resulted in a 4:00 a.m. race through Gainesville to take Kevin to the ER. Although we later concluded that he had a little-known tick and meat allergy, the experience made me wonder how much we can ever know about the sources of our food.

My interest in canning and desire for safe and local food point to widely held and complicated concerns about the safety of our food supply and what some consider to be misplaced nostalgia. Our canning instructor repeatedly reminded us that many people have died or become seriously ill from poorly canned foods: poorly processed green beans become poison, despite their nutritional content. Industrial canning and freezing technologies have given us both safe foods and varieties of foods that even my parents could not imagine as children—year-round strawberries. Nostalgia for repetitive and sometimes toxic diets of yore would be misplaced; even though Kevin and I mostly eat seasonally available foods, I appreciate the newer varieties of foods that I can both grow and buy from our farmers' market. Despite the massive economic and environmental failures of industrial agriculture, it's true that fewer people die from poorly canned green beans today. On the other hand, massive recalls of peanut butter, meat pumped full of antibiotics and hormones, and pesticide-laden vegetables point to very real concerns about the safety of our industrial food supply. Along with residents of intentional communities and fellow members of Grow Gainesville, I seek the middle path: I am not nostalgic for my grandmother's childhood diet nor do I wish to remain trapped in a highly centralized and toxic industrial agricultural system. Instead, I prefer to "face forward" to a decentralized and flexible food system that is responsive to my specific bioregion and that draws upon past wisdom yet embraces innovation and creativity.

Small economies and intentional communities experiment with new or revived modes of production. At the same time, they must be accountable for their products, so must find a balance between the freedom to produce and food safety regulations. Many intentional communities—now and historically—have supported themselves with micro-industries and have created their own physical infrastructures, and today exist as test beds for accommodations between safety regulations and the freedom to produce. Intentional communities and localized economies offer levels of trust and accountability that small towns have historically provided because, in small and localized economies, residents generally knew all links of production. Today's highly efficient and centralized agribusiness supply chains have made it much more difficult to trace food contamination. Similarly, small communities encourage accountability because the victims would be your neighbors rather than faceless statistics. Many residents of intentional communities share our general ambivalence about regulations; they, too, want both safety and the freedom to choose. However, their small size and emphasis on participatory democracy provide them the opportunity to confront this dilemma directly.

Few people are likely to pick up and move to an intentional community, whether urban or rural, but, as test sites or social laboratories, they can stimulate us to imagine different ways things could be. Further, they can draw attention to regulations that need to be updated, such as restrictions on cottage food industries. These small, cohesive communities provide a lens into the performance of social change, and their experiments demonstrate alternatives enacted in specific contexts and geographies. Since they are willing to engage in and demonstrate the complicated and messy processes by which residents translate abstract ideals into specific practices, including governance, food, structures, and communication, intentional communities have much to teach us about nonviolence, voluntary simplicity, and civic engagement.[19]

Transplanting the Seeds

As I spent time in different communities, participating in activities and engaging in wide-ranging conversations, I continually wondered how I could bring home what I was learning. Living out values requires trade-offs, and residents in the communities I visited had to decide how to interpret and enact their values in the context of their geographic, cultural, and ethical frameworks. Nonetheless, I had taken to heart their integrated approach to nonviolence, self-sufficiency, and voluntary simplicity and recognized possibilities for those of us in cities and suburbs. Like writer David Leach, I also "aspire to live more intentionally" within my own community: "I realize that maybe I don't need to sell my house, flee the city again, and live off the grid to save the planet. I belong to the 99%—the vast majority who make our homes in communities more conventional than a commune, an ecovillage, or cohousing."[20]

I attended a workshop led by Leach where we brainstormed about how we could make our suburbs more sustainable and community oriented. In groups of six, we first listed existing resources, such as libraries, bike trails, and green space, and then discussed possible retrofits, such as linking neighborhoods and tool-lending libraries. I think the potential of the suburbs surprised all of us.

Even though I love Dancing Rabbit, I am not ready to leave Florida—and my job—and move back to the cold Midwest. Nor am I ready, at this stage of my life, to live in an intentional community, but I wonder whether there are ways to do both: to enjoy community benefits and maintain an independent home. As I stated in my letters of introduction to the communities, I was not seeking to join one of them, but rather to learn more about them and how I might live out some of these ideals at home. Gainesville already boasts many innovative programs, ideas, and communities that draw upon values of sustainability, nonviolence, and voluntary simplicity.

In my visits, residents asked me about Gainesville, what sort of city it is and what opportunities already exist there. Gainesville hosts the University of Florida (UF) and Santa Fe College. Like places such as Madison, Wisconsin; Asheville, North Carolina; and Portland, Oregon, cars in Gainesville sport bumper stickers like *Be the Change* and *If anything can go well, it will* because students and residents of Gainesville tend to be conversant in the language of social change. Gainesville sustains organizations, neighborhoods, and communities that reflect this constellation of Gandhian values, including the Civic Media Center and the River Phoenix Center for Peacemaking. Gainesville's many religious organizations, churches, temples, synagogues, and mosques organize food- and justice-related programs. For instance, members of UF's Muslim Student Association feed the homeless in downtown's Bo Diddly Plaza.

With visions of New York's SoHo, property owner Chris Fillie spurred an arts and micro-industry renaissance in SoDo (south of downtown), a slightly rundown Gainesville neighborhood.[21] He established Porters Community Farm in the adjacent Porters neighborhood to showcase sustainability and urban agriculture with the help of the Florida Organic Growers and the Food Sovereignty Solidarity Working Group of Gainesville.[22] Fillie drew on existing grassroots networks in this area, efforts that reflect local initiative, unlike the high-end city and university-sponsored Innovation Hub several blocks to the north. In 2015, two artists opened the SoMa Art Media Hub to facilitate collaboration between local artists, and the nearby First Magnitude Brewing Company has become a community gathering spot.

The Citizen's Co-op, a community-owned market that opened in 2011, partners with Blue Oven Kitchens, a nonprofit, certified, commercial kitchen and kitchen incubator, and is dedicated to a "whole-system approach to the sustainable growth of the North Central Florida food system."[23] Nearby, the well-established Civic Media Center and Library serves as an "alternative library, reading room, and infoshop for activists working to create more just and sustainable communities."[24] The more recently founded River Phoenix Center for Peacemaking runs programs that help participants heal from violence and establish pathways for nonviolent communications (NVC) among groups and individuals. For example, in January 2013, I participated in a two-day NVC seminar that taught and reinforced communications skills that have proven critical in the success of groups such as Dancing Rabbit. Not surprisingly, several of the NVC participants had been or were living in an intentional community, and one participant, Mary Aplin, was in the process of creating a cohousing community in Gainesville. Speaking with them reinforced what I had learned in my visits: the bundling of the values demonstrated by Gandhi has proven potent.

Meeting participants in the NVC seminar demonstrated one instance of how new ideas circulate among people and communities. In the NVC workshop, those experienced in intentional communities shared their insights with the rest of us and advised Aplin about establishing Gainesville Cohousing (http://www.gainesvillecohousing.org/). As I witnessed how ideas are shared and adapted, I realized that I could contribute to the tradition of spreading ideas among communities and beyond.

Ina May Gaskin of the Farm, for example, helped mainstream midwifery and home births in the United States. In 1971, Ina May and Stephen Gaskin drove from California to Tennessee to establish the Farm, an intentional community that fits many stereotypes of the communes of the 1970s.[25] Gaskin believed that birth should be a "sacrament" and, without formal training, she and five other women began a midwifery practice. In 2011, she won the Right Livelihood Award for her "work teaching and advocating safe, woman-centered childbirth methods," and midwives are now a routine choice for many women.[26] Similarly, Belfast relies upon the expertise and collective wisdom of the now-adult children of intentional communities and homesteads established in the 1960s and 1970s who now run organic farms and CSAs.

Dancing Rabbit cofounder Cecil Scheib provides a contemporary case in point of this iterative circle of feedback and circulating ideas. After living in Dancing Rabbit for fifteen years, he moved to New York City in 2007 to become the director of energy and sustainability at New York University (NYU). In 2012, Scheib left NYU for the Urban Green Council to improve New York City's sustainability efforts. The alumni magazines of both NYU and Stanford University, Scheib's alma mater, featured his work in sustainability at Dancing Rabbit and NYU, which illustrated concepts of energy conservation and their practical applications to hundreds of thousands of alums, students, and their parents. Both magazines credited Scheib with massive energy savings for NYU and New York City, the equivalent of "taking 25,000 New York City homes off the grid for a year," according to NYU's publication, and both magazines note that Scheib's impact extends far beyond NYU.[27] In a 2014 visit to Dancing Rabbit, Scheib, now a Dancing Rabbit board member, credited Dancing Rabbit with providing him the credibility and practical foundation to bring his work to a larger, more mainstream arena.[28] Additionally, Scheib's work—and the work of other previous Rabbits—provides feedback and inspiration for current Rabbits.

The dialectical process of circulation and assessment generates innovations built around alternative forms of communities. The Transition Network founded by Rob Hopkins and Naresh Giangrande of the United Kingdom, for example, helps towns resiliently transition to reduced fossil fuel usage. While the focus is not residential per se, the Transition Network's approach recognizes the necessity of collective action. In 2010, Micanopy, Florida, a small rural town ten miles south of Gainesville and the location of the 1991 film *Doc Hollywood*, became the sixtieth Transition Town in the United States and the first in Florida. According to the Transition Micanopy website,

> It all starts off when a small collection of motivated individuals within a community come together with a shared concern: *how can our community respond to the challenges, and opportunities, of Peak Oil and Climate Change?* The Transition Towns website admits: "We truly don't know if this will work. Transition is a social experiment on a massive scale. What we are convinced of is this: if we wait for the governments, it'll be too little, too late; if we act as individuals, it'll be too little; but if we act as communities, it might just be enough, just in time." It's hard to imagine a more visionary yet practical approach to the dire challenges that face us in the years ahead.[29]

Micanopy has emphasized food and agriculture, hosting permaculture and reskilling workshops and partnering with groups such as the Co-op and Blue Oven Kitchen in Gainesville.

Similar to Transition Towns, Resilience Circles, also known as Common

Security Clubs, demonstrate yet another form of nonresidential intentional community that has arisen in response to economic insecurity, environmental concerns, and the fraying of social ties.[30] According to the Resilience Circle website, "Resilience Circles are small groups of 10–20 where people come together to increase their personal security through learning, mutual aid, social action, and community support." The instability and fears spawned by the 2008 Great Recession prompted these groups to form and provide emotional—and sometimes financial—support for members. One group, called the "Neighbors," composed mostly of women over sixty, formed prior to the Common Security Clubs in response to climate change, but today they provide support when members are ill and share skills and goods.[31]

I was familiar with Sarah Susanka and Kira Obolensky's book, *The Not So Big House,* which illustrates comfortable, cozy, and efficient homes. Instead of featuring large but useless spaces like big entryways, Susanka and Obolensky focus on warmth and connection and building features such as reading nooks. Similarly, the Tiny House Movement advocates "smaller spaces and simplified living" in homes of one hundred to four hundred square feet, as opposed to the typical American home of twenty-six hundred square feet.[32]

I came across the concept of pocket neighborhoods in architect Ross Chapin and Sarah Susanka's coffee-table book, *Pocket Neighborhoods,* while perusing the library at LA Eco-village. Susanka's foreword to *Pocket Neighborhoods* suggested that the characteristics of her not-so-big houses could be scaled up to neighborhoods. The book beautifully illustrates the possibilities for neighborhood enclaves as small as four or six houses.[33] According to Chapin's pocket neighborhoods website, pocket neighborhoods

> are clustered groups of neighboring houses or apartments gathered around a shared open space—a garden courtyard, a pedestrian street, a series of joined backyards, or a reclaimed alley—all of which have a clear sense of territory and shared stewardship.
>
> They can be in urban, suburban or rural areas. These are settings where nearby neighbors can easily know one another, where empty nesters and single householders with far-flung families can find friendship or a helping hand nearby, and where children can have shirttail aunties and uncles just beyond their front gate.[34]

These neighborhoods-within-neighborhoods help foster community while preserving privacy, offering an important middle ground. Many times I have joked with friends about all of us living in the same neighborhood, sharing gardens, but occupying separate houses: the concept of pocket neighborhoods gives me a name for this idea. In fact, because not everyone is in a position to move, the authors of "What Are the Boundaries of an Intentional Community?" consider the potential of a geographically dispersed but virtually connected community.[35] This idea takes on an even greater significance for me as my friends and I confront the challenges of aging. We wonder whether we could "age in place" as a group, retaining our privacy but sharing some services and appreciating the safety and security of nearby friends.

I visited most of these communities several times, and in each visit I saw them growing and moving closer to their goals of sustainability and nonviolence. Growth inevitably brings new challenges. For example, Dancing Rabbit has had to balance rapid growth with upholding its core mission, yet the residents' struggles hold lessons for us as they demonstrate their choices and the necessary trade-offs in deciding what to build and what to plant. The residents of these communities have sought to incorporate abstract values into the fabric of their lives and communities. With an eye to the future, they also draw on the experiences of the communities and homesteaders who have gone before.

2

Standing on the Shoulders of Giants

Gandhi said we needed a million experiments in nonviolent living so someone might figure it out.
—Ethan Hughes, Possibility Alliance

SINCE ITS FOUNDING, in part, by members of religious communities like the Quakers seeking freedom from oppression, the United States has long served as a safe haven and testing ground for individuals and intentional communities seeking to create alternatives to existing social, economic, and ecological lifeways. Writing about the communes of the 1960s, religious studies scholar Timothy Miller states that "much of what the public at large (and sometimes the communards themselves) regarded as new and sometimes shocking about 1960s communal life was not new at all, but merely a recapitulation of themes that had long danced across the American communal stage. The youth of the 1960s were not the first to be infected with back-to-the-land romanticism; in fact that theme has been a major American communal staple."[1]

Intentional communities demonstrate a confluence of old and new, originality and recapitulation in that they continually revisit American themes of self-reliance within the context of their specific temporal, spatial, and cultural geographies, so that they are at once novel and traditional. Contemporary environments—physical, social, and economic—make these communities unique and particular to our times, but we can trace threads of continuity to earlier individuals and communities that have provided lessons and inspiration.

Contemporary intentional communities rest on the shoulders of giants, including the long history of US intentional communities from the Shakers to the communes of the 1970s, homesteading gurus Helen and

Scott Nearing, and individuals such as Gandhi, Dorothy Day, and Wendell Berry. The FIC has a large database, including its own Wiki site, to help communities share ideas and expertise (http://wiki.ic.org/) about topics such as governance, finance, and conflict resolution that can lead to success or reduce chances of failure. Further, a number of books illustrate the goals, successes, and pitfalls of other communities. For example, Twin Oaks cofounder Kat Kinkade's *Is It Utopia Yet? An Insider's View of Twin Oaks Community in Its Twenty-Sixth Year;* Ecovillage at Ithaca cofounder Liz Walker's *Ecovillage at Ithaca: Pioneering a Sustainable Culture;* and Dancing Rabbit resident Ma'ikwe Schaub Ludwig's *Passion as Big as a Planet: Evolving Eco-Activism in America* illustrate how these communities have negotiated these topics in their own specific contexts.

Most communities draw from multiple sources. Even Catholic workers look to a range of thinkers and doers beyond Dorothy Day and Peter Maurin. Alan Keitt of Cobb Hill, a cohousing community in Vermont, cited a range of sources: "It's a little bit of fertilization. Dana Meadows was one of the bees, and the Leopolds were a pervasive influence due to family connections in Madison. Meeting Thomas Berry and Miriam McGillis was another huge influence. So you get little grains of pollen when you rub up against people."

An eclectic range of sources and inspirations has helped these communities create resilient social, communications, and governance structures, learning lessons from the past while continuing to question both past and present practices. Nonetheless, contemporary communities must address lingering suspicions about communal movements fostered by the cult controversies of the 1970s.

Ghosts of the 1970s

Writing about intentional communities in Vermont, journalist Katherine Flagg illustrates concerns that met the founders of Cobb Hill: "When participants in Cobb Hill Cohousing approached the town of Hartland with their plan, they faced questions such as 'Do you wear robes?' and concerns about potential secret ceremonies in the woods. (For the record, they don't appear to engage in either practice.) When the group of idealistic young people behind Blue Moon Cooperative approached the town of Strafford in the 1980s, they had to convince town officials they wouldn't be a repeat of an actual commune that preceded them there in the 1960s."[2]

Despite their best efforts, intentional communities still swim upstream against the ghosts of the 1970s, when fears about cults and communes were rampant. When I was a teenager in 1970s suburban New York, my parents and teachers repeatedly warned us about cults, and we heard endlessly about indoctrination and deprogrammers. My friends and I dared ourselves to peek into the gated estate of the Reverend Sun Myung Moon—home of the Moonies—in Tarrytown, pleasantly terrified that we might be grabbed and indoctrinated, yet both my brother and I went to school with Moon's children. We also dodged the Hare Krishnas selling flowers and copies of the *Bhagavad-Gita* in Grand Central Station, more bemused than scared.

Intentional communities, new religious movements (NRM), and communes proliferated in the 1960s and 1970s, in part due to the large population of youth seeking alternatives to the perceived conformities of the 1950s. Some religious groups, such as ISKCON (the International Society for Krishna Consciousness) and the Moonies, were described as cults, especially in the media. In the context of the 1960s and beyond, the term *cult* was typically applied to groups that were insular, had a charismatic leader, advocated beliefs and practices far outside of the American Judeo-Christian mainstream, and encouraged members to break relationships with outsiders.

The FIC recognizes that intentional communities frequently become embroiled in the controversy over cult because these communities, like cults, question mainstream values and propose alternatives to existing lifeways. Yet many of the markers used to identify cults are overly general. According to the FIC Wiki page on cults and intentional communities:

> People who see "cults" as a major social menace often draw up lists of generalizations by which a savvy observer should be able to identify evil groups. The problem is that the items on those lists almost always apply just as fully to good, healthy groups as to problematic ones. Consider these items from the typical cult-hazard list:
> - "A 'cult' has a strong, powerful, dominant leader." But that doesn't identify inherently dangerous situations. Alan Greenspan, the head of the Federal Reserve System, is enormously powerful and makes decisions that deeply affect the lives of all of us, so is he automatically a "cult leader"?
> - "'Cult' members often cut off ties with their birth families and old friends in favor of total dedication to the 'cult.'" Actually,

that's just what Jesus advised his followers to do; see Matthew 19:29 and Luke 14:26.[3]

The article goes on to suggest that instead of relying on generalized markers, we should use common sense, trust our instincts, and keep our options open.

Fundamentally, the distinction is not so much theological but instead revolves around questions of leadership, democracy, and transparency. For instance, consider whether residents are expected to follow a leader, or a small group of leaders, without question, and how the group is governed. Anthropologist Margaret Hollenbach gives a pragmatic perspective. In 1970 she joined a commune, the Family. She eventually left the group and recounted her experiences in her book *Lost and Found: My Life in a Group Marriage Commune*. For her, defining whether the group is or was a cult is far less important than asking, "How closed is the group?" and "How easy is it to leave the group?"[4] Groups that encourage residents to cut off ties with family and friends or those that purport to have all the answers often pose a danger to participants. Consider the mass suicides of members of the People's Temple and Heaven's Gate, whose leaders were obeyed without question.

Intentional community expert Diana Leafe Christian addressed the cult question in her book *Finding Community*. Sixth on her list of the "Ten Most Common Fears about Joining a Community" is "I don't want to live in a hierarchical system or follow a charismatic leader," and seventh is "I don't want to have to think like everybody else. What if it turns out to be a cult?" She addresses fears regarding mind control, charismatic leaders, and governance and cites the FIC's webpage demonstrating that, in 2006, over two-thirds of the communities listed had democratic governance systems. Moreover, few communities have conformist "hive mind," but instead are open to incorporating a wide range of ideas and practices. Christian continues, citing Tim Miller and the FIC's assertion that the word *cult* is not helpful because labeling a group a cult has become shorthand for either "not liking or not understanding a group's practice or behavior." For this reason, religious studies scholars have largely abandoned the term and instead use NRM language. Ultimately, both Christian and the FIC encourage people to avoid the ambiguous word *cult* and use straightforward descriptive language instead; for example, if a group is "lying, manipulative, emotionally abusive," describe it as such.[5]

The intentional communities I have explored have not cut themselves off from broader society, but instead actively engage with their neighbors and others. These communities emphasize shared governance and transparency, and their experiments generally aim to increase civic engagement, not reduce it. Nonetheless, no community is perfect, and individual perceptions of a group and its policies vary. As the FIC states, "People have different needs. One person's great communitarian or religious experience can be another's worst nightmare."[6] Some people migrate in and out of communities at different periods of their lives, depending on their needs at the time. For example, baby boomers who experimented with community life in their youth, especially women, as they age now seek out the social life and assistance that different forms of community offer.

Rethinking Success and Failure

Thousands of intentional communities and homesteaders have come and gone, prompting accusations of failure, but communities disband for many reasons, including economic failure, poor governance, and personal conflicts. In *An Unconventional Journey: The Story of High Wind from Vision to Community to Eco-Neighborhood,* Lisa Paulson narrates a painfully honest account of High Wind's thirty-year lifespan, from idea to dissolution. A 1976 visit to the Findhorn Community in Scotland inspired cofounder Lisa Paulson to develop sustainable living patterns in Wisconsin. Lisa and Belden Paulson received a $25,000 grant from the US Department of Energy to build an experimental passive solar bioshelter. Volunteers appeared to help build the structure, and in time, the Beldens realized that they had become—unintentionally—an intentional community. The group subsequently developed social and governance structures. In 1991, in response to internal pressures and increasing numbers of visitors, High Wind disbanded as an intentional community and relabeled itself an ecological neighborhood.[7] The new community founded an affiliate group, the Plymouth Institute, which continued outreach and began subscription farming, feeding over eight hundred families in the greater Milwaukee area.

The Paulsons established High Wind because they wanted to test and demonstrate sustainable living concepts to US residents. They did so as streams of visitors arrived at their doorstep to learn about the community, and they continued to educate the public after they transitioned to an eco-neighborhood through the Plymouth Institute. Was High Wind a success?

If longevity is the sole criterion, then High Wind failed as a community. The founders intended, however, to introduce sustainable living to the United States, and they succeeded in educating large numbers of visitors about sustainable building. High Wind and similar communities, regardless of their longevity, have prompted the circulation of new ideas and alternatives so that their influence extends far beyond their walls, which could be viewed as a marker of success.

Writing about Catholic worker communities, which tend to come and go according to local needs, sociologist Paul Stock suggests that the language of process and context can help us rethink criteria for success and failure.[8] Intentional communities arise in response to contemporary social issues, and needs change over time. Asking why communities fail or cease to exist, perhaps because of personality conflicts or poor locations, offers insight into the historical, social, and economic conditions of these communities and the usefulness of their experiments.

Scholars and community residents themselves have noted that intentional communities function as social laboratories that test new ideas and innovations. Media specialist and resident of multiple intentional communities Jesse Drew argues that "communes and collectives provided the critical mass, the people power, and the collective wisdom to test out ideas in practice, not just in theory."[9] What happens to these ideas next? These communities are educational and demonstration sites, and many visitors, both short- and long-term, come seeking ideas and inspiration to take home. For instance, I ate breakfast at Dancing Rabbit one morning with a young mother from a small, rural town outside St. Louis who wanted to start a co-op selling organic foods. She stayed overnight at the Milkweed Mercantile, Dancing Rabbit's bed and breakfast, to see what she could learn about the community and the process of owning a store. Those of us at the table brainstormed with her about getting support in her hometown, and she left with a number of concrete ideas.

The constant interactive flow of residents, visitors, and guests creates a dialectic in which ideas circulate, both online and in person, and people can adapt and transform concepts according to their specific circumstances. These ongoing relations can help us reevaluate what might constitute success or failure for intentional communities. For example, the average stay in an intentional community is four years, a relatively short period. Some intentional communities disband after as little as one year, although others can last for as long as twenty-five years. If longevity represents the primary measure of success, often intentional communities can be characterized as utopian failures.[10] However, perhaps a more appropriate measure might be the flow of ideas and what these communities have taught us.

Lessons Learned from the Farm

The Farm in Summertown, Tennessee, is one of the best-known intentional communities, and its experiments continue to provide important lessons for other such communities and those interested in alternative lifestyles. The Farm began in 1971 when people in a caravan of sixty buses and other vehicles arrived in Tennessee, purchased land, and began building. From 1968 to 1970, San Francisco State University English professor Stephen Gaskin had been teaching "Monday Night Class," whose participants created the Farm's philosophical underpinnings encoded in "agreements."[11] The agreements included nonviolence, vegetarianism, no social hierarchy, and voluntary poverty. The Farm functioned as a commune for thirteen years.

From 1975 to 1980, approximately fourteen hundred people lived at the Farm, and the large numbers sometimes strained residents' abilities to follow the original agreements:

> During the years of peak population, the middle to late 1970s, most houses, some of which were customized tents, had four or more families, i.e. couples with two to four children, a few single men and women, a single mother or two, some with several kids, maybe an "adopted" teen-ager.
>
> Living with that many people was, to put it mildly, intense; but then add in no electricity; a sporadic running water situation, no flush toilets, meals for forty having to appear from "scratch" three times a day and whew, it could tend to the stressful and no-fun side of the meter. But when it was working it was like an adrenaline rush, manic gleams in our eyes sharing a secret—This is a blast![12]

Rupert Fike's *Voices from the Farm: Adventures in Community Living* is a collection of vignettes like this one that illustrate life at the Farm from its inception to its later reorganization. It is striking how well the Farm functioned, given the large numbers of well-intentioned but untrained youth who built and governed the community and provided a range of social services to those in need. In 1983, under financial and social pressures, the

Farm reorganized as a cooperative, required $100 per month rent, and gave residents a choice between simple membership or participation in the Second Foundation, a 501(d)3 communal society. Legally, income-sharing communities are structured as "apostolic communities," a 501(d)3 category the IRS formed to accommodate monastic organizations.

The Farm as a community is especially important because it paved the way for the communities that exist today. Twin Oaks Communities Conference speaker Lyle Estill, founder of Piedmont Biofuels and author of *Small Is Possible: Life in a Local Economy*, commented that there is a "huge heart feeling for the Farm" because it has been a beacon of possibility for other communities, both in its original intention and its adaptation to current circumstances. The Farm and the other communes of the 1970s instruct us about a host of issues, including the need for transparent governance, planning, and membership policies.

For some, it is heartbreaking that only a tiny core of income-sharing communards remain at the Farm, and the predominance of penny loafers over bare feet speaks volumes about changes in the Farm's demographics. While some lament the Farm's socioeconomic changes, the community has adapted to contemporary challenges and now thrives, albeit in a different manifestation. In a presentation to the International Communal Studies Association, Farm resident Albert Bates discussed the Farm's transition to an ecovillage in the 1990s. In 1993, residents created the Farm Ecovillage Training Center, which hosts courses in permaculture, alternative methods of ecological construction, midwifery and health care, and sustainable forestry. These courses provide income for the community and employment for the Farm's young adults. The ecovillage also addresses a social problem posed by Bates: how does one keep a twenty-year-old interested in a community that was based in the values and symbols of the hippie cultural milieu of the 1960s?[13] While not all residents applaud the Farm's changes, the transition to ecovillage has brought vitality and financial stability to the Farm, and its continuing evolution demonstrates resilience and the ability to meet new challenges. As such, the Farm continues to be a model to other communities.

Building Social Capital

The presence of homesteaders or residents of older communities—even if those communities have disbanded—provide social capital for new communities. First, older communities and homesteaders offer friendly networks for services and goods, and second, many previous communities have demonstrated that intentional communities can be valued neighbors. Belfast reaped the benefits of the 1970s back-to-the-land movement when hippies and college students flocked to Maine, drawn by the ecology movement and Scott and Helen Nearing. The Nearings homesteaded and lived off the land in rural Vermont during the 1930s and 1940s. They chronicled their homesteading experiments in *Living the Good Life: How to Live Simply and Sanely in a Troubled World* and many other publications, and the example of their lives drew a new generation of homesteaders to the rural Northeast in the late 1960s and early 1970s. Their experiments in homesteading illustrated how individuals and families could *live* their dissent from US consumer culture.[14] Many of the homesteaders' children remained in the area, a receptive audience for yet another generation of homesteaders and communards.

Coleen O'Connell of Belfast Cohousing and Ecovillage in Belfast, Maine, noted how previous generations of homesteaders and intentional communities created the social capital that allows Belfast to thrive:

> This area of mid-coast Maine around Belfast had about ten hippie communes in the early seventies and late sixties. They would come up and buy a hundred acres, or their families would have a hundred acres and a farmhouse they had owned forever. The young college kids would come up, take over, and live there, raising their own food with *Mother Earth News*.
>
> That community of aging hippies is still here. They raised their kids here, and the kids grew up. Some of them are running CSA farms. The communes broke up, but many of the residents are here. Their children grew up here and started the farmers' markets and the Belfast Co-op, the first co-op in the state in 1973. The Co-op is a third space. If you want to meet somebody, they'll say, "I'll see you at the co-op." This town has attracted agriculturally focused, grow-your-own, self-sustaining people. That was why I moved here.

Belfast area residents, often the children of the 1970s homesteaders and communards, established farmers' markets, the co-op, and local dairies, all of which attract like-minded newcomers and provide them with a socioeconomic infrastructure and moral support.

The previous generation of homesteaders and communards—and their children—began what we might call a virtuous circle, in which existing people, goods, and services encourage individuals to create new businesses and services that, in turn, draw a new generation, excited by the promise of living off the land. When I walked through downtown Belfast early one morning in June, I saw numerous storefronts that embodied this spirit, including an artists' cooperative and the Green Store, a "general store for the twenty-first century." O'Connell continued: "This area is ripe with a generation and now a second generation of people. We have all these young, young farmers coming down and young couples with babies. It's the second wave of the back-to-the-land."

Maine Organic Farmers and Gardeners Association (MOGFA, http://www.mofga.org), a well-respected organization in Maine and in the organic farming world, trains young farmers from Maine and beyond. Apprentices work and learn on Maine farms for room and board, and MOGFA's reputation carries status in the farming world. MOGFA, the Belfast Co-op, and the availability of fresh food influenced Belfast Cohousing's decision to settle there.

Existing communities also draw individuals and newly developing projects that form clusters of communities and people with similar values. For instance, the Possibility Alliance settled in close proximity to the three communities of Red Earth, Dancing Rabbit, and Sandhill, and homesteaders and small communities such as Butterfly Hill Farm settled just down the road. In February 2014, two residents of White Rose Catholic Worker House in Chicago announced their intention to move to La Plata, Missouri, at the behest of their friends at the Possibility Alliance: "The move comes in response to the invitation of our campañeros at the Possibility Alliance (PA) to partner with them as a neighboring project. The folks at the PA run a joyful community farm dedicated to 'integral nonviolence,' including electricity and petroleum-free living and gift economy. We are inspired, encouraged, and challenged by this budding relationship and opportunity to put down deeper roots towards the ever-stronger call we feel to live in a land and craft-based society built on love."[15]

In some cases, community clusters coalesce as smaller communities bud off from a larger community when it grows too large for some residents. For example, the Hutterites, a communal Anabaptist group, had a tradition of splitting off into daughter communities when a community reached 150 to keep the communities manageable. Although both Acorn and Living Energy grew out of Twin Oaks in Louisa, Virginia, they have slightly different emphases. The Living Energy Farm (http://www.livingenergyfarm.org/) is a zero–fossil fuel community and focuses on energy issues. Acorn focuses on food and agriculture. These communities are located near Twin Oaks and help each other when the need arises; for example, Twin Oaks assisted when Acorn's seed-storage facility burned down.

Previous intentional communities have often paved the way for newer communities, demonstrating that they both contribute to the larger community and make good neighbors. Creating these relationships takes a concerted effort because existing communities, whether rural or urban, can be suspicious of newcomers' values and motives. Since many intentional communities question existing social values, including gender roles and capitalist economic systems, their existence poses an implicit threat to the mainstream. However, that is their role—to test alternatives—and those who are invested in existing financial or social systems or those who mourn the passing of what they perceive as traditional values may, indeed, feel threatened.

In rural regions, shared appreciation of rural culture and local economies creates mutual trust and respect. Our tour guide at Twin Oaks said that the community's rural neighbors appreciate its presence in part because Twin Oaks is getting young people interested in farming and agriculture and thus, in some ways, validating their rural lifestyle. Although Twin Oaks feels extremely remote, it is situated midway between Richmond and Charlottesville, Virginia, both growing cities. In areas threatened by encroaching development, farming-friendly intentional communities have made good neighbors and have created strategic alliances.

Dancing Rabbit, Sandhill, and Red Earth in Rutledge, Missouri, have worked hard to collaborate with their Amish and Mennonite farming neighbors, including developing a farmers' market, purchasing goods, and inviting them for tours of the communities. Every September, Dancing Rabbit hosts an open house, and the entire community participates by cleaning and preparing the campus for hundreds of visitors. Guests go on tours, stopping at different stations where Rabbits explain the community's experiments in energy, building, and governance. Local Mennonite families come every year to see what the community has done since the last open house, such as constructing new homes or expanding agricultural areas. The Mennonites in this area are Old Order Mennonites who wear conservative dress somewhat similar to the Amish, but they use tractors, allow electricity in their homes, and interact with the public through

Solar cooker on display at Dancing Rabbit's open house

their businesses. Since the Missouri Mennonite community members have traditionally been small farmers, Rabbits say that their Mennonite neighbors appreciate their small farms and methods of animal husbandry, and Dancing Rabbit actively cultivates these relationships.

Residents of the Possibility Alliance in La Plata, Missouri, forty miles away, also work hard to respect their Amish and Mennonite neighbors' values and ethos regarding dress. My visitor orientations at both the Possibility Alliance and Dancing Rabbit stressed that we should dress appropriately. For example, we were asked to avoid wearing revealing tank tops when in sight of their neighbors and when shopping at Zimmerman's Store, a Mennonite-run grocery store in Rutledge. By taking care not to offend their more conservative neighbors, the communities can build relationships based on their shared values on food and farming.

Nonetheless, despite the best efforts, misunderstandings occur, as illustrated by an exchange in the fall of 2013. One thirty-something Rabbit was paying for her groceries at Zimmerman's Store when the Mennonite woman who was checking her out commented, "It must be hard." Puzzled, the Rabbit asked, "What must be hard?" When the checker replied that sharing your husband would be difficult, she realized that their Mennonite neighbors assumed that all Dancing Rabbit residents were polyamorous. Although some Rabbits do experiment with polyamory, and the community is open to a range of social formations, polyamory is neither a norm nor required.

Lessons Learned from the Past

Contemporary intentional communities, from communes to cohousing, draw upon a long history of intentional communities in the United States and, in particular, upon lessons gleaned from communities and movements popular in the 1960s and 1970s. The Possibility Alliance, Dancing Rabbit, and the other communities described above learned important lessons from their predecessors about the need for robust governance and educational structures. These communities at once look back to earlier generations and move forward to new forms of living, working, and eating together based on voluntary simplicity, nonviolence, and self-sufficiency.

Creating structures that facilitate nonviolent communications, for example, helps them live out their values of nonviolence, and designing educational programs around appropriate technologies and basic skills advances their goals of regional sufficiency and sustainability. Whereas communities in the 1960s and 1970s assumed that skills such as communication and building would emerge organically, contemporary communities often create programs and workshops to teach these skills to both residents and the public. For instance, many intentional communities of the 1970s attempted to transcend gender roles and aimed for racial and class equality, yet despite their efforts, some fell back into traditional gender roles and remained the province of the white middle class. Despite the rhetoric of gender equity, it was inevitable that, without training in basic cooking or building skills, for example, men and women would fall back on existing strengths. Achieving racial and class parity remains a challenge, but communities have made progress regarding gender equity, both in terms of women in leaderships roles and women working in areas such as building. Some progress must be attributed to broader social changes over the past forty years, but community programs that teach women building skills, for example, empower women to take on nontraditional roles.

Communities today can also draw upon the collective wisdom and experience provided by the FIC, whose website includes a communities directory, a wiki, and blogs on relevant topics. The FIC website, in addition to other social media resources including Facebook, provides potential residents and others information unavailable to seekers of earlier generations. This continually updated database helps communities both learn from the past and addresses contemporary challenges on issues such as gender, aging, and sexuality. Few intentional communities of previous generations addressed aging because most residents were young and healthy, nor did they discuss LGBTQ, a term that did not exist in the 1960s and 1970s, but today's communities—and the general public—must adapt to the needs of these populations. Communities that emphasize radical democracy and nonviolence are also well positioned to respond to emerging needs, to parties who are not yet "at the table," in philosopher Catriona Mortimer-Sandiland's words, and just as aging and LGBTQ are contemporary concerns, future communities will look to today's communities for guidance on emerging social issues.[16] As bellwethers for social change, intentional communities create innovative responses to emerging social questions. In short, these communities are living out the notion of being the change they want to see in the world.

3
Choosing a Life

It is an experiment with creating an example of a different way to live that is in harmony with nature, that uplifts all life, and that is enjoyable and good.
—Dan Truesdale, Possibility Alliance

AT THE START OF this project, I had no idea whom I would meet when I began visiting intentional communities. I had scoured the Web for information and read mission statements, bios, and blogs from a variety of intentional communities and residents. One kind of intentional community, the ashram, had been part of my field research in India, where retreating from society either temporarily or permanently is a religiously and culturally sanctioned practice. These Indian communities tend to be austere and their members celibate, and the residents focus inward, removing themselves from worldly temptations. However, in the context of my US research, I was interested in communities that were testing new models of living such as incorporating voluntary simplicity into their ordinary lives that could be adopted and adapted by others not residing in such communities. Consequently, I sought communities that integrated voluntary simplicity practices rather than communities based on the ascetic practices I had seen in India.

Voluntary simplicity comprises a set of values that can be interpreted differently by various populations. In the United States, for example, voluntary simplicity means one thing to an individual who experienced the Depression, such as my father, something entirely different to a generation of digital natives for whom an iPhone is essential, and quite another thing in the practices of an intentional community. I wanted to explore who populated these communities and investigate how they practiced values like voluntary simplicity.

When I set out for northeast Missouri to visit the Possibility Alliance and Dancing Rabbit Ecovillage, I was both nervous and excited. In retrospect, I should not have been surprised that baby boomers and millennials comprised significant percentages of the residents of intentional communities. Many millennials, shaped by the recession and our current fetishization of entrepreneurship, are eager to throw off the corporate shackles that bound their parents and create different lifeways. Their ease with communications technology enables them to create networks across time and space, and virtual organizations such as CouchSurfing, WWOOF (World Wide Opportunities on Organic Farms), and Next GEN North America have enabled young Americans to meet and inexpensively test new locations and new communities. One young woman said that she thought the FIC was too static and dated to keep up with the dynamic interactions forming around electronic communications.

Numerous baby boomers, especially those born in the early years of the boom, said that they saw living in community as a continuation of their youthful activism. One cohousing resident stated that he and his wife hated suburban life: "I think partly because my wife and I both came out of the sixties, and we lived in all types of group situations, with and without clothes."

Further, baby boomers do not want to age as their parents did, and for some, this means forging new paths for their retirement years. Many boomers now embark on second careers or join the Peace Corps, viewing their senior years as a new challenge rather than a time to slow down. Aging in community presents its own sets of challenges, as residents of Dancing Rabbit discussed in the Q&A sessions of their visiting program. Dancing Rabbit does not yet have the infrastructure or health-care resources for an aging population, although some communities, such as Twin Oaks, have built on-campus health-care facilities. Similarly, like their baby boomer predecessors, millennials who have been shaped by the Great Recession are seeking new patterns for living and working, and marketing research identifies millennials as "community-oriented, virtual and physical."[1] This population has embraced social entrepreneurship and social networking, and many are engaged in what could be termed the "new new economy," that is, an economy characterized by collaboration, creativity, and small-scale entrepreneurship. Although people of all ages live in intentional communities, boomers and millennials constitute a large portion of the demographic and influence the direction and character of their communities.

One obvious critique of intentional communities, especially rural ones, is the lack of race and class diversity; not surprisingly, the white middle-class is well represented in these populations. That residents of these communities have chosen voluntary simplicity or, in some cases, voluntary poverty highlights an important point: these individuals have chosen this lifestyle, and so have had the financial and/or the social resources to make this decision. Further, sociologist Jade Aguilar argues that, not surprisingly, race and class shape how people understand "living simply."[2] Most communities expressed the desire for greater class, cultural, and racial diversity, but acknowledged the reality that sites such as the rural Midwest do not usually attract nonwhite or less well-to-do residents. Further, as Lois Arkin of LA Eco-village stated, while communities might see themselves as open and welcoming to all, outsiders might not view them in that light.[3] It is difficult to find statistics about the demographics of intentional communities, but the communities themselves continue to wrestle with racial and cultural diversity, as demonstrated by the March 2015 panel discussion "Building Diversity in Intentional Communities."[4]

Joining a community can be expensive, and some communities require significant upfront investment; residents of Ecovillage at Ithaca (EVI) purchase their homes, a requirement that prices the community out of the reach of many. Other communities, including LA Eco-village, Lost Valley Educational Center in Dexter, Oregon, and Dancing Rabbit, have structured their costs and fees in ways that may support more diversity.

Urban organizations, such as the Catholic worker houses, are more likely to bring in different demographics, whether as residents or partners in some capacity. The Catholic worker house in Gainesville, for example, holds monthly roundtables and potlucks that facilitate dialogue among populations such as students and the homeless who typically do not interact. Catholic worker houses often run on donations or exist on previously purchased lands, so they remain affordable to a broader social range.

The demographics and emphasis on values such as voluntary simplicity expose these communities to charges of elitism, similar to critiques that movements such as Slow Food are elitist. While allegations of elitism might be legitimate—many communities are, after all, economically exclusive—

that does not negate the salience of their goals and values. Organic agriculture, for example, has been similarly criticized as elitist, but instead of questioning the legitimacy of organic agriculture, perhaps we should ask why organic produce isn't priced so that all income levels can afford it. Further, traditional agriculture has always been organic by default, and peasant farmers in countries like Mexico prefer organic agriculture for environmental, religious, and economic reasons. Community residents do not demand that everyone adopt voluntary simplicity, but they recognize that members of the white, professional middle class consume far more than their fair share, so they seek to mitigate some of this damage. Ultimately, however, the poor and marginalized bear the burden of unsustainable practices, so while I would not argue that sustainability should be the province of the white, I do think those of us who are middle or upper class should acknowledge our responsibility and act accordingly. I further suggest that we have much to learn from reflecting on the values and practices of some intentional communities.

Living Values

Regardless of their demographics, people come to intentional communities to live out their values and see how abstract values emerge in practice. Eric Anglada of New Hope near Dubuque, Iowa, commented, "It's all about integrating practice with theory. Peter Maurin loved books, but he lived the voluntary poverty and nonviolence." My conversation with Anglada echoed those with other Catholic workers who stressed the importance of practicing and modeling values such as the Works of Mercy, not just talking about them. Doing as opposed to talking yields at least two benefits: first, modeling practices demonstrates that they are doable; and second, demonstrated practices are more compelling than lectures. Alice McGary of Mustard Seed in Ames, Iowa, noted, "Hospitality and the Works of Mercy are about social change and the dignity of every person." As they live their values and practice the Works of Mercy, these residents create social change by recognizing the dignity of all humans, rich and poor.

Dave Wilcox, a practicing Quaker and father of Possibility Alliance resident Sarah Wilcox-Hughes, echoed Anglada's stress on practicing their values and noted that nonviolence involves the entire biotic community. "Gandhian nonviolence works in conjunction with my Quaker principles of simplicity and peace. But peace and nonviolence doesn't only deal with my relationship to other human beings. It has to do with the land and with other beings." Living in these experimental communities enables residents to test the boundaries and practicalities of translating their values into practice. Doing Gandhian nonviolence or Works of Mercy creates new patterns of interactions with other beings, both human and nonhuman, and these ideas—their benefits and shortcomings alike—become manifest in the building, growing, and governing practices of these communities.

Sarah Wilcox-Hughes elaborated on the process of living values: "It's a process of both stripping down and adding on. We strip off our old shell and learn skills so we can move on and replace them with a new culture. It's helpful to see other projects because it's accessible if you can read about it or if you can imagine it. We know that we can live without refrigeration, and human beings have for centuries, but to actually see it when we went to France, suddenly we knew we could do it because we had lived that way in France."

Practices that might seem impossible in the abstract become doable when demonstrated, and the obstacles no longer seem insurmountable. Demonstration and educational programs reveal that new lifeways are not only possible, but they are enjoyable also. For example, in Gainesville, programs teach skills such as how to grow some of your own food and how to commute by bicycle, instruction that not only creates newly skilled workers but also empowers people and builds community.

Locating Communities

How do you find an intentional community? Numerous resources, including books and websites, address almost all aspects of finding, joining, and living in community. The Fellowship for Intentional Community website (http://ic.org) lists a range of resources about intentional communities in the United States and abroad, including a database of communities categorized by geographic region and type of community (for example, ecovillage, commune, or religiously oriented). These communities span a range of views and practices, from ecumenical spiritual to libertarian to new monasticism, and many emphasize sustainability, especially in terms of food and agriculture.

The FIC website includes an interactive form that identifies possible communities to explore based on a list of preferences, including shared meals, decision-making style, and spiritual practices. For example, when I requested a suburban, partial income-sharing community with one shared meal a week, about twenty communities popped up. Listings in the database are voluntary, and any existing or forming community can upload its information and self-identify as an intentional community. As such, this database is limited to communities that want to be found and identified. Some groups, therefore, such as group residences in urban and suburban regions that violate existing zoning laws, may prefer to remain under the radar. Each entry includes a description of the community, contact information, and information for visitors and potential residents. The FIC directory, available in both print and digital form, listed more than 2,500 communities in 2015, up from 1,600 in 2013 and 350 in 1992, and the numbers are likely to increase as interest in these kinds of communities grows.[5] Sorting through so much information can be confusing even after you make an initial list based on criteria such as geography or decision-making style. My initial list of twenty suggestions still seemed overly broad, and it was difficult to choose based on available information.

The comprehensive FIC website lists multiple varieties of intentional communities, many of which have vastly different goals and lifestyles, from income-sharing egalitarian communes to cohousing to religious or spiritual communities. Several of these subgenres also have websites and organizations specific to their goals. The Federation of Egalitarian Communities (FEC; thefec.org), a "union of egalitarian communities which have joined together in our common struggle to create a lifestyle based on equality, cooperation, and harmony with the earth," provides information about egalitarian communities—what most of us think of as communes—and their governance structures. The Cohousing Association of the United States website (http://www.cohousing.org/) presents comprehensive information, and the Catholic worker website (http://www.catholicworker.org/communities/directory-picker.html) maintains a directory of Catholic worker communities. NASCO (North American Students of Cooperation; www.nasco.coop) details information and resources about student housing cooperatives, where many communards first experience living in community.

Despite this wealth of information, it can be challenging for people who want to know more about or perhaps join an intentional community. Diana Leafe Christian is a well-known and respected authority on intentional community who maintains a busy speaking and consulting schedule. She is the author of *Creating Life Together: Practical Tools to Grow Ecovillages and Intentional Communities,* and in her book *Finding Community: How to Join an Ecovillage or Intentional Community,* she suggests questions to separate the "wheat from the chaff," some as simple as evaluating photos on the community website.[6] What do the people look like, for example, and does the infrastructure look well maintained? She identifies potential red flags such as overly long and theoretical names like Living Adherents of the Divine Order or Acolytes of Angelic Actualization,— although of course these communities might be the right place for some people.

These directories, books, and websites help narrow down the dizzying array of intentional communities, but the best way to get to know a community is to visit and meet the residents.

Visiting Communities

Many communities welcome the general public on scheduled occasions such as tours, workshops, or extended formal visits, and the FIC site describes each community's policy toward visitors and new members. Dancing Rabbit's Milkweed Mercantile B&B offers guests a window into ecovillage life, and New Eden in Escondido, California, advertises the opportunity to "Experience True Hippie Living" on Airbnb. Lost Valley Educational Center in Dexter, Oregon, offers educational and recreational opportunities to the public, and one member surmised that almost everyone in nearby Eugene had visited the community at some point. Dancing Rabbit, LA Eco-village, and Sirius lead afternoon tours that are open to anyone and provide a brief glimpse into community life but require little time or emotional investment. Catholic workers, through their mission, engage the public through hospitality programs, roundtable discussions, and volunteer opportunities. Many cohousing communities give tours and invite potential residents to community events and potlucks. These educational opportunities allow communities to showcase themselves to their neighbors and others interested in community.

Every Labor Day weekend, Twin Oaks opens its campus in Louisa, Virginia, for the annual Twin Oaks Communities Conference (www.communitiesconference.org). The conference brings together communities seeking residents, visitors seeking communities, and the curious, like me—I met three other authors when I attended in 2013. At that conference, participants chose workshops on topics such as legal issues facing communities and conflict resolution. Saturday morning featured a meet and greet in which a representative from each community had one minute to introduce him- or herself and the community. The conference organizers had not placed restrictions on the kinds of communities represented, so some were well established, some were still in the process of forming, and several consisted of one person, some land, and an idea. After representatives of the thirty or so communities had spoken, they staked out spots at picnic tables where, for the rest of the morning, visitors and community representatives interacted. For visitors and community residents, the meet and greet served primarily as a venue for gathering information and testing the waters for a good fit for potential community residents—a first step in the mutual vetting process.

Conference participants were invited on tours of Twin Oaks (www.twinoaks.org), Acorn (www.acorncommunity.org), a Twin Oaks spin-off; and the newer Living Energy Farm (www.livingenergyfarm.org), which aims to use zero fossil fuels. I especially appreciated the community tours because uninvited guests are typically not welcome to wander about at will. Although each of these communities identifies as an educational and demonstration community, they nonetheless have had to create rules and boundaries for visitors in order to maintain some privacy.

Both the FIC and the Cohousing Association of the United States maintain calendars of educational events, tours, and conferences to strike a balance between community and visitor needs. Conferences and tours help community seekers determine which communities might best fit their individual needs—no one "perfect" community exists; communities reflect and serve the strengths and needs of their residents. After information seekers or community seekers have identified one or several potential communities, their next step is to arrange to visit.

I learned about the visitor process when I began fieldwork for this book. I had received funding from the University of Florida to begin my study in summer 2011, and I thought the cluster of four Missouri communities would be a good place to start, particularly since I was looking forward to returning to the Midwest. Doing fieldwork in the United States was an exciting departure for me. I had done a yearlong research trip to north India for each of my two previous books, and much of my fieldwork involved conducting interviews, visiting temples, and participating in village life. When in 1991 I arrived in Vrindavan, a small pilgrimage city in a rural region in north-central India, for my dissertation research, few people had telephones, and you could simply show up on someone's doorstep. Since I was asking about Krishna, the beloved cowherd-boy deity of the region, I was typically welcomed and fed tea and snacks. Perhaps this ease of access made me overly casual about making initial contacts with these US communities. Although I knew that visiting communities would not be a matter of merely stopping by, I did not anticipate how much I would learn about the communities from the very process of requesting invitations to visit.

Although all of the communities I considered gave tours or demonstrations that were open to the public, simply touring a community would not be enough because I wanted to conduct participant-observation field research. This meant that I would need sufficient time to interview residents and to observe and participate in daily life within the communities by, for example, working in their gardens, helping to build straw-bale houses, and participating in seminars on nonviolent communications. In addition to being a researcher in this project, I was also an actor and a participant. This meant that my ongoing, evolving question shifted over time from "What is my role?" to "How can I help these communities?" to "How can I bring this home?" to "What can I do promote the spread of intentional communities founded on what I value?" In my letters to communities, I had offered help in the form of my labor, but when I visited, I realized that I could also help them connect with other communities and spread information between communities and beyond, and this became a main purpose of this book.

Most communities hold visitor programs with an orderly application process for visitors, especially those who want extended visits or who seek to join the community. So I wrote detailed letters of introduction that explained my reasons for wanting to visit and hoped they would be interested in me. In my letters I expressed my professional and personal interests in intentional communities and described my recently published book, *Growing Stories from India: Religion and the Fate of Agriculture*, which asks how we might create a sustainable food system that is equitable for multiple populations. *Growing Stories* focuses on our stories about food, but I wanted to learn how these communities ate and understood and translated concepts such as voluntary simplicity, self-sufficiency, and nonviolence into practice. I knew that many communities, especially smaller groups such as the Possibility Alliance, emphasized bread labor, the assumption that everyone must physically contribute to supplying their basic needs, rather than simply buying someone else's labor. In this vein, I offered my own bread labor, citing my interests in both contributing my gardening skills and learning new skills in areas such as building.

My letters also expressed my personal interest in the goals of these communities and how my stakes in the outcome of this new project differed from my previous research. Although I care deeply about Radharaman Temple and my friends in Vrindavan, my work in that project was not intended to advance a goal other than to explain a particularly compelling religious tradition to a relatively select group of interested readers. For this project, however, I was—and remain—committed to the outcome. That is, I would like to live in a society that reflects a constellation of Gandhian values, and I am committed to the process. So my letters to the communities made clear that although I was not necessarily looking to join their community, I hoped to learn from them and wanted to implement some of what I learned in my hometown.

Later, during visits to these communities, I learned that offered labor such as mine often proved to be a hindrance to residents who were actually trying to get some work done. For example, Alice McGary of Mustard Seed explained that I would need instruction to learn how they did laundry, and she patiently taught me proper hoeing technique so that I could help plant carrots. I realized that, like many visitors to communities that emphasize self-sufficiency, I had never developed the requisite specialized self-sufficiency skills and that, for anything other than mundane tasks, my labor required an investment on the part of the community residents in my education. In retrospect, I suspect that my letters were met with some eye rolling, yet nonetheless I received invitations to visit. These generous invitations demonstrate a graciousness and willingness to reach out for which I am grateful.

Joining Communities

Joining a community is a serious decision for both the individual or family and the community itself, so guest or visitor experiences can last several weeks. Many people visit several communities prior to finding a good fit, a practice advocated by Diana Leafe Christian in a section entitled "Don't Marry the First Community That Asks You."[7] When I attended the Communities Conference at Twin Oaks, a resident of the Red Clover Collective, an urban community in Baltimore, Maryland, likened the process to an extended dating period. Personality quirks and traits emerge over time and often only in stressful situations, so an extended probationary period protects all parties from the consequences of a hasty decision. Christian's book *Finding Community* provides pertinent information about all aspects of finding and joining a community for visitors and potential residents, including how to be a "great guest," how to assess communities, and how to understand the experience. For example, in the section "Come Here, Go Away," she explains that although communities welcome visitors, they can be overwhelmed and must find a balance between privacy and welcoming guests.[8]

In general, the more tightly knit the community, the more extensive the mutual screening process is. For example, tightly bound income-sharing communities such as Twin Oaks and Sandhill need to ensure that residents fit the community. Cohousing communities, on the other hand, which are structurally similar to homeowners' associations (HOA), are less able to screen and block residents if their properties are listed publicly.

The vetting process goes both ways, and potential residents should ask hard questions of community residents. Residents and potential residents are sizing each other up for the possibility of a long-term relationship. During Dancing Rabbit's guest period, visitors and residents gathered for Q&A sessions where visitors fire questions at residents. Assembled in the community house, we sat in a large circle on chairs and sofas. During one of my visits, a middle-aged female visitor asked what life would be like for a single, fifty-something woman. A young couple asked how children were educated. One man asked how differing political views were tolerated. At the Communities Conference, Laird Schaub, a well-known speaker and facilitator for intentional communities, urged potential residents to ask hard questions such as "What is the process, if any, to revoke community membership?" If a community does not have clear and transparent policies to handle difficult situations, conflicts will be even worse in times of emotional stress. Dancing Rabbit manages this process in part by posting an article, "How to Become a Resident and Member of Dancing Rabbit," on its website that clearly outlines the residency and membership process and provides links to relevant information (for example, the membership agreement).[10] This parallels the clear, orderly policies and processes other intentional communities provide about joining.

Nonetheless, vetting new residents is not a science, and the process can be difficult for both sides. Alyson Ewald of Red Earth in Rutledge admitted, "We're trying to figure it out, and I don't think there's any way to avoid people being on pins and needles: 'Are they going to accept me?' Because it's not open membership and we decide who gets to live here, we are in this position of power. And it's been quite uncomfortable at times for everybody." I attended a few visitor programs that seemed to me like summer camp, but I was not seeking membership. Had I been, I imagine that my experiences would have been markedly different.

When I visited Dancing Rabbit, I understood why the vetting process was so important. Dancing Rabbit is a small community, with about fifty residents during my first visit in 2011, and residents work hard, building houses and growing food. Hosting visitors takes a great deal of time away from what residents need for basic subsistence and mental energy. Community life can seem exotic to visitors who are curious about alternative ways of living, and they may ask about different aspects of community life: "What do you eat?" or "Can a straw-bale house meet code requirements?" Although residents of demonstration communities enjoy sharing aspects of their lives, accommodating even small numbers of unplanned guests can overwhelm the community; imagine guests walking around your home, peeping in the windows. For visitors like me who seek longer visits and for people who are seeking a community, Dancing Rabbit, like many communities, holds five one- to three-week visitor periods in a year.

People who want to visit submit introduction letters. The visitors' committee reads these and creates groups of about ten people, aiming to balance different ages, goals, and backgrounds. More casual visitors like me might only stay a week, while visitors who are considering full-time residence are encouraged to come for the entire three weeks.

During visiting periods, current residents interact with visitors during meals, activities, and work parties to vet potential residents and assess their potential fit and contributions to the community. Our visitors' cohort had two liaisons who answered questions about Dancing Rabbit and helped us process ideas and practices that we might not understand otherwise. What is a humanure toilet, for example? (Humanure is composted human waste.) The liaisons also offered feedback on the visitors' behavior, which was especially important for those seeking membership. Intentional communities, because of their autonomous nature, attract idiosyncratic individuals, including those who are not comfortable with mainstream life and want to live in a community with a shared ethos and set of values. The liaisons helped potential residents begin to transition to community life and become acculturated to Dancing Rabbit's lifestyle.

Dancing Rabbit structured the visitors' period so that potential residents can understand Dancing Rabbit "culture" and what it would mean to live, work, and play in that community. The highly structured first week included talks on issues such as conflict resolution, Dancing Rabbit history, and alternative building techniques, all necessary to live successfully at Dancing Rabbit. These talks helped us learn about life at Dancing Rabbit, and also more about the specific interests of different residents. One Rabbit led my visiting group on a land tour to teach us about the native birds and plants of this midwestern prairie and to describe his particular agricultural ventures, including a vineyard and hoop house. We participated in work parties such as weeding a neglected garden and plastering a straw-bale house. Most Rabbits participate in food co-ops (for example, the vegan Bobolink co-op and the Outdoor Kitchen during warm months), so meals for visitors rotated through the co-ops; we ate different meals with different co-op members.

The Rabbits kept us busy with activities and social opportunities, but it was always fun. Tony Sirna said that visitors should have the "time of their lives," and I loved the time I spent at Dancing Rabbit, whether working or playing. Evenings featured community-wide activities, some of which were weekly get-togethers. I especially enjoyed Wednesday Night Sings, where each person could suggest a song for the group to sing. I learned some new songs and sang songs I remembered from summer camp. On my first visit, I taught residents the final verse of "Plastic Jesus," and the group was singing it when I returned the following year. I also enjoyed, but did not participate in, the "No-Talent Shows, which showcased highly talented musicians as well as elementary school gymnasts. In addition to providing entertainment, No-Talent Shows demonstrate how Rabbits support each other, especially the resident children. All these activities provided opportunities to meet and converse with Rabbits and see them socializing informally.

By the third week of the visitor period, little formal structure remained. Visitors had begun to establish ties with individual Rabbits and to determine whether and how they might live in the community. At this point, visitors who wanted to join Dancing Rabbit initiated the six-month residency, the first step toward membership, by writing a letter of intent to the Dancing Rabbit Membership and Residency Committee (MARC). Dancing Rabbit's website says that letters of intent should discuss why prospective members want to live at Dancing Rabbit; what they can contribute; and how they intend to meet their physical, financial, and spiritual needs there.[10] Then MARC would schedule an interview, open to all Rabbits, with the potential resident to address possible concerns and begin a prolonged conversation about membership. The new resident could then apply for membership after six months.

Sharing Spaces

"I could never live like that," friends often commented when I brought up intentional communities. "Live like what?" I asked one of my friends from Ames as we drank coffee on a warm fall Iowa morning. We were sitting just outside her back door on the driveway she shares with her neighbors. The two houses and garages enclosed the end of the driveway, making a small courtyard that abutted her garden. I knew that we shared goals about sustainability and building community, so I was eager to hear why she thought she couldn't live in an intentional community. She lived alone in a single-family house and valued her space and privacy and, not surprisingly, said, "I like my own space. I don't want to be right on top of everyone else." I empathized with her. Even though I value community, I lived alone until I met and married Kevin. I'm not sure I would want to share my house with someone other than Kevin. I explained that most residents of intentional communities in the United States also value their personal space and that most communities must somehow accommodate this need. After all, open space and personal freedom loom large in the North American psyche. Homesteading, home ownership, even having your own room as a child reflect deeply held values of freedom and independence. In most cases, I would rather sleep outside in my own tent than share a room with someone other than Kevin or a good friend.

I explained to my friend that the communities I visited demonstrated a range of living options, on a continuum from individual rooms in income-sharing communities to individually owned stand-alone houses in ecovillages and cohousing communities. Twin Oaks, for example, offers each adult a single room, an arrangement that admittedly is not ideal for families with children. LA Eco-village, in urban Los Angeles, features cost-controlled apartments around an enclosed central courtyard that has several seating areas shaded by an assortment of fruit trees. Most cohousing communities, whether urban or suburban, provide multiple housing options on their campuses, including apartments, stand-alone houses, and duplexes. Different communities offer varying amounts of personal space, from rooms to apartments to single-family homes and the amount of available personal space is certainly a determining factor in selecting a community. While I have been content in a single room for extended periods of fieldwork in India, now I want a single-family home, or at least a duplex, with space for a garden.

Our house in Gainesville is not large by American standards. We live in a three-bedroom concrete block house and use the two smaller bedrooms as home offices, with Kevin's office doubling as a guest room. The rest of our living space is open, with plenty of room for two people and two cats. Further, our year-round warm climate means that we can use our outdoor space all year. Our house backs up onto a five-acre lake, and when we sit on our back porch looking out across the lake, we see mostly trees. Our neighbor's house on the other side of the lake seems distant, and the lake dulls the road noise. It feels like we are in the country, and it is hard to believe that our house is less than a half mile from two major roads in Gainesville. I can ride my bike to both downtown Gainesville and the University of Florida in under fifteen minutes. So although I live in the heart of the city, I have the illusion of space, and access to space, even shared space, appealed to me when I visited communities.

Shared resources or space is a sine qua non for most intentional communities. Common houses, courtyards, and outdoor seating areas, for example, encourage the informal socializing that strengthens personal relationships and community ties. For both residents and visitors, shared spaces means that they gain comfortable and safe access to far more space than most individuals could afford on their own. Even as a visitor, I always felt like I "owned"—even if temporarily—more space than the room or tent that was officially mine. While visiting LA Eco-village, I frequently relaxed in the interior courtyard, where enthusiastic gardeners tended a variety of fruit trees and vegetables. As I basked in the soft Los Angeles sunshine, passing residents occasionally stopped to chat, and one of the gardeners proudly gave me apples and figs. My studio apartment, a unit set aside for short-term guests, was spacious, in a 1920s building originally designed for employees and visitors to the local mineral hot springs on the block in the early part of the twentieth century. But how much time did I want to spend alone in my apartment? LA Eco-village's courtyard, as well as its community room and library, gave me far more space than my studio apartment and the chance to visit with residents. Although I could hear Los Angeles traffic noises from my room, the courtyard seemed like an oasis from the city.

I experienced a similar openness and freedom in many of the communities I visited, a freedom to enjoy and explore places beyond what was assigned to me. Even when I stayed in a single room in Cherith Brook in downtown Kansas City, Missouri, I had the run of the entire downstairs of the rambling Victorian-style house. Of course, in LA, Kansas City, or anywhere, I could have gone and sat on a park bench outside of the community space, and I have often done that. However, in the LA Eco-village courtyard I felt like I belonged and, as a fifty-plus woman, I felt safe. Had I sat on a park bench, I would have been much more guarded and less likely to engage in random conversations, which is one reason I have always appreciated B&Bs, for their protected shared spaces and opportunities for conversation with other guests. These experiences helped me think about my need for personal space.

Perhaps I would be satisfied with less private space if I had more access to shared space. Residents of intentional communities have privileged access to shared space over providing more personal or private spaces. Again, intentional communities vary considerably in the amount and type of personal and private space granted to individuals and families, and the amount of space varies within communities as well. Dancing Rabbit offers multiple housing options, ranging from split-level, single-family homes to small apartments housed in repurposed grain bins. LA Eco-village offers a range from studio apartments to two-bedroom apartments that are comparatively generous spaces for the dense urban area. The shared spaces and community resources available to residents, though, reduce needs for personal space in creative ways. LA Eco-village and many cohousing communities designate guest suites for short-term guests, whether they are visitors to the community or family members or friends of the residents. While I would like a designated guest room in my house, Kevin and I host guests only several times a year, so a shared guest room in a common house would be sufficient for our needs. Similarly, access to a large common kitchen would facilitate my large-scale cooking projects, such as, for example, when I can fruits and vegetables. Some intentional communities offer daily or weekly community meals that can take the pressure off individual kitchens and cooks if they choose to partake in those meals, and some community residents do not have individual kitchens.

Questioning How Much Community We Want

Sharing space and resources leads to some obvious benefits, including increased access to resources and informal socializing, but sharing also raises concerns about shared responsibility and the larger question of how much community we want. Cohousing communities and some ecovillages might be loosely bound where residents meet weekly for meals, while Catholic worker houses and small communal groups work and eat meals together.

While I often claim that I would like stronger community ties, I'm not exactly sure what I mean by that. Journalist Katherine Flagg writes that living in community requires participation and work. "These communities seek to strike a balance between individual privacy and group engagement. Is the result a 'Kumbaya'-singing utopia, or an overcrowded hell? The answer, of course, depends on the resident. Intentional communities aren't for everyone, their advocates say, and even the most picturesque ones demand that residents shoulder a heavy share of hard work and pragmatic responsibility."[11]

Intentional communities lie upon a spectrum of community engagement, and potential residents must consider how much they want to interweave their lives with others. At minimum, most communities require attendance at community meetings or potlucks; LA Eco-village, for example, requires members to participate in at least one potluck or community meeting and/or one work party per month, hardly an onerous burden, though much greater participation is expected. Residents hold community meetings every Monday night, potlucks every Sunday night, and generally one or two work parties per month. In this respect, LA Eco-village seemed comparable to some of the cohousing groups I visited, which also have minimal participation requirements. Residents of Cobb Hill in Hartland, Vermont, have community work obligations; for example, residents must help cut the firewood that the community uses for heating. In addition to official community gatherings, residents engage in less formal, and often spontaneous, gatherings; for example, meeting neighbors on the path or in the common house can lead to dinner or drinks. Well-designed infrastructure with crisscrossing paths and cozy seating niches facilitates the repeated and spontaneous interactions that build familiarity and comfort.

Cohousing communities function similarly to homeowners' associations, although homeowners' associations do not require hours of community service. In both cases, residents agree to abide by community by-laws and covenants, but elected governing boards can seek and make changes in the by-laws according to community desire. The covenants and by-laws ensure that the community is filled with like-minded members, or at least residents apprised of the rules and requirements for participation. Nonetheless, ensuring full participation is a challenge for loosely bound communities

Path and houses at Cobb Hill

such as cohousing communities. In *The View from #410: When Home Is Cohousing*, founder and resident of Cambridge Cohousing in Cambridge, Massachusetts, Jean Mason laments that there always seem to be 10 percent who do not participate.[12] I heard similar numbers echoed in conversations with residents of other communities, and from my observations, I might offer a higher percentage. Enforcing participation in community life is a perennial problem for intentional communities, especially cohousing communities structured as homeowners' associations, even among residents who self-selected, in part, because they wanted stronger community bonds. In any case, enforcing participation or disciplining a resident is bound to stir up conflict that most would like to avoid.

Cohousing communities tend to have fewer community obligations than most other intentional communities. In most cases, residents of cohousing

Balcony at Daybreak Cohousing designed for social interaction

communities own their own houses and property, they hold jobs outside of the community, and their lives are equally intertwined with friends and obligations beyond as well as within the community. Further, joining a cohousing community might be as simple as meeting community residents, learning the rules, and buying a home, and living in community could require as little as a few shared meals a month and several hours of community service. Many cohousing communities are designed to facilitate social interactions. At Daybreak Cohousing in Portland, Oregon, the window over each unit's kitchen sink—where residents tend to spend a significant amount of time—faces the external walkway so that residents literally see their neighbors come and go. A drawn shade signifies that residents are busy and do not want to be disturbed.

Other communities, including Catholic worker houses, home-sharing communities, and income-sharing communities, weave together facets of residents' lives much more tightly. Their residents spend a great deal of time with each other, much more than most people spend with friends, neighbors, or even our families, something that became especially clear when I spent several days at the Cherith Brook in an unseasonably cold and wet April.

For three days, I lived in one of Cherith Brook's two "Christ" rooms that abutted the kitchen in the main house of the campus. Sometimes visitors like myself occupy the Christ rooms, but more important, Christ rooms offer comfortable and dignified housing to those in need, so they might house someone just evicted from their home or a woman fleeing domestic abuse. "Did you take me in when I was homeless and a stranger?" Dorothy Day cites as a biblical mandate to house the poor, because "heaven hinges on the way we act towards Him in his disguise of commonplace, frail and ordinary human beings."[13] So, according to Dorothy Day, every home should have a Christ room, and now most, if not all, Catholic worker houses do have Christ rooms available. Since my room was right off the kitchen, I was aware of the comings and goings of the others living in the house. Jodi and Eric Garbison and their two children lived upstairs, and three other residents lived in the apartments across the courtyard. These residents did not eat all of their meals together, but their lives were deeply intertwined. While I was there, each morning, at least two residents coordinated the guests and volunteers who participated in their daily breakfast and shower program, and all residents cooked and attended the Thursday evening community meal that served approximately fifty people. Three times a week, they held morning prayers, and once a week, they coordinated their schedules and discussed community and individual well-being.

Balancing different needs was complicated, one resident explained, because families and single twenty-somethings lead very different lives even when they are explicitly living out shared values. In the short period I lived in this community, I saw that they did more activities with each other than many of us do even with our spouses. The tightly knit lives of this community echoed one of the most-invoked fears about intentional communities—the loss of personal space and autonomy—and, in fact, finding a balance between personal autonomy and community life is an ongoing challenge for most communities.

Income-sharing communities, organized as 501(d)3 societies, such as Sandhill and Twin Oaks, illustrate the most tightly interwoven lives of intentional communities. Sandhill and Twin Oaks are communes: residents work for the community and in return receive housing, food, clothing, and medical care. While people might socialize outside of the community, most facets of residents' lives revolve around community life. Twin Oaks' rural community of Louisa lies approximately halfway between Richmond and Charlottesville on I-64, and while the town boasts a small downtown strip, there are few stores and restaurants either there or on the neighboring highway exits (a lack I discovered when searching for gas). The community sends weekly vans to both Richmond and Charlottesville for travelers and shopping excursions, but many residents find little reason to leave the Twin Oaks campus. Residents fulfill their weekly work obligations at Twin Oaks in a variety of tasks, their meals are provided, and most of their recreation needs are met there. For example, Twin Oaks has its own swimming hole, and musicians can join one of several musical groups. "Shoppers" can choose new outfits free of charge in the Commie Clothes area, and riders on the vans traveling to Charlottesville and Richmond bring lists of items requested by others. While Twin Oaks' level of interweaving lives might strike some as suffocating, our tour guide explained that, to him, this system represented freedom.

From cohousing to income sharing, intentional communities exemplify a broad spectrum of community life, ranging from full engagement to occasional potlucks. Communities vary in both their formal and informal expectations of participation, and potential residents can explore and see which communities best fit their needs and expectations. Residents' needs and expectations of their communities also change over time. Younger single residents might be heavily invested in community life, but maintaining that level of participation seems onerous to young families. Communities like Sirius have adapted by creating associate memberships for individuals and families who want to maintain or establish more informal relations with the community. A number of associate members, many of whom are former members, have purchased property adjacent to Sirius and created the Hearthstone Village neighborhood so that they can participate in Sirius but bear fewer obligations.

Keeping Company While We Age

On the opening night of the annual Twin Oaks Communities Conference in 2013, participants gathered in the Pavilion for the evening program. The words "Living together is an art," painted in bold letters on the eave of the

Pavilion at Twin Oaks Communities Conference

open-air wooden structure, set the tone for the program. After a round of announcements and awards, author Karen Bush led the group in an exercise about the benefits of living together. Bush's coauthored book *My House, Our House: Living Far Better for Far Less in a Cooperative Household* had recently been published, and I had read about her experiences in home sharing in a recent issue of the *AARP Bulletin*.[14]

The audience, comprised mostly of twenty-somethings and boomers, mirrored the demographic of conference participants and, indeed, reflected the broader population mix—boomers and millennials or, perhaps, hippies and hipsters—living in or seeking community. I had thought that most people associate the idea of intentional community with communes, like those formed by baby boomers in the 1970s, but I had not anticipated the level of interest in cooperative living expressed by boomers in 2013, including those like myself born at the end of the baby boom generation. During this weekend and over the time I conducted the rest of my fieldwork, I spoke to many fifty-somethings and older folks who were either looking to create a cooperative community of some sort or seeking to live in one. In fact, when I discussed my project in any number of groups, whether at conferences or in random conversations, I got the most enthusiastic responses from baby boomers. For instance, on a Paddle Florida trip in the Florida Keys, I fell into conversation with a sixty-something retired nurse living in Melrose, Florida. She pointed out, as others have before, that her generation began their adult lives as activists, seeking alternatives to mainstream living, and now many are returning to their roots, adapting their activism to address their concerns about aging.

Running counter to the American dream of autonomy and single-family homes, older women and female baby boomers are seeking cooperative living arrangements. In an article in a 2013 *AARP Bulletin,* author Sally Abrahms highlights Karen Bush's experiences with her two housemates and writes that home-sharing websites, meetings, and workshops are becoming increasingly popular in the United States. While motivations range from financial necessity to a desire for connection, fundamentally, the social connections benefit residents physically, emotionally, and socially. Abrahms quotes Marianne Kilkenny, founder of Women Living in Community: "Women have a yearning for community and connection, and that's why the home-sharing movement will change history. It's about choice. Women don't want to count on their kids or be a burden. This is an alternative."[15]

In break-out sessions at the 2013 Twin Oaks conference, Bush and Annamarie Pluhar, author of *Sharing Housing: A Guidebook for Finding and Keeping Good Housemates,* spoke of a loneliness epidemic among aging populations, especially women, and noted the high proportion of individuals in single-family dwellings. While many older Americans wish to age in place, research by University of Florida gerontologist and geographer Stephen Golant suggests that communities such as "elder villages" offer community engagement and help residents maintain independence for longer periods.[16]

For several reasons, including financial ones, more women seek community living arrangements, but men, too, seek out the company of others. During the 2013 conference, I had several conversations with a seventy-one-year-old man who lived in a nearby city. He came to the conference because he was concerned about climate change and wanted to learn about growing food and homesteading. Most important, though, he had been living in his neighborhood for fifteen years, always trying to be a good neighbor. When a tree fell on his house during a storm and none of his neighbors stopped by to check up on him, he decided to explore options for a more tightly knit community or at least a means to build stronger social ties with others.

While home-sharing arrangements can be defined as intentional communities, they still closely resemble mainstream American life. Each household develops its own rules about guests, divisions of household labor, and eating arrangements, and in most cases, each resident controls his or her own finances. In short, these home-sharing arrangements are not communes or income-sharing communities.

"I do not want to live in a retirement village." That sentence was a common refrain I heard when speaking with boomers in intentional communities, even those living in communities designated for those aged fifty and older. In fact, I found myself explaining several times that Florida, although it is sometimes called God's waiting room, is not simply one sprawling retirement village. These boomer residents contrasted what they understood life to be like in retirement communities with their socially active and communally engaged lives in their chosen intentional communities. For example, intentional communities require participation in community activities, from committee work to labor, the latter ranging from cooking group meals to stacking firewood. My tour guide at Two Echo in Brunswick, Maine, a retiree, commented, "This place keeps you young because it keeps you busy, and you're moving more than you normally would be if you just have a single-family house." Cohousing communities, which also closely replicate typical US housing patterns, are increasingly popular with baby boomers. As Jean Mason notes, cohousing communities come with a social contract, and cohousing residents opt for closer community bonds of socializing and, more important, obligation and assistance.[17]

The presence of children draws many residents to multigenerational communities. Two residents—one retired and one working age—of Two Echo stated that "[we] both like living here because children are here. . . . I love having kids here. As a matter of fact, my parents retired to Florida and after they died I swore that number one, I would never set foot in Florida again, and number two, I would never live in that kind of community."

In fact, when I arrived at Two Echo (http://twoecho.org/community/) on an unseasonably hot Saturday in May, several families were busy setting up a birthday party for a six-year-old boy. My tour guide, a retired woman on the membership committee, had graciously offered to show me around the community. During my tour of this small community, I saw a collection of mostly freestanding houses, a well-used community building, and food gardens, both small kitchen gardens adjacent to some houses and larger gardens outside the housing area on the edge of the community. Unlike many communities, Two Echo, founded in 1991 and situated on ninety-five acres purchased in 1996, did not resemble a work in progress. Additionally, because the land will be conserved, no more houses will be built in the community. Walking paths led to neatly painted single-family homes that were slightly smaller than most American homes, and, as in many cohousing communities, residents did not park their cars at their houses but in lots at the community entrance. Heating a home for a Maine winter is difficult and expensive, and residents use a variety of methods to reduce their use of fossil fuels, including interior storm windows and heat pumps.

As we walked around the community and into the common house where the birthday party would be held, my guide greeted the children and told me a bit about each one. Her appreciation of the children paralleled what I had seen at other multigenerational communities where many of the older residents were enthusiastic about the community's children. As Coleen O'Connell of Belfast Cohousing in Belfast, Maine, pointed out, the children "can have ten instant grandmas," an arrangement that mutually benefits those grandmas, parents, and children. However, she recognized that "it's been difficult for the families that joined to see so few families with young children joining and a lot of retiring people joining because they didn't want to be in a retirement community."

Finding the right balance between generations is a challenge, and most multigenerational communities work hard to attract families with children. From my observations, it seems fair to say that while children are a draw for both seniors and other families, few families seek out communities where residents are disproportionately over fifty. Since cohousing communities tend to be more expensive than other intentional communities, they face the greatest challenges in maintaining demographic balance and sustaining the community. One resident of Two Echo remarked, "In terms of sustainability, if everyone ages out at the same time, at some point you're going to have a problem getting things done. At my parents' community in Florida, they all bought in when they were very young retirees, but they all aged out at the same time."

However, not all retirees want the noise and chaos that comes with children, and many cohousing communities restrict their residents to those aged fifty and above. While some communities simply want to avoid children, most restricted communities aim to accommodate the different needs of aging populations. One representative, Roger, spoke about Elderspirit Community at the Communities Conference at Twin Oaks, and I later sought him out to learn more about his community.

Elderspirit Community in Abingdon, Virginia, a cohousing community for seniors, serves only residents who are fifty-five or older; and in 2013, 25 percent were over eighty. Described at the Communities Conferences as "aging in community... with spirit," Elderspirit Community blends goals of spirituality and ecology. "We envisioned a community of elders who would live and age together and have support in their final years. We then discussed and wrote our values that included walking a spiritual path, taking care of ourselves and one another, living simply, and respecting the earth."

In the fall of 2013, forty seniors lived at Elderspirit, with thirteen owner-occupied units and sixteen reserved for low-income residents. The community received HUD funding, which placed some restrictions on occupancy, but Roger noted that "low income" did not mean poverty but included those who could afford "eating out and travel to Europe." Elderspirit Community's population illustrates two trends and challenges in senior communities. First, Elderspirit Community's gender balance—only four residents were men—supports anecdotal evidence that women, who tend to live longer than men, disproportionately seek out community-based living situations, and second, even relatively low-cost communities are beyond the reach of many North Americans, a fact that worries many baby boomers whose retirement funds plummeted in 2007.

Margaret Critchlow, a retired anthropologist, established Harbourside, a senior cohousing facility in Sooke, British Columbia. Critchlow designed Harbourside to meet the needs of seniors who are independent but may need some assistance, such as in making minor repairs or carrying heavy groceries. I met Critchlow at a conference on intentional communities held at the Findhorn Foundation in Scotland. In her conference talk she noted that assistance with basic tasks could prolong independent living for years, helping residents "age in place" in a setting that is both ecologically and socially sustainable. Potential residents are required to complete Aging Well in Community, a two-day course at nearby Royal Roads University, before they can enter this community that emphasizes cooperation, social connections, and mutual obligations. Harbourside's FAQ describes the concept of co-care to potential residents. "Co-care is a grassroots model of neighbourly mutual support that can help reduce social isolation and promote positive, active aging. It encourages independence through awareness that we are all interdependent. In a cohousing community, giving and receiving co-care is entirely voluntary. We may choose to support each other through such activities as doing errands, driving, cooking, or going for a walk with our neighbour. We believe that being good neighbours helps us age well in community and have fun doing it."[18]

While Harbourside plans to have three below-market units to house "helpers," most care will be mutual, based on bonds of friendship and care that constitute, in Critchlow's words, "a natural insurance policy, as we used to do in communities."

Harbourside's mutual-aid plan aims to address one considerable challenge of intentional communities: what happens when residents become too infirm or incapacitated to carry out their community responsibilities. Of course, this question also applies to those of any age who become temporarily or permanently disabled. In general, intentional communities depend upon their residents to perform bread labor and to participate in committees and governance, and in many communities, the labor is difficult (for example, all Cobb Hill residents help carry and stack the firewood that heats their houses all winter). Similarly, the Rabbits of Dancing Rabbit carry five-gallon buckets of waste as part of their humanure system, and Rabbit Kurt Kessner lamented, "I can't do some of the physical stuff I was doing twenty years ago or even five years ago."

In the mainstream US economy, assuming we have money, infirmity presents less of a problem; we outsource numerous forms of labor, from dog walking to home repair. In reality, the more physical the task, the more likely it is to be outsourced. I dug up much of our yard for garden beds, but the pleasure of knowing I did the work myself was compromised by the physical toll. And hiring someone to do the work costs less than physical therapy.

Despite the comparative economic advantages of outsourcing, many communities aim for egalitarian and nonhierarchical social and labor structures. Buying your way out of labor would implicitly violate the spirit if not existing covenants of the community. Even if community residents adapt their individual homes and lifestyles to accommodate increasing needs, they still must consider their roles in the community. So while intentional communities provide some security in terms of aging or disability, these communities and their residents must decide what levels of participation in community labor are acceptable.

Residents of both Cobb Hill in Hartland, Vermont, and Pioneer Valley in Amherst, Massachusetts, are beginning to address the challenges of aging, such as what happens when residents can no longer function in the community or on the land. Cobb Hill and Pioneer Valley both consist of well-constructed homes, with a mix of singles, duplexes, and triplexes; an interior walking path; and road access to the rear. Like Two Echo, common houses occupy the heart of the community, providing a central place for residents to eat and mingle. Both Cobb Hill and Pioneer Valley were built in hilly areas, affording beautiful views of the New England landscape, but creating difficulties in the region's long snowy winters. Bruce Chernoff, president and CEO of SCAN Foundation, which focuses on long-term health-care issues, calls it the 70-70-70 conundrum: "Seventy percent of people over the age of sixty-five will need some form of long-term-care supports as they age," he says. But when you look at polling, "roughly seventy percent of Americans don't actually think they're likely to need it, and roughly seventy percent think Medicare will probably cover it when they get there." The problem, of course, is that "those last two seventy percents are not true."[19]

Cobb Hill and Pioneer Valley residents recognize that, in time, they will need to adapt their lifestyles, but to what? they wonder. Peter Jessop, a longtime Pioneer Valley resident, commented,

> We have a little more trouble with workdays these days when we have a whole day set aside. They're not as well attended as they used to be and we don't get as much stuff done because we're not in our forties anymore. We're in our fifties, sixties, and seventies. We're looking at each other, asking who is going to mow the lawns here? Who is going to shovel the snow all winter long? Who's going to do all that work? Some of us will have to figure out how to age someplace else because we don't have a good plan here for making this place handicap accessible. And if you were in a wheelchair here, you couldn't get around very well. It's going to be a challenge to get all the work done.

Judith Bush, a long-term resident and membership coordinator of Cobb Hill, shared Jessop's concerns in regard to her community:

> We haven't developed our social contract about aging here. The subset of us who are older are in a fairly long-standing conversation about that topic from the perspective of: would we want to remain here as individuals? The geography of the place can become challenging for anybody with mobility problems, old or young. We haven't buckled down as a whole community and talked to each other about limits and expectations. Do you expect the community to do your unit's share of moving wood if you cannot?
>
> What's the community going to lose if there are X number of people who can't pull their weight? Then the person must decide, am I comfortable living here? There's an inner process and a community process.

Adapting facilities to the needs of a less mobile population at both Cobb Hill and Pioneer Valley would be difficult for several reasons. Changing the campus requires consensus and, for Pioneer Valley, permission from the town zoning board. Further, both communities lie on steep hills that can be treacherous in snow and ice. Ideally, they would build small residences onto or near their common houses, but in both cases, available space is so far from the common house that these residents would be isolated from the rest of the community. Jessop said that "a small group of us just made an offer on nine acres, and one of the concepts would be an over-fifty-five cohousing. It's a flat field. All handicap accessible, and close enough for a sister community."

Determining the format and governance of such a community presents a challenge because cohousing communities are typically considered and designed over time and with deliberation by residents, a process that should include ample time for reflection and consensus among residents. But, as always, there are trade-offs. Judith Bush noted, "Senior communities are a vibrant subsegment of cohousing. The classic cohousing model calls for resident development, but some cohousing developers are architects or proponents, and they come into a new group and fast-track the process. However, it compromises the learning, because they are facilitating your discussions."

The popularity of senior cohousing could lead to shortcomings in design and governance. Some communities take years to spring into being while residents debate, seek equity, and confer with others; however, some seniors might not be willing or able to spend years mulling over plans.

Currently, few intentional communities are designed for impaired mobility regardless of its cause, and some design impediments reflect conflicting goals of sustainability and access. For example, buildings in several ecovillages have incorporated high thresholds for heat retention and air tightness that do not accommodate people who use wheelchairs or have muscle fatigue. Geographer Amita Bhakta, who has cerebral palsy, wrote that her "floppy muscles" made it difficult to step over these high-threshold doorways. Most sustainability-focused intentional communities design around their natural geographies and incorporate permaculture principles to some degree while working within natural constraints. Bhakta asserts: "Nature itself can make the environment more difficult to pass through, for both wheelchair users and those with mobility disabilities. This restricts participation in a wider range of eco-living activities and can mean that sustaining the natural environment can exclude disabled people from involvement in community activities."[20]

Bhakta articulates the inherent tensions within ecovillages and sustainability-oriented intentional communities between sustainability and disability. Communities that encourage or require bread labor (such as building, agriculture, and energy production or maintaining natural features such as unpaved roads) make it difficult, if not impossible, for aging or disabled people to live there.

The issue of aging in community emerged frequently at the 2013 Twin Oaks Communities Conference, and one of the workshops focused on aging in community and home sharing. For example, Karen Bush acknowledged that the shared four-bedroom colonial walk-up, which had served the three housemates well for nine years, would not be adequate in the coming years and that they were looking for the next step. Later, in a workshop on income-sharing egalitarian communities, a young woman asked what happened when you are old or frail. Laird Schaub of the Federation of Egalitarian Communities replied that aging is a big issue for everyone and that communities have different answers, so you need to ask to find out which offer satisfactory answers for you. As an income-sharing egalitarian community, Twin Oaks meets all of its residents' cradle-to-grave needs: this is communism with a small c. Residents generally perform forty-two hours of work each week, but those who are fifty or older subtract one hour for each year above fifty from the requirement. Nonetheless, the Twin Oaks community balances for age by restricting applications from "pensioners" older than fifty when the average age among members rises above forty.[21] However, because Twin Oaks counts so many activities as labor, even aging people should have no trouble performing the requisite amount of work. Further, as our tour guide claimed anecdotally, Twin Oaks residents are generally healthier than the average American because their lifestyle is so active.

Our Twin Oaks tour guide brought us to the community's new hospice, where we sat in air-conditioned comfort and peppered him with questions. Residents had wanted to care for a dying resident on the premises and therefore built the facility, which included a hospital bed and a motorized wheelchair. The accommodation allow residents to die in their community rather than in a hospital. Although they will bring in outside medical personnel when necessary, residents can fulfill their labor credits by caring for their friends and colleagues. Of all intentional communities, Twin Oaks boasts one of the most advanced on-site healthcare facilities, but others are certain to follow its lead. Income-sharing communities such as Twin Oaks might be especially motivated by its cradle-to-grave commitment, but communities such as Dancing Rabbit, which seek to be full-service villages, are bound to consider these kinds of support structures as their residents age. Miccosukee

Land Co-op near Tallahassee, Florida, which celebrated its fortieth anniversary in September 2013, recently added facilities for aging.

As Schaub suggested, community solutions to aging vary according to the community type and its residents.[22] Most residents of intentional communities are not wealthy, and some fall below the poverty line—sometimes intentionally, like Catholic workers. Other residents have worked in alternative economies or alternative currencies, so they can well provide for their food, clothing, and shelter needs within the community, but do not have dollars that translate outside the community. For example, one Rabbit replied to a visitor who asked about the ability to retire after working at Dancing Rabbit that "your Dancing Rabbit income would allow you to live well in that community, but not outside in the mainstream." Egalitarian communities like Twin Oaks offer a freedom that stems from full security, but few communities offer care of that magnitude.

In a workshop on community and legal issues, one participant asked whether we could create an affordable middle ground between Twin Oaks and expensive continual care retirement communities such as Oak Hammock in Gainesville. He wondered if we could create programs like Vista or AmeriCorps to merge senior wisdom with youthful energy. More young people, twenty-something millennials, seem to be drawn to community life and, as social entrepreneurs, are creating innovative solutions to a range of social problems. Also, if retirees increasingly seek multigenerational living situations, as Phyllis Korkki suggests, perhaps the mix might generate novel solutions.[23] For example, Hope Meadows, an intergenerational community with twelve families, fifty children, and sixty seniors in Rantoul, Illinois, pairs senior "grandparents" with families with children to "adopt." This innovation offers reduced rent to the senior residents in return for their volunteer grandparenting.[24]

Boomers to Millennials

Today, intentional communities appeal to a broad range of people, from creative energetic hipsters to activism-oriented baby boomers. While aging boomers are increasingly drawn to shared living arrangements, communities often struggle to attract young families, who might be put off by the disproportionate numbers of boomers and child-free twenty-somethings. However, the social cohesion and support do attract young families as well as single women over fifty who recognize the mutual benefits of such communities.

Whether they live in communes, cohousing groups, or ecovillages, residents of these communities realize that they are creating new pathways both for themselves as individuals who seek to create their own ways of being in a community context and for their chosen communities, which model options for others who seek the same kinds of community.

Many residents of intentional communities never imagined themselves living in community, especially older Americans raised on the dream of a two-car garage attached to a single-family home. Whether driven to home sharing by the desire for companionship or by financial necessity, many older women have appreciated the benefits of sharing their homes with others and have learned how to maintain privacy in the context of shared space. Living in community requires social skills around conflict resolution, which is a challenge, but pays dividends in reducing the loneliness and isolation experienced by many seniors in single-dwelling residences. Individuals and families joining intentional communities must decide the extent to which they wish to interweave their lives with others.

Inviting others into shared living space—whether a home or an ecovillage—demands serious thought and an extended vetting period. Both residents and potential residents need to understand how others respond to a variety of circumstances and must agree on approaches such as individual property, work requirements, and group participation. Thus, most communities have a formal process by which residents and potential residents can suss each other out, and making participation requirements and community values transparent helps avoid unnecessary conflict. While most people would like to avoid disputes, this vetting and sorting process raises questions about the extent to which we surround ourselves with like-minded people. In tightly bound communities, consensus and governance are already difficult even among residents who share values, and gaining consensus about issues such as sustainability among a representative sample of Americans might be impossible. Nonetheless, given concerns about the growing polarization of the United States, are intentional communities one more instance of "gated communities," despite their intentions of broad engagement with the public?

Despite the inevitable sorting, intentional communities showcase processes, lifestyles, and governance skills that can benefit everyone. Women working to create home-sharing agreements might find they have much in common with communities that have created robust governance structures, and aging residents of cohousing communities might appreciate the social fabric of Twin Oaks. Even if community residents might align on more overtly political aspects of gender and environment, shared experiences across communities, such as aging, might generate broader alliances and coalitions. Regardless of how much residents choose to interweave their lives with others, these communities—from ecovillages to home-sharing agreements—are creating new forms of American culture based on community, resource sharing, and mutual support.

4

Creating Cultures

It's creating a culture instead of fighting against systems we don't agree with. It's creating a new system and culture that we can live in and that work.
—Sarah Wilcox-Hughes

SARAH WILCOX-HUGHES and Ethan Hughes founded the Possibility Alliance because they wanted to be the change they wanted to see in the world by creating the culture they desired and not simply complaining about the world they live in. Similarly, Alline Anderson, a longtime resident of Dancing Rabbit, said, "It has to start somewhere, with someone. I'm not trying to change the world personally. I don't think I have that power. I'm trying to find a way to live my life in a way that feels in alignment with my values. I'm trying not to use more than my share. I'd like to be contributing to the solution, not the problem."

What Anderson, Hughes, and Wilcox-Hughes share with their friends and colleagues living in community is the goal of creating cultures that enable them to author their own lives. They seek the freedom to find their own paths by experimenting with and intentionally living out a set of ideals.

People find and join Catholic worker houses, ecovillages, and cohousing communities because they seek to create different lifeways and patterns. Most residents of intentional communities share critiques of mainstream society—for example, the waste and anomie associated with sprawl—and they also share social anxieties engendered by modern life and, more recently, the extended economic malaise that the United States can't seem to shake. Intentional communities aren't about escapism or running away from individual problems; residents work much too hard for simple escapism. Instead, they seek to live with intention, asking what a good life is and producing the lives they wish to lead.

Nonetheless, most community residents hail from the middle class and acknowledge the privilege that enables them to reject the mainstream and design new communities and alternatives. Residents of these communities have been able to choose voluntary simplicity, for example, and most see this choice as enriching their lives. Poverty and unemployment, however, have coerced millions of North Americans into involuntary simplicity and have forced difficult choices: between milk and medicine, for example. Few community residents are forced to make those choices.

Defining Freedom

For many people, intentional community delivers the exact opposite of freedom, especially if we define *freedom* in the context of individual rights. For example, many intentional communities have requirements, rules, and covenants that are often far more restrictive than those of homeowners' associations. When I bring up the topic of intentional communities, I hear a range of responses from "I could never live like that" to "Only community can save us" and everything in between. Although some people understand—and actually experience—community as oppressive and recoil from the rules and social obligations, others find liberation in communal obligations and relations. For some, living in community provides the freedom and autonomy to pursue alternatives that are not possible in the mainstream.

Our fifty-plus tour guide at Twin Oaks espoused the latter point of view. During our one-and-a-half-hour tour, we walked through the many buildings and open spaces of the Twin Oaks campus. The community's buildings, homes, and fields occupy over 350 acres of rolling countryside, giving Twin Oaks the air of a rural retreat. The unpaved roads showed the effects of recent summer storms, and we dodged puddles and mud as we learned about the community, the small businesses that keep it afloat, and the labor that living at Twin Oaks involves. Almost everything we saw—buildings, agricultural fields, and pathways—was the result of the labor of past and present residents.

Twin Oaks residents perform forty-two hours of labor weekly and must abide by community rules, but the community meets all of its residents' needs, including health care and education. For our guide, the security provided by Twin Oaks freed him from worries about access to health care that plague many Americans. Currently, as Americans are engaged in rancorous debates about health care and the appropriate relationship between government and individuals, tightly bound and self-insured communities such as Twin Oaks demonstrate one community alternative to this vexing social problem. Many people, even those living in community, have a more ambivalent relationship with rules. For example, Alline Anderson of Dancing Rabbit found the many community rules to be cumbersome, even though she helped design those rules.

Rules or no rules, community residents recognize that intentional communities provide them the physical, social, and emotional sustenance to live out their values. A boomer-aged psychiatrist who recently moved to Sirius noted that his sustainability goals were achievable only in community. "It's the camaraderie. I sold a big house in the suburbs to reduce my carbon footprint, and I couldn't do it without changing my lifestyle. We're not off the grid, but we're close to it. We grow much of our own food, and the garden is such an important part of our life here. I wouldn't have that if I wasn't in community. The main thing is the people, but I also needed the lifestyle of being closer to the earth and a smaller carbon footprint."

The Valhalla Movement, a community near Montreal officially launched in 2012, links community, sustainability, and freedom in what its members call "freedom culture," which they define as "a collective state of being that empowers and encourages all individuals to contribute their unique gifts to the world. Through ecologically sustainable lifestyles, economic self-reliance in local communities, and global collaborative action for the benefit of all, freedom culture can become the new normal."[1]

Although the Valhalla Movement has a physical location near Montreal, its members understand themselves as a movement, providing links among individuals and communities. Sustainability, Valhalla states, produces freedom because "when you provide your own food, water and energy, you do not need to work in order to survive. You OWN your life! Consequently you have more free time to dedicate towards helping the world. Right now the world needs people who can dedicate their lives to bringing about change."[2]

I met an energetic twenty-something representing the Valhalla Movement when we were both visiting Sirius in October 2013. Members of Valhalla Movement have traveled to intentional communities around the world documenting stories and achievements, hoping to "proliferate 'freedom culture' by igniting a global passion for sustainability, self-reliance, and collaborative action," as stated on the Valhalla Movement's website. The boomer from Sirius and the millennial of Valhalla exist on different ends of the community spectrum, both generationally and in regard to technology. The boomer gave away his TV and, like most Sirius residents, avoids the demands of email and Facebook, while the Valhalla Movement team embraces emerging forms of communication media that most of her generation are fluent with. However, both these individuals and their respective communities link community and freedom, where living in intentional community creates the freedom to "own your life."

That freedom, as espoused by the Valhalla Movement, brings up questions about the nature of work or labor. Providing for your own food, water, and energy needs, members claim, eliminates the need for work, presumably meaning paid labor. However, the reality of owning your life then constitutes bread labor—contributing to meeting your own basic needs. Valhalla's point of view carries the implication that this is not work, but bread labor often means tasks that demand the physical labor that most of us identify as work or, at least, sustained effort. Mark Becker and his fellow Possibility Alliance residents specifically draw upon bread labor—and its rich history—to describe both how they produce their food and how this labor enacts a social ethic. The "Possibility Alliance Mission Statement and Guiding Principles," written and signed in 2007, declares:

> We will practice "Bread Labor," a term embraced by Leo Tolstoy, later adopted by Gandhi. The principle is that everyone who is able should assume a share of the physical work to provide life's basic needs. When people avoid this necessary work, their share of the work unfairly shifts onto the shoulders of others (usually the poor and oppressed). Tolstoy and Gandhi saw in this the root of all oppression. We will produce as much as we can to provide our basic needs on the land and work with our own hands in our gardens, orchards, and forests. Each day we will move closer to self-sufficiency, and until we are completely self-sufficient, we shall get our resources as locally as possible (within biking distances and within our bioregion).[3]

History of Bread Labor

Becker and others use the term *bread labor* to describe what I think of as extreme DIY—do it yourself—a lifestyle-changing form of DIY that

Possibility Alliance daily schedule, including bread labor

extends beyond the contemporary trendiness of such projects. Cable TV schedules, for example, are crammed with DIY shows and competitions and, thanks to Amazon's one-click purchasing option, my own bookshelf groans with home and gardening books. While many do-it-yourselfers enjoy honing their skills as a hobby, others create their own food, clothing, and shelters out of financial necessity. However, the ways Becker and others speak of bread labor reflects the term's origin as an ethical stance: simply living off of the physical labor of others is wrong. Ethan Hughes quoted Lanza del Vasto (1901–1981), the founder of the Community of the Ark, as an inspiration.

> Work with your hands. Don't force others to work for you. Don't make others into slaves, even if you call them paid workers. Find the shortest, simplest way between the earth, the hands, and the mouth.... Do it yourself. Show that it is possible to live this way.
>
> Then you know at once what are the true needs and what are fantasies. When you have to sweat to satisfy your needs, you soon know whether or not it's worth your while. But if it's someone else's sweat, there is no end to our needs. We need cigarettes, beer, cars, soft drinks, appliances, elec-

tronic devices, and on and on. . . . Learn to do without. . . . Learn how to celebrate . . . prepare the feast from what your own hands have grown and let it be magnificent.[4]

Tolstoy popularized the term *bread labor*, which was created by Russian writer T. M. Bonaref, arguing that everyone should perform some bread labor—some physical work—to support his or her own existence, whether growing food, building shelter, or making clothes—rather than living off the labor of others. Although bread labor is more an ethical than an economic stance, it doesn't mean that each person must be self-sufficient by individually fulfilling his or her own needs. Instead, performing bread labor ensures that we recognize the work that produces our food, homes, and clothing and that acknowledges that we all rely on others. Further, doing our own sweeping and cleaning, for example, inculcates the humility that none of us are above these essential, but often denigrated, chores.

Mohandas K. Gandhi adopted this concept in his campaigns for Indian independence and the freedom and dignity of Indian peasants. He founded the Tolstoy and Phoenix ashrams in South Africa, utopian farm-ashrams that emphasize the dignity of human labor and promote bread labor, the idea that all people should contribute their own labor for goods consumed.[5] Gandhi demanded that all ashram residents share in the labor of cleaning the latrines, causing tension with high-caste Hindus who typically avoided work deemed polluting. Although Gandhi borrowed the concept of bread labor from Tolstoy, he stated that the third chapter of the *Bhagavad-Gita*, a central Hindu text, reflects the principle that food eaten without sacrifice, or bread labor, is stolen.[6] Even today Gandhian intentional communities require four hours per day of bread labor.

Although the term *bread labor* is not popular in the United States, the subset of the population familiar with Catholic workers or Helen and Scott Nearing is likely to be familiar with the concept, if not the term itself. In the 1930s, Catholic workers founders Dorothy Day and Peter Maurin incorporated the term and concept of bread labor into both philosophy and practice, and bread labor became a critical part of Maurin's agronomic university plans.[7] Maurin developed the concept of the agronomic university as a pedagogy that would both provide the poor with salable skills and dignify their labor.[8] Maurin hoped to create a green revolution (as opposed to a bloody, red revolution) that would bring a blend of physical and intellectual labor to the land and promote skilled agrarian communities, a plan remarkably similar to Gandhi's.⁹ Today, following the Rockefeller Foundation–funded Green Revolution program in the 1970s that emphasized chemical- and water-intensive industrial agriculture, most associate the term *green revolution* with the high-input, high-yield monocultures that have overrun the US Midwest and much of the world. Maurin, on the other hand, envisioned a democratizing and ecologically sound green revolution that would bring material, spiritual, and intellectual benefits to the poor.

Similarly, the gurus of homesteading, Helen and Scott Nearing, adopted bread labor when they began homesteading in the 1930s. They also required that residents work four hours of physical labor daily.¹⁰ Today, residents of intentional communities, who typically hail from the US middle class, have adopted the term and adapted it to the twenty-first century. While many might not directly attribute the phrase or concept of bread labor directly to Tolstoy, the term circulates among communities, especially Catholic worker communities, and has been brought back into circulation by the Jesus Radicals, a network exploring links between Christianity and anarchism.¹¹

Producing Your Own Life

I met Mark Becker when I first arrived at the Possibility Alliance in May 2011. I was disoriented from my drive through rural northeast Missouri. Missouri's county roads wind through the countryside along streams and farmsteads, and the steep rolling hills unsettled me—it felt like riding a roller coaster but without the tracks to guide the car. Yellow signs alert drivers to the presence of horse-driven buggies, and I didn't want to meet either a buggy or a pickup truck cresting one of these blind hills. Ethan Hughes had given me excellent directions, and I was relieved when I saw the Amish homestead that housed the Possibility Alliance. While Amish homesteads are typically painted white, Hughes and Wilcox-Hughes chose a taupe/lavender to blend with the taupe and mauve hues of the prairie landscape. I was relieved to have arrived, but nervous because the Possibility Alliance was my first community visit, and I wasn't sure what I would find.

I found Becker, a slight twenty-seven-year-old originally from Iowa, wearing what looked like a pair of homemade pants. At first, I couldn't get the image of a scarecrow out of my mind. But later, after many conversations and singing with him on the steps of the front porch, I struggled to recall that first impression. No matter what he was doing, whether making bread in the cob oven or hoeing rows in the garden, he did it cheerfully. More than anyone else, Becker embodied the phrase "joyful productivity" that graced the calendars of several communities, including the Possibility Alliance and Sirius. I sought him out for conversation many times during my time at the Possibility Alliance. One morning, he spoke of his personal goals and what he hoped to accomplish there. I later heard his concerns about food, social justice, and the freedom to produce your own life echoed in conversations with individuals in a number of communities.

> Food production is a really important piece. Peter Maurin said that you don't set a man free by breaking his shackles, you set a man free by connecting him with his destiny. Our destiny is to be creative people, doing the work that serves each other and serves the good of the people, not just the work that keeps these things moving.
> Bread labor, with a particular focus on food production, is my first step. I want to produce my own clothing. I want to produce my own life. And this is not just as a utopian vision, but I want to show that a joyful, vibrant life of fullness in every aspect that humans need is possible without this system of violence that we've created. So I hope that through work, through bread labor, and through service, we can connect with people in need.

Becker and the other residents grew a significant portion of their own food. Because the Possibility Alliance began on an existing homestead, residents could focus on food and agriculture rather than buildings or infrastructure. When I visited, they had already created several garden areas and cleared land for a Peace and Permaculture Center. Their plentiful meals and well-stocked cellar belied the reality that growing food is hard work. It is tempting to romanticize this labor. Working outside in the fresh air sounds especially appealing after a long day glaring at my computer, struggling to produce intelligible prose. One morning Becker and I, along with six other residents, prepared one of the newer fields for potatoes. From 9:00 until noon in the hot sun, we dug trenches and built rows in the hard-packed soil. The Midwest's 2012 drought was just beginning, and the heavy clay soil was difficult to break up. After lunch, we worked until dinner. They had planned to have a garden party, but it was too hot even for fun. We worried that the forecasted rain wouldn't come and that all of that hard work would be in vain. As I hoed with the others, I silently thanked

Alice McGary of Mustard Seed for teaching me how to use a hoe correctly, but despite my improved technique, I still ended up with wrist pain and a bloody blister. We completed only six rows that day, and I knew that after I left, the group would continue tilling, planting, tending, and, eventually, canning.

Why today, when we have HyVee, Publix, Amazon, and global supply chains, would Becker and residents of many other communities want to grow their own food, make their own clothes, and build their own houses? Let's step back from Becker and look at how bread labor, independence, and community reflect larger social anxieties. Few individuals possess the skills to grow, sew, and build what they need. These tasks are time and labor intensive, and economists argue that doing rather than purchasing is incredibly inefficient. However, residents of communities such as the Possibility Alliance have chosen this DIY lifestyle, so their rationale must go beyond economic or circumstantial necessity. Becker identified his efforts at food production as the first step toward the freedom to produce his own life and to create his own destiny.

Consider our consumer choices and freedom, taking the example of food available in a ubiquitous North American grocery store. In Gainesville, where Publix stores conveniently appear about every twenty blocks, snack aisles overflow with varieties of chips, pretzels, and popcorn. Every year new flavors created in sophisticated laboratories and produced in huge factories lure us toward the interior aisles—where we can choose, say, between Doritos and Cheetos—and away from the healthier foods that line the outer edges of the stores. This overflowing abundance and apparent variety illustrate one aspect—or perhaps the illusion—of freedom and choice: the assumption that consumers enjoy a multitude of options. I argue that this is a false assumption about freedom and food. We can choose anything we want, as long as a corporate entity has decided to provide it.

Supermarkets project the story that we are free to eat what we choose and that the abundance of food available for quick purchase frees us for more productive endeavors, whether work or leisure. True, buying food at Publix, especially prepared foods, would free me for hours of biking, kayaking, and writing, but I wonder whether I would have truly chosen or merely succumbed to the seductive pull of corporate food production, complete with attractive packaging supported by billion-dollar ad campaigns.

The choices available to me reflect a level of privilege that not everyone shares. Many people in the United States do not have easy access to well-stocked supermarkets. Approximately 23.5 million urban and rural residents live in food deserts, defined by the USDA as "urban neighborhoods and rural towns without ready access to fresh, healthy, and affordable food," who face the challenge of making healthful and economical meals from foods available at convenience stores.[12] When fast food outlets populate each block in a food desert—a food swamp—unhealthy food choices become the default, and the people who live there, often already trapped in cycles of poverty, must bear the additional burden of the health consequences of eating convenience foods.

Bread Labor, Food, and Freedom

Now let us consider the freedom of growing your own food. For one, individuals and communities seek the freedom to grow and eat the foods they want, not simply the foods that are marketed to us. Growing food can also be a step toward food security, community development, and improved health by, for example, providing easier access to vegetables.

While grocery stores now sell a variety of prepared and fresh foods, growing food allows some control over food choices even though it brings its own seasonal and geographic constraints. Today, most stores have responded to burgeoning consumer demand for local and organic foods, but consumers must rely on stores' willingness and ability to provide these products, especially less profitable products, such as heirloom tomatoes with shorter shelf lives than commercial varieties, rutabagas, or cardoons.

Food freedom encompasses freedom from violence and unsustainable practices. Becker, like many residents of sustainability-focused intentional communities, lamented the systemic violence of our contemporary food system. Farmers, scientists, and writers such as Wendell Berry, Wes Jackson, and Fred Kirschenmann have documented how large-scale industrial agriculture has devastated rural economies and poisoned soils and water. Almost a century ago, Gandhi argued that true freedom lay in our ability, as individuals and communities, to provide for our own needs, especially food, clothing, and shelter, and that we must break the chains of dependence on centralized forces such as governments and corporations. Gandhi feared that cravings for consumer products would bind newly independent Indians to those who fulfilled their desires, and he under-

Baltimore Free Farm/Horizontal Housing

stood these ties as a form of violence. Today, Gandhi's prescient warnings seem to have foretold the junk food industry's ability to prey on the inherent human yearning for fats and sugars. Michael Moss describes the research and marketing behind flavors and food products we (are supposed to) crave, such as the aforementioned Doritos.[13] Similarly, Marion Nestle explains the corporate control of our food system.[14] I have never eaten Lunchables, and I hope I never will, but some reptilian part of my brain lights up every time I eat Doritos, so I understand the compulsion.

The salads, bean soups, and home-baked breads served at Possibility Alliance seemed a world apart from the processed foods, even the healthier options, sold in supermarkets and convenience stores. While Becker and his colleagues had less variety than is available to shoppers in grocery stores, they also were free from the constraints of mainstream choices and desires.

Growing food and supporting similarly minded growers and producers create alternatives, even in urban areas and food deserts. While many communities like the Possibility Alliance have settled in rural regions so they have the acreage to farm, urban communities like LA Eco-village and Baltimore Free Farm have stepped up to address food desert challenges. The LA Eco-village Food Lobby, a bulk food micro-industry, brings bulk foods to LA Eco-village and their neighbors in Koreatown. Similarly, situated in the historic North Baltimore Hampden neighborhood, Baltimore Free Farm and the nearby Ash Street Community Garden both provide garden space in this working-class neighborhood and donate fruit and vegetables to their neighbors. Further, Baltimore Free Farm residents do "food rescue" each Wednesday, reclaiming three hundred to five hundred pounds of food that would otherwise have gone to the landfill. Bread, fruits, and vegetables near or just past their expiration date might be unsalable, but they are safe and edible.

Trade-offs: Food Freedom or Outsourcing Your Life

Does growing our own food or making our own clothes make sense when we could invest that time and effort into income-generating activities that allow us to purchase those essentials? Quoted in a *New York Times* article, Columbia University economics professors Jon Steinsson and Emi Nakamura argued that engaging in subsistence activities does not make sense, demonstrating that outsourcing almost any chore, ranging from cleaning to sorting old photos, leads to subsequent income gains if the time is invested in career-related activity.[15] I suspect most economists would agree with Steinsson and Nakamura, who cited the principle of comparative advantage, and, in fact, most people routinely outsource jobs ranging from food production to car maintenance. Indeed, nearly all global corporations learned the economic benefits of outsourcing long ago, which is why most consumer goods available in the United States are not made here but rather in other countries where labor and environmental laws are less stringent.

Interestingly, immediately after I read this article about the benefits of outsourcing, my eye fell upon another that offered a different take on work, money, and freedom. Jim Sollisch wrote about his millennial musician son who makes just enough money to get by and save a little, but lives the "life of a millionaire retiree."[16] That is, he does what he loves. We have no scale other than the IRS scale—that is, money—as Sollisch points out, to measure a successful lifestyle. So how do we account for residents of communities who enjoy the trappings of a middle-class lifestyle on $10,000 per year? Perhaps we could turn to other scales, such as the World Happiness Scale, which indicates that greater wealth does not necessarily correlate with greater happiness (http://worldhappiness.report/).

Nonetheless, while home cooking, canning, and making your own clothes provide some measure of freedom from corporate America, these activities tend toward gendered roles and restrictions our mothers and grandmothers sought to escape. For many women—and, later, men—TV dinners and prepared foods provided an escape from kitchen drudgery, so these foods do illustrate a form of freedom. After all, after a day of work, it is far easier to order a pizza than make a nutritious home-cooked meal. Nonetheless, the labor of preparing food in more traditional ways falls disproportionately on women. Most intentional communities strive to renegotiate gender roles so that neither men nor women are trapped in traditional roles. As Rebecca Gould notes in *At Home in Nature,* the homesteading populations following Helen and Scott Nearing also held those goals, but typically families lapsed into traditional roles, especially after children came. However, she continues, it is important to consider *how* individuals perform activities such as cooking because, for many homesteaders and community residents, cooking and canning are themselves forms of resistance to commercial culture.[17] Ironically, while religious and cultural conservatives might hold that women belong in the kitchen—and some women agree—other women use cooking and canning as means of resisting existing food cultures.

These articles demonstrate some of the trade-offs inherent in bread labor and alternative lifestyles. Intentional community residents spend many hours fulfilling basic needs, such as producing food that could be obtained more efficiently at Wal-Mart. Their labor produces little economic benefit in the context of the US economy, but, like Sollisch's son, they have enough money, though not much extra. However, these communities emphasize values such as sustainability, voluntary simplicity, and equity, and producing their own goods enables them to live these values. They believe that purchasing food or other goods at conventional grocery stores or Wal-Mart or Target feeds an exploitive system in which low-wage workers in the United States and abroad manufacture cheap products for US consumers. Performing bread labor is one means to resist the system and live the life and values they cherish.

Bread Labor for a New Millennium

Mark Becker and others who embrace bread labor and related values swim upstream against a culture that lionizes efficiency and our mass-produced, profit-driven consumer culture. Although the work is difficult, Becker is enhancing his farming skills and deepening his relations with nature and with others. More important for Becker, though, his bread labor gives him control—authorship—over his life and frees him from the constraints of mainstream society. His bread labor and voluntary simplicity are means to a vibrant life, not guilt-induced deprivation. Further, he is crafting his life both in a community setting and in engagement with the world outside his community; he is not isolated.

Residents of intentional communities perform bread labor, in part, to resist inequitable and exploitive economic systems, and they aim to create systems that are sustainable in terms of economy, equity, and ecology. Both Possibility Alliance and New Hope near Dubuque, Iowa, draw upon the concepts of bread labor and the agronomic university to frame their practices. Eric Anglada brought Maurin's plan to life in 2010 when he created Growing Roots at New Hope Catholic worker farm, a twenty-eight-acre, four-family community farm. Although New Hope is not far from Dubuque, the steep narrow roads made the region seem remote; to call my husband, each morning and evening I climbed over a mile up the hill to gain cell phone access. Anglada writes that a group of Catholic workers met for a week and labored to "dig deeper into the intellectual, spiritual, and agrarian core of the Catholic worker—and explore its meaning today."[18]

> Each day we awoke at 6:30 a.m. to milk the cow, feed the chickens, take a walk, or pick berries, then came together at 8 a.m. to pray the Daily Office and eat breakfast. The next three hours were devoted to the "intellectual," during which Michael Baxter and Sheila McCarthy, both from the Catholic worker house [South Bend Catholic Worker] in South Bend, Indiana, led us in discussions on various topics, including "The Intellectual Foundations of the Catholic Worker," "Alisdair MacIntyre and Permaculture," "Peter Maurin, Tradition, and Herbal Medicine," and "The Integrating Visions of Hildegard of Bingen and Ade Bethune." After lunch and a leisurely rest, we devoted another three hours to engaging creation and our bodies. The work was varied, ranging from splitting wood and weaving baskets to harvesting vegetables and identifying wild edibles in the woods. The close of the day found us around the bonfire, playing music and singing.[19]

In late spring 2012, I attended a weeklong permaculture class hosted by Anglada and New Hope that followed a similar structure. We camped in the area that doubled as our classroom. The class mixed discussions of permaculture principles with design exercises in which we considered how to use the land's natural features to fulfill the farm's goals. We learned that, according to permaculture principles, features should fulfill multiple goals, so we debated how the existing spring could function as a natural refrigerator and fishing hole, among other things. Several of my classmates had just returned from a Jesus Radicals gathering, and I learned about a group of self-described anarchists who are striving to live out Jesus's gospel, a radical stance in today's capitalist economy. During class discussions and in the evenings sitting around the fire, the Jesus Radicals and the Catholic workers taught this religious studies professor a great deal about compassion, open dialogue, and living the world you wish to see.

Adam Campbell of the Possibility Alliance, although not a Catholic worker himself, taught the course, and most of the other participants were affiliated with the contemporary Catholic Worker Movement. Anglada noted the current strength and growth of the movement, which had virtually been given its last rites in the 1980s, as explored by author Dan McKanan.[20] Anglada and I discussed challenges facing bread labor and craft culture in our contemporary socioeconomic context.

> There is good interest in the Catholic Worker Movement, but it is hard to view them as more than token gestures in a lot of ways. But in a lot of ways, everything we do is sort of a token gesture. Making candles and making soap are important, but it's hard to envision economies built around those things. For the last several generations, capitalism has commodified everything we did to meet our own needs. We pay for services that we ourselves or a community or a village used to do ourselves. And so hand-dipped candles and making soap are novelties. We're not pure or perfect and that's not what we're searching for. It's just trying to have integrity about our daily lives. Food is the most direct and in many ways the easiest way to do that.

All the Catholic workers I spoke with emphasized the difficulty and slow pace of social change, but agreed that living their values sustained Peter Maurin and Dorothy Day's vision. Anglada, though, acknowledged that slow change through living and demonstrating the change is part of Catholic worker spirituality. "Day's favorite saint was Therese of Lisieux, a conservative, traditional young woman who you wouldn't necessarily associate with

Dorothy Day. Day was an anarchist, but Therese of Lisieux was all about the little way. We embrace the fact that we're doing small actions and hoping that these actions add up to a bigger movement. It is a spiritual thing—we're not going for a mass movement or some giant reform."

Alice McGary of Mustard Seed articulated the movement's goals and her rationale for acting on these principles. Mustard Seed is one of the smallest communities I visited, both in acreage (eleven acres) and number of participants (four to five residents). The acreage, near Ames, Iowa, sits on the edge of a larger farm, and although Mustard Seed did not own the land, McGary and her husband had built a small house there. Mustard Seed is well known in Ames and publishes a newsletter, the *Catholic Worker Farmer*, which reaches beyond Ames and Iowa. McGary said,

> Solidarity with the poor, voluntary poverty, nonviolence, the works of mercy, hospitality, education about social justice, the land ethic that Peter Maurin taught, distributive economics and this idea of land and craft, and this model of doing work because you believe in it, not because you're getting rewarded for it. We're turning our economic models upside down by making that switch. It's a foreign switch and hard to communicate and model to people, but it's really important to me. This work is important and we want to do it, because it's serving the greater good, and I have a passion about it. And I feel like it needs my soul, and I'm willing to do it not for pay. I'm choosing. I do not want to do it for pay.

Like Becker, she emphasized that the work is not drudgery, but service to others: "The work is also really important. Our work is a service to each other, and it's not that I'm suffering through drudgery in order to get what I want. I do think that the actual physical work and the fruits of our labor are really vital to what we're about."

For Catholic workers and Possibility Alliance residents, the term *bread labor* evokes a legacy of thinkers including Gandhi, Tolstoy, Peter Maurin, and Dorothy Day. Bread labor is a service to others and a means of deepening community bonds. Whether community residents consciously use the term or not, for most, their work and participation in these communities, fulfilling essential needs, offers freedom from the emotional and social demands of mainstream society. Since they labor for themselves and their chosen communities, not corporations, universities, or governments, they perceive—as does the Valhalla Movement—that in performing the labor of self-sustenance, they own their lives.

5

Asking What's for Dinner

In solidarity with our street friends, I eat what is present. Solidarity is transformative for all of us, so I will eat dumpstered supreme pizza if that is what is available.
—Eric Garbison, Cherith Brook Catholic Worker

RESIDENTS JOIN sustainability-focused communities because they hope to translate values such as voluntary simplicity, self-sufficiency or interdependence, appropriate technologies, and integral nonviolence, including nonviolent communications, into practice. Food is the most direct and, in many ways, the easiest way to practice these values on the personal, community, and ecological scales. However, practicing nonviolence raises questions—for example, what counts as nonviolent food and what is meant by voluntary simplicity? These questions and the choices that result reflect decisions about food that many people make on a daily basis; for example, are cage-free eggs worth the price?[1] (I think so.) Books, newspaper articles, and movies have persuaded North Americans that eating is not a neutral act; each forkful raised to our lips qualifies as a vote for a food system. I purchase and drink Organic Valley milk because I value hormone-free milk and because Organic Valley's cooperative structure benefits farmers and rural regions. I also purchase local produce to benefit producers in my own Alachua County. The proliferation of food labels suggests that more and more people use ethical and environmental criteria to guide what and how they eat. For example, a Fair Trade International label (http://www.fairtrade.net/) indicates that farmers, workers, and producers received a fairer price, and the Certified Humane seal (http://www.certifiedhumane.org/) ensures humane treatment of farm animals.[2] That meaningless designations, such as "100 percent natural," have also proliferated indicates that more and more consumers care about how their foods were grown, slaughtered, and produced. Navigating and prioritizing the values inherent in various labels can be difficult and disorienting. For example, is it more important to eat local or organic?

For individuals or families, deciding what to eat can be complicated and stressful, so it is clear that feeding large groups of people means that conflicts are all but inevitable. For residents of intentional communities who join to live out values around nonviolence, sustainability, and cooperation, food and eating can be both highly gratifying and problematic in terms of practicing nonviolent communication. Communal meals, even if they are only monthly potlucks, can strengthen community bonhomie, and most communities consider some shared meals essential for their existence as a community.

Most of the communities held shared values on the importance of local and organic foods, or at least what they perceived as sustainably produced foods. Choosing local foods benefited their own internal economies (for example, micro-industries such as cheese making) or their neighbors'. Most grew food organically or generally purchased, if possible, organic foods. Communities or individuals that ate meat typically chose humanely raised meats or, in some cases, had access to hunted meats, such as venison or fish. Deciding what to eat and determining who decides what to eat are more difficult, in part, because these decisions require that residents translate values such as nonviolence or hospitality into specific food practices and communication practices, which means making trade-offs.[3] The decisions must address questions such as: How it is possible to eat nonviolently? How we might eat and produce food in ways that are sustainable and just for the earth, animals, and people? For individuals and communities that protest the systemic violence of industrial agriculture, what constitutes nonviolent food and agriculture? These questions extend from a central question: How should we think about food and nonviolence?

After all, eating is inherently violent: something must die so that we can eat. One way of addressing this question is to consider the connotations of ahimsa, an Indian word that is often translated as nonviolence. The Sanskrit word *a-himsa* (literally, no harm) implies abstaining from harmful action, meaning that we should eat, breathe, and work in ways that cause minimal harm to other beings. Jains, for example, do not eat root vegetables to avoid the inevitable violence and karma that result from killing the plants and microorganisms in the soil. Nonviolence is a call to action, not simply a lack of action or withdrawal, and these communities are actively rethinking all aspects of life, including food production, using the rubric of nonviolence. Because discussions about what we should eat reflect cultural and religious norms, communities continually reassess what it means to eat less violently and what it means in their specific contexts.

Humane Eating: Coffee, Chocolate, and Meat

Possibility Alliance residents interpret and enact nonviolence through their modes of growing and eating food. Like many intentional communities, they grow virtually all of the food they eat, although they receive some food in trade or gift from friends and family. Several neighboring homesteaders had settled on Frontier Lane to be part of Possibility Alliance's larger community orbit, and they contributed both food and expertise in food production. During the summer, residents fish in their small pond. Their chickens, which roam freely around the homestead, provide eggs and occasional meat, such as the chicken dinner I ate with them during a Friday evening Shabbat. Breakfast consisted of grains flavored with fruit, milk, and syrup; lunch and dinner featured salad greens, soup, homemade bread, and a cooked vegetable. Most of us combined all of our food into one bowl, combining soup, salad, vegetable, and bread into one tasty pile, with some of us eating with hand-carved spoons. Both of my visits took place in May and June when the first greens could be harvested; later in the summer and fall, meals would include peppers, cauliflower, and many other seasonal vegetables from their gardens. Canned produce from the previous year filled the cellar and supplemented meals in early summer.

We ate most of our meals outside, shaded from the sun that had just begun to climb toward its summer heat. One table is always set aside for anyone wishing to eat in silence, but during my meals there, we all sat together to socialize over the meal. The residents had built an outdoor kitchen with a cob oven constructed from locally available natural materials such as clay, straw, and earth, and a niche for a rocket stove. Rocket stoves are highly efficient stoves that use small pieces of wood to produce high temperatures and were designed for less developed countries. The cob oven was adorned with a yellow and black salamander made of earthen pigments, reflecting the founders' belief that beauty and creativity are essential aspects of sustainability and human life.

Outdoor kitchen at the Possibility Alliance

As in other communities I visited, before we ate each meal, the cooks announced the contents of the meal and its origins. These meals reminded me of the elegant Farm to Fork meals that I have attended at Swallowtail Farm, just north of Gainesville, where local chefs showcase their skills using Swallowtail Farm's produce. Although in a less elegant fashion, Possibility Alliance residents ate like Farm to Fork three times a day, from winter scarcity to summer bounty.

Ethan Hughes and Sarah Wilcox-Hughes consider the Possibility Alliance an experiment in interpreting integral nonviolence in an American context, a concept I will discuss further in chapter 6. Integral nonviolence illustrates Gandhi's understanding that nonviolence must be practiced in all aspects of life, from the personal to the political, and that nonviolent practice requires a personal inner transformation.[4] The wheel of nonviolence, which I saw depicted on walls at both the Possibility Alliance and Cherith Brook, illustrates this holistic approach to nonviolence.

This comprehensive understanding of nonviolence encompasses more than simply the exterior practice of abstaining from violent actions; nonviolence must become essential to one's being, an orientation that shapes

Asking What's for Dinner   111

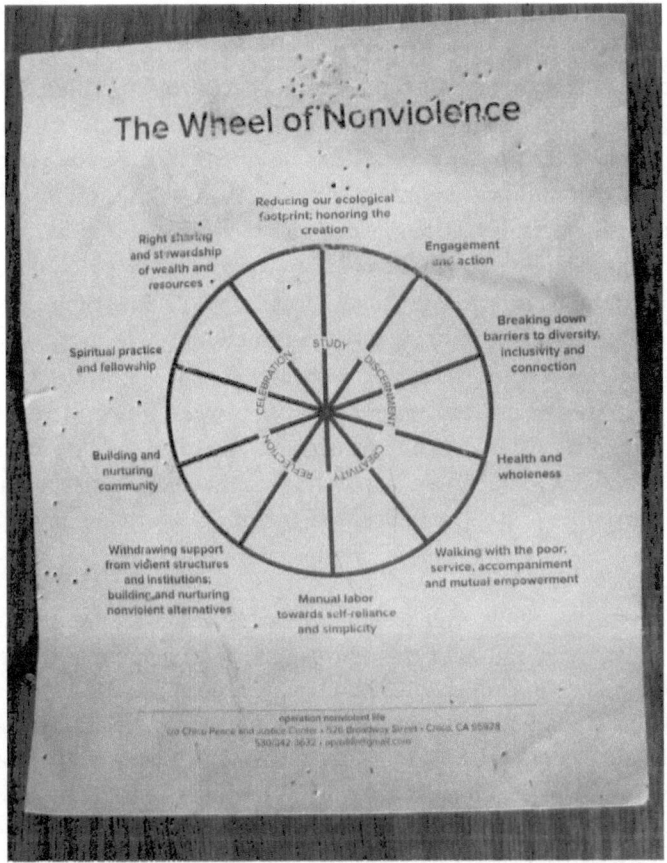

Wheel of nonviolence

all relationships. Several Possibility Alliance residents stated that any violence present in one's self or in relationships inevitably seeps into practices such as agriculture, so inner work is necessary to remove the internal roots of violence or anger.

Many residents had taken or were planning to take courses in nonviolent communication or participate in restorative justice circles, a process that focuses on the individual needs of both victims and offenders, or receivers and authors, in the context of the community (http://www.restorativejustice.org/). Inner nonviolence means developing compassion toward opponents and understanding the roots of their actions, even while fighting those opponents—a practice that requires self-discipline. These beliefs echo Gandhi's emphasis on personal transformation as the first step to social transformation: one must recognize the humanity of all people and cultivate an inner peace, rather than harbor feelings of hatred or revenge. Inner peace or compassion, not self-righteousness, facilitates humility.

In conversations I had with the residents and interns as I worked alongside them and in later interviews, they emphasized the primacy of nonviolent communication, interpersonal relationships, and inner transformation. These conversations helped me recognize the importance of the clustering of Gandhi's values; concepts of sustainability, nonviolence, and voluntary simplicity are inextricably linked. In deliberations about the relationship between food and violence, Possibility Alliance has moved beyond questions of organics and vegetarianism to incorporate less frequently recognized aspects of political economy, such as inequitable production regimes for coffee and chocolate.[5] Residents of the Possibility Alliance have joyfully chosen, as Ethan Hughes terms it, to abstain from chocolate and coffee, both tropical foods that are grown in environmentally destructive and oppressive conditions. He explains:

> Here at the Possibility Alliance we think sacrifice is a good thing. According to the *Oxford Dictionary*, sacrifice is giving up something of lesser value for something of greater value. So I give up chocolate, which has an amazing culinary history and is delicious, but is of lesser value to me than eating bioregionally. Eating bioregionally has less impact on the biotic communities of the earth. What is of greater value for me than eating chocolate is to live in a world where 7 billion people can be fed without collapsing earth's ecosystems, and where no one is in the hot sun picking cacao for the rest of their lives to export to me. Transformation does not come from thinking, "I'm eating chocolate; I'm bad," rather it comes from remembering the most important things—my values, convictions, and vision for the world.

Eating a vegetarian meal followed by chocolate and coffee, Hughes explained, would be to fail to follow through on responsible food choices, in which the social, political, and environmental costs of producing and transporting these goods must be taken into account. One's inner transformation comes from consciously choosing the nonviolent path, recognizing that food choices have environmental and social consequences, and reframing what constitutes abundance.

Similarly, the Possibility Alliance's abstention from the fossil fuel economy exemplifies its refusal to contribute to inequities perpetuated by the oil and gas industry, both in the United States and abroad. Possibility Alliance residents are well aware of the embedded energy bound up in their own infrastructure and that of their modes of transportation (for example, the energy required to produce their bicycles and farm equipment), but they cook, grow, and transport their food without using fossil fuels. Like Gandhi, they incorporate a broad range of social, political, and economic factors into their assessment of violence and, like residents of other intentional communities, facilitate conflict resolution in neighboring communities.

However, both Ethan Hughes and Sarah Wilcox-Hughes emphasized Possibility Alliance's experimental nature—acknowledging that the community did not have all the answers but instead was exploring how to live and eat as nonviolently as possible. As an experiment in integral nonviolence, Possibility Alliance seeks to address violence in all aspects of eating, growing, and producing food, and the residents' efforts reflected Gandhi's understanding that nonviolence is not easy or simple. Instead, they maintain that we all should contemplate what nonviolence might mean in any given context, such as considering the broader effects of actions, even those performed with nonviolent intentions.

Possibility Alliance sets a high standard that few are likely to follow, and others working toward similar goals of nonviolence might make different choices, such as choosing fair trade or direct trade coffee to support small farmers in developing nations rather than abstaining from coffee entirely and thus withdrawing from an important market for those producers. These choices lie on a continuum, so choosing to eat nonviolently—however someone defines it—for just one meal a day or week still makes a difference.

Most discussions about food and violence center on meat because deliberations about meat point to larger conversations about food in the contemporary United States. Residents of the Possibility Alliance and many other communities, if they are not vegetarians, eat meat that has been raised in what they perceive to be a humane fashion. Possibility Alliance residents, for example, eat fish from their pond and occasionally slaughter their chickens. This stance reflects the choice of a small, but growing, population of North Americans who base their meat choices on *how* the animal was raised and slaughtered and view humanely raised or hunted meat as a less violent, or at least more humane, choice—hence the term *happy chicken*. (While this option does seem less violent in the meat-oriented United States, the vegetarian residents of Brahma Vidya Mandir, a Gandhian ashram in Paunar, Maharashtra, find any meat consumption to be violent.) Similarly, most Dancing Rabbit and Possibility Alliance residents, if they are not vegetarians, eat meat that has been locally raised, reflecting an emphasis on local economies and bioregionalism, the idea that social and environmental policies should reflect the bioregion.[6]

Guests and Hosts: Catholic Workers and Hospitality

I visited a number of Catholic worker houses and farms, including Cherith Brook, that share many of the Possibility Alliance's values and goals, especially service to the poor and educating for self-reliance. When I volunteered at these houses and farms, doing laundry, preparing food, and gardening, for example, and in discussions with Catholic workers, I discovered that their ethos of hospitality and service adds yet another dimension to the issue of food and violence.

Ethan Hughes directed me to Cherith Brook because of that community's efforts to integrate sustainability and nonviolence initiatives into an urban context. Founded in 2007, Cherith Brook is located in an impoverished, historic neighborhood in northeast Kansas City, Missouri—the driver of the airport shuttle asked me several times if I really wanted to be dropped there. Cherith Brook owns two buildings that are separated by a large yard and parking lot. One building is a large brick house with a wraparound porch, and the other has a kitchen, shower, and eating area in the front and apartments for workers in the rear. Like many older buildings, they are slightly run-down, but the wooden trim and older windows give the buildings character, even a shabby gentility.

The community has established an extensive garden, beehives, and chicken coops that contribute to its hospitality mission. Gardens irrigated by large rain barrels adorn the front and side yards, and painted wooden doors serve as a fence to demarcate the backyard. The doors and artistic labels in the gardens help offset the grimness of the surrounding neighborhood. Residents obtain eggs from their chickens that roam in the backyard, although occasionally one escapes into the driveway. Solar panels, rain barrels, and shared housing contribute to Cherith Brook's sustainability efforts and differentiate its buildings from the others in the neighborhood, and the mural painted on a wall visible from the street announces the community's presence.

Mural at Cherith Brook Catholic Worker House

Like most Catholic worker houses, Cherith Brook feeds and clothes those in need. According to the Cherith Brook website, "Our daily lives are structured around practicing the works of mercy as found in Jesus' teachings. We are committed to regularly feeding the hungry, clothing the naked, giving drink to the thirsty, welcoming the stranger, visiting the prisoner and the sick in the name of Jesus."[7]

Cherith Brook also includes what I call a *shower mission* in its hospitality program. Many guests, in fact, know the house as the Shower House. Initially, the Catholic workers planned to provide meals and roundtable discussions, as do most Catholic worker houses, but one day someone knocked on their door and asked if he could take a shower and change clothes. From this demonstrated need, Cherith Brook developed a morning program in which guests not only eat breakfast but can also shower and receive clean, fresh clothing. As cofounder Eric Garbison states, "What I've learned from Dorothy Day (a founder of the *Catholic worker movement*) is that the world is a sacrament. . . . Part of volunteering here is taking turns eating with everybody, sitting down. That for us is Eucharistic. . . . And sometimes we talk about the showers being a baptismal experience because every morning, somebody says, 'I feel like a whole new person. I feel like a human being again.' Well, isn't that what baptism's all about?"[8]

The shower mission exemplifies the Catholic worker emphases on serving and providing hospitality to the poor, no questions asked, and on human dignity, recognizing that clean clothes are essential not only for our well-being but also for full engagement in society. The community also holds monthly women-only shower sessions that become beauty parlor events of sorts.

The first time I volunteered for the morning shower program, I arrived late, around 9:00 in the morning, when breakfast, showers, and clothing exchange were already in full swing. I had visited the community in the calm of the previous afternoon and had not anticipated the swirl of activity that greeted me. I took a deep breath, walked in the door to the Shower House, and was immediately drafted for laundry duty. For the next three hours, I shuttled dirty clothes down to the efficient front-loading washer in the basement and clean clothes up and outside to the clothesline. The communal closet, like those in numerous other intentional communities, was full of clothing of all sizes for both men and women and was where, in solidarity, the residents also "shopped." The basement was crammed with well-labeled supplies in case toiletry or other items or sizes ran out.

After the guests signed the shower list—only the first twenty got showers—they waited in the dining room to be called to enter one at a time for their turn. The guests were a mix of black and white, reflecting the neighborhood's racial composition, and approximately three-fourths were men. The line between guest and host is blurry—many volunteers are also guests—but only Cherith Brook residents or volunteers accompany guests to the communal closet so they can choose clothing without coercion, a freedom especially important for women, who otherwise might be pressured by boyfriends or pimps. After having selected an outfit and basic toiletries, each guest is ushered into one of two shower rooms, both full bathroom size, and given a maximum of twenty minutes to shower and change. Outside the shower rooms, guests use mirrors and racks holding hair dryers, gels, and combs to finish getting ready.

Selection of toiletries at Cherith Brook Catholic Worker House

Depending on their place in the shower line, guests ate breakfast before or after their showers. Cherith Brook's gardens provide some food, but most of supplies come from donations from stores, restaurants, and individuals. When I visited, Cherith Brook served breakfast five days a week and dinner on Thursday nights. Most of the donated food goes into the breakfasts and dinners served to guests, but the breakfast area also contains a shelf holding vegetables, bread, or salad greens guests can take home. To the extent possible, the workers prepare healthy meals with salads and vegetables, and each table holds a bowl of fruit, including bananas, apples, and oranges. Nonetheless, since the bulk of the community's food comes from donations, members have far less control over their food choices than communities that grow their own. When we went to pick up donations at Constentino's Market, a high-end grocery store in downtown Kansas City, we sifted through the offerings in the carts, choosing bread and bagels and rejecting piles of cakes, pastries, and doughnuts. Workers avoid foods that are high in sugar and fat, but must be mindful of the preferences of their guests, who might choose white bread over whole wheat.

When we returned, we stored the food in industrial-sized refrigerators, moving the oldest donations to the front.

The refrigerators were packed with boxed salad greens, vegetables, and tomatoes, and part of my job in preparing breakfast was determining what produce was still fresh and edible. Breakfast at Cherith Brook often includes soup and salad in addition to more typical breakfast foods because some guests might otherwise not have access to fruits or vegetables. I opened and washed each of the plastic boxes of salad, tossing some in the salad bowl and some in the compost. At first glance, I wondered how many leaves would be good enough to eat, but as I sorted through the greens, I realized that most of the lettuce was fresh and edible. When I commented on how much edible food is thrown away, one resident recalled a similar experience with a group of student volunteers. They were amazed that they could make and eat a meal composed of what had been considered trash. One resident explained, "We get a lot of resources from the grocery store, things that they throw away. We really don't need to buy much food-wise, and a lot of resources are donated for our hospitality work. We try to encourage each other to use the resources that we have and not get new stuff, if it's not totally necessary."

While Catholic workers abhor waste, in part, due to their choices of voluntary poverty or voluntary simplicity, their efforts also reflect values of sustainable food systems. Residents of Cherith Brook do not buy meat, but will eat and serve meat that is donated to them, whether that meat is hunted or farmed. One self-described "opportunivore" said the community members felt best about the hunted meat donated to them each year. In this case, they must balance their goals of reducing food waste with those of eating sustainably produced foods. Recovering food wasted at the end of the supply chain, whether tossed out by stores or rotting in our own vegetable bins, is one step toward a sustainable food system.

Cherith Brook held a community dinner every Thursday evening followed by a hootenanny on the porch, and every third Friday featured a roundtable discussion. I first joined a community dinner on a cold and dreary April night. About twelve guests arrived early to socialize on the house's wraparound porch, drink coffee, and use the bathroom. At around 5:00 p.m., when the thirty to forty mostly male guests had arrived, all of us assembled, sat in a circle holding hands, and introduced ourselves, and then a guest said a blessing, a routine that the group typically followed. As I helped serve the meal, which consisted of a spaghetti casserole, a broccoli and cauliflower mix, and garlic bread, I recognized many of the guests from that morning's shower. After we had served everyone, we joined the guests at the tables for food and conversation. Each table seated about six to eight, so it felt like a family meal. The meal brought together a population that varied according to age, socioeconomic status, and race, and the small tables fostered face-to-face conversations. At our table, the conversation ranged from the mundane—the garlic bread needs more butter—to serious discussions about the trials of getting enough food while living on the street. Because many guests and hosts came to this dinner weekly, the meals facilitated long-term relationships and friendships and offered some stability to those living on the street or in otherwise unstable living situations.

Like Cherith Brook, the Gainesville Catholic Worker House, affectionately called the Green House, also provides hospitality and opportunities for both scheduled roundtable discussions and less formal interactions. Catholic workers founded Gainesville Catholic Worker in 2000 and open their home to serve homemade organic meals to people in need, many of whom lived in Gainesville's tent city, a community of homeless people settled in nearby woods, which since has been disbanded. The green, two-story house sits in downtown Gainesville, so it is easily accessible for many people by foot, bus, or bicycle. The property has a small chicken coop in the back and herbs growing in pots scatted about the front yard. The kitchen is set up to accommodate the volunteers who help prepare meals.

Gainesville Catholic Worker holds monthly potlucks and roundtable discussions and serves lunch on Wednesdays at Dorothy's Cafe. Most of the food is locally sourced, a combination of food from the community's own garden and from a nearby partnering micro-farm, Black Acres Farm, which holds workdays on most Thursdays and Saturdays. Worker volunteers occasionally glean extra produce, such as citrus, from willing neighbors, and the house receives donations of surplus produce from nearby small farms and individual gardeners.

Gainesville Catholic Worker's monthly roundtable discussions, one of the three planks of Maurin's thought, bring together diverse populations to explore contemporary social issues.[9] Like Cherith Brook, the house announces its programs and discussion topics on its website, but information also travels by word of mouth. The regularity of the schedule helps because many guests have only sporadic access to computers. Invited leaders moderate roundtable discussions on topics that tend to focus on relevant social issues, primarily to engage a broad audience, which includes students and homeless individuals.

Sitting with the guests engaging in conversations breaks down us-versus-them barriers and shows respect for guests as persons, not recipients of services. I attended one discussion facilitated by Occupy Gainesville members, and my Religion and Food class hosted a discussion about sustainable foods and the people who produce our food.

Gainesville Catholic Worker residents practice an ethic of care and justice informed by Catholic social thought. They serve shared sit-down meals, complete with tablecloths and candles, which provide their guests moments of dignity and respect that are not often present in their lives. Their goal is to serve just meals that nourish body and soul:

> Meals that are just are also mindful of the system that produces them. Our current food system has shifted during the last fifty years from a network of predominantly family owned farms ... to the current globalized system where a very few corporations own, manage and profit from the production of food. People who don't live near the farms and have no vested interest in the well-being of the community usually run these "agri-businesses." Profit is the bottom line, and consequently, the environment suffers as topsoil is depleted and run-off from pesticides and fertilizers pollutes local waterways. In addition, migrant workers and slaughterhouse workers are underpaid and working in dangerous workplaces. If our meals are to do justice, they must strive to sustain a system that treats both workers and the earth with justice.[10]

Like Possibility Alliance and Dancing Rabbit, Cherith Brook and Gainesville Catholic Worker incorporate concerns about labor and political economy in addition to health and sustainability when gathering, cooking, and eating their meals. In short, they actively translate their values into practice.

Translating Values

Although these communities strive to practice a shared set of values, they perform these values according to their own ethical, geographic, and community contexts. Different communities emphasize disparate priorities and criteria in making their food choices. Like residents of Dancing Rabbit and Possibility Alliance, Gainesville Catholic workers share concerns about meat and its production. However, they also consider their primary mission to be that of hospitality to the poor, so they practice compassion for the needs of the diverse populations they serve. They reject the violence associated with factory-farmed meats, but they cannot afford locally raised or organic meats, so they serve only vegetarian meals. Although a few guests might grumble at the imposition of vegetarian meals, those who eat at the Gainesville Catholic Worker House have chosen this particular experience. Gainesville serves numerous food options to the homeless or otherwise needy, and those who desire meat can get it fairly easily.

Cherith Brook, on the other hand, serves meat to guests and residents who eat meat, and my conversations with residents gave a different perspective on the role of meat. People who come to Cherith Brook have few other food options, and they tend to want meat. Their guests, one resident explained, perceive meat as a luxury, a rich person's food, and they relish this opportunity to eat typical American meals. That many guests consider vegetarian meals an imposition reflects the continued prominent role of meat in the North American diet.

Although some Cherith Brook residents and volunteers themselves prefer a vegetarian diet, the vegetarian option invokes a tension in commensality. One resident said, "When we serve breakfast it's often with meat. Sometimes I wish I could eat the same food as our friends from the street because I wonder if that makes us different. 'Oh, I can't eat the food that you're eating because I . . .' So there's tension sometimes." She worried that when residents and volunteers do not eat the meat, guests might perceive this choice as a sort of snobbery, as in "Isn't our food good enough for you?"

Breaking bread with their neighbors and guests brings Cherith Brook closer to its goal of solidarity with the poor, but choices around meat introduce tensions in relations between hosts and guests. Resident Eric Garbison recognized the tensions between fellowship and vegetarianism and said that he saw opportunities to "witness both practices with grace and mercy. They [the residents of Cherith Brook] are called to serve and offer choices to those who have few choices." So Catholic worker communities must balance their compassion for animals with their compassion for the physical and emotional needs of their guests.

Meat is only one aspect of the relationship between food and violence. The communities I studied embody Gandhi's understanding that centralization is a form of violence and that self-sufficiency and self-rule are intimately linked with—and rely upon—concepts of nonviolence and decentralization.[11] Similarly, the Sisters of Providence in Ontario and the women religious of Genesis Farm in New Jersey provide "sanctuary" for heirloom seeds and their genetic "scriptures" as a means of enacting environmental justice.[12] In this vein, to protect local agrarian knowledge, rural communities maintain seed banks of varieties that were adapted to local conditions. Residents of these communities lament the growing corporate control over our food supply, and their efforts to create seed banks, diversify their local food economies, and establish a measure of regional self-sufficiency are attempts to create alternatives to the dominant food paradigm.

These communities, in theory and in practice, critique industrial agriculture as a form of systemic violence on human and nonhuman communities. Like many other communities, they also identify a range of practices as violent, including application of toxic pesticides and unfair labor regimes as well as other, less visible practices, such as increasing corporate control over political and educational institutions, privatization of germplasm, inequitable financial structures, and policies and procedures that perpetuate poverty.[13] Cherith Brook "strives to be a 'school' for peacemaking in all its dimensions: political, communal, and personal, working constantly to undo poverty, racism and militarism."[14] Its hospitality programs, including meals and showers, extend to the personal level by giving people a much-needed sense of dignity.

Further, these communities consider the political economy of food and whether the food they consume and serve to others was produced in a sustainable or equitable manner. Decisions to abstain from coffee or chocolate reflect the growing awareness of the social consequences of food production. So in addition to asking if food is organic, many now ask whether the laborers were paid a fair wage. For example, they seek fair trade coffee and chocolate and locally grown options that recirculate money within the region. So, for Possibility Alliance and the other communities, nonviolence, equity, and voluntary simplicity mean not only asking what or how much stuff we need, but also how workers or producers are treated.

Community practices of voluntary simplicity, self-sufficiency, and nonviolence demonstrate how residents of these communities consciously integrate these values into their daily lives to reveal a range of interpretations and alternatives. While many people, whether living in community or not, might agree that values such as nonviolence are important, what these values mean in practice varies according to specific circumstances. The communities discussed here hold relatively similar values and practices, while communities in different religious, geographic, and cultural circumstances (for example, Jains or Inuit people) would likely manifest a different set of practices and interpretations of food and violence.

Eating Together: Balancing Community and Individual

Every Tuesday, residents of neighboring communities Dancing Rabbit, Sandhill, and Red Earth gather for a tri-community potluck. Dancing Rabbit and Red Earth are adjacent to each other and are easily reached by foot on the well-worn path that links them. For the three-mile trip to and from Sandhill, most travelers carpool or cycle, the predominant modes of transportation for all three communities. When I was there, after some time spent socializing and finding a spot for food contributions, the group held hands and circled up. After a number of announcements, we went around the circle and announced our contributions. I attended these potlucks during visitor periods when guests and interns expanded the populations, so we newcomers also had a chance to introduce ourselves to the group. Then we lined up at the tables, groaning with dishes: beans, salads, and breads.

I attended one community potluck at Dancing Rabbit and one at Sandhill. In both cases, I spoke with residents—adults and children—who were otherwise busy with work and school during the visitors' sessions. Visitors and residents heaped their plates and sat down at the random assortment of tables set up outside for the occasion. After eating, I better understood the point of announcing our contributions. All of the food was homemade, much of it was homegrown, and some dishes were cooked using alternative energy, such as solar ovens. Each dish reflected sustainable values as well as ingenuity and creativity in cooking and growing, and each dish incorporated a significant amount of labor. I was slightly embarrassed by my own contribution of a purchased pie, but I consoled myself that I had purchased it from a local Mennonite family.

Most intentional communities emphasize shared meals as an essential component of community building and cohesion. The kitchen is considered the heart of many homes, and for intentional communities as well, kitchens and shared meals represent the pulse of a community. Small and tightly bound communities such as the Possibility Alliance and some Catholic worker groups share most of their meals, while larger communities such as ecovillages and cohousing groups might hold weekly or monthly community meals. In smaller communities, rotating groups of cooks might prepare a meal for the entire community, while larger communities tend to have potlucks. One common feature in many, though not all, communities is that, prior to a meal, the group circles up, holding hands, and says a blessing of gratitude for the food and the occasion. Then the cooks announce the food and its origins or production, and everyone eats.

Eating community meals can be an incredibly cohesive experience, but deciding what to eat and how often to eat together can be divisive. And, in addition to environmental and social concerns around food, the community must deal with health concerns, such as food allergies and intolerances. A friend reported that her cohousing community was wracked with tension over whether community meals should be gluten free. Then there is the question of how much togetherness people want. Residents of intentional communities must decide how often to eat together while balancing community social needs with the needs of individuals and families for privacy and independence.

The community food practices of Dancing Rabbit, one of the larger intentional communities, demonstrate a robust and resilient approach to food and other matters of governance. In Dancing Rabbit's early years, it had one food co-op which, according to resident Alline Anderson, cost $5 per day and required cooking approximately one dinner and the next day's lunch once a week.[15] The low cost and pooled labor made sense, especially when the new residents were building the original infrastructure; nobody wanted to cook after a day of labor.

As Dancing Rabbit's population has grown and developed, as intended, smaller communities and co-ops have formed within the community according to shared views on issues such as income, housing, and food. These varied approaches to food, preparation, and eating accommodate various food practices and social arrangements. Some communities within Dancing Rabbit require greater commitment; for instance, members of the communal building Skyhouse, situated at the heart of Dancing Rabbit's campus, share income and live together. Rabbits join food co-ops to share the work of food production and preparation, and it is not difficult to change co-ops. Homes at Dancing Rabbit are tiny and close together, and many do not include kitchens, so for many Rabbits communal cooking is essential. All members of the different communities and co-ops are somehow affiliated with Dancing Rabbit, whether as residents, interns, or work exchangers ("wexers"), but not all Rabbits join co-ops or communities.

The number of food co-ops varies from year to year. In 2013, Dancing Rabbit had seven. Because Dancing Rabbit does not have one generalizable eating style or rule, the dietary practices of the co-ops vary greatly. For example, some co-ops eat meat, while others are vegetarian or vegan. Bobolink, which eats in Skyhouse, focuses on local and vegan foods.[16] Ironweed has a large garden and its kitchen boasts "chicken TV," a window in the shared wall between the kitchen and chicken hutch. The chickens warm up the kitchen and provide entertainment as well.

Most Rabbits grow some portion of their own food, and the percentage is increasing as more residents finish building their homes. To achieve a modicum of self-sufficiency as well as sustainability, most residents preserve either home- or locally grown foods to last through the winter, and others have developed micro-industries, such as baking bread or making mozzarella cheese. Eating simply is time-consuming and laborious, as one Rabbit stated, but her dislike for processed foods and factory-farmed meat overcame her desire for convenience. Rabbit Alline Anderson put it this way:

> We cook with whole foods. So during the summer, we pickle and can and preserve a lot of the produce from the garden, which all takes time. It's how we choose to live; I'm not complaining. I like cooking like this. One time I got really annoyed with all of it, and I just thought, "Forget it, I'm just going to go to the store and buy packaged pre-made food. I'm just going to buy it." So I went through the frozen food section and there was Stouffer's lasagna, and well, I make better lasagna than that. And the bread, well, I make better bread than that, and besides, I know what is in it. And the chicken, well, I thought, "I can't buy that chicken, I know how that chicken was raised, in a little tiny cage with no beak." And so I came home with nothing and I thought, "Man, I'm screwed. My own ideals are getting in the way."

Even if they aren't vegetarians, most Rabbits prefer to avoid factory-farmed meats, and inevitably the issue of hunting arose. Rural northeast Missouri teems with deer and rabbits, and few people—Rabbits or others—look upon these animals sympathetically because they destroy the gardens and eat the food that Rabbits depend on. During the Q&A period in my visitor session, a bearded thirty-something veteran from Mississippi asked about Dancing Rabbit's approach to hunting. Over the previous several days, he had engaged in heated discussions with members and visitors on sensitive subjects, such as military force and organic foods, so I was especially curious to hear the Rabbits respond to his question. Several Rabbits chimed in, noting that they had no rules against hunting, and that several residents had been trapping rabbits without much opposition. While residents would likely resist guns, in part due to the noise, some had been considering bow hunting, an activity that would require deliberation. Trapping or hunting the prolific deer and rabbits that decimate their gardens would barely reduce their population, and the combination of animal protein and saved produce would enrich their food supply and variety.

Sustainability-oriented Rabbits eat humanely, but generally are pragmatic in their attitudes toward animals; they do not romanticize animals, and none screamed about "killing Bambi." I visited one couple that had recently moved from Chicago and finished building their house. She had just skinned a chicken for the first time. She said that "both my husband and I felt since we had eaten animals it was important to understand the killing and prepping process. It was our responsibility."

Rabbits have started animal-based micro-industries; for example, some are keeping goats for milk products. The Critter Collective, a group of six Rabbits, advertised "critter internships" for 2014, described as a "reality check for those who still think living off the grid at an ecovillage is all cozy firelight and frolicking naked with butterflies in the meadow at dusk." Critter interns would manage the growing collection of Muscovy ducks, goats, and sheep, tasks the Critter Collective describe as "the more hardcore side of ecologically friendly living."[17] Both Sandhill Farm and Dancing Rabbit residents said that they had shifted from vegetarian to omnivore over the years. One Sandhill Farm resident thought, "The earlier generation was more likely to be vegetarian or vegan, but maybe my generation is over that."

Dancing Rabbit cannot, at this point, fulfill all of its food needs, and even the sustainability-oriented Rabbits occasionally crave chips and other processed foods. Dancing Rabbit's on-site bed and breakfast and store, the Milkwood Mercantile, stocks organic products such as Annie's Homegrown and organic/fair trade chocolate and sells a mix of organic and nonorganic beer and wine. On Thursday nights Milkwood Mercantile hosts pizza night, an event that draws residents, guests, and neighbors for custom homemade pizzas.

Still, when they purchase food, Rabbits must choose between the ecological, social, and economic benefits of local versus organic, a long-standing topic of debate in environmental and agrarian thought. Milkweed Mercantile co-owner Kurt Kessner wondered, "Should we shop at the local grocery store for what's left and try to buy as much organic as we possibly can? Here's the ecological trade-off: do we drive an hour into Kirksville to get organic vegetables from California or do we buy off the shelf in Memphis just ten minutes away? We decided it's a smaller ecological hit just to go to Zimmerman's store or the grocery supermarket in Memphis."

Asking What's for Dinner 127

Milkweed Mercantile welcome sign

Zimmerman's, a local grocery run by Mennonites, in addition to stocking the more traditional dietary preferences of the rural Midwest, also carries foods (such as tofu) that cater to Dancing Rabbit preferences but are increasingly becoming mainstream. Dancing Rabbits' ecological covenants and sustainability guidelines emphasize reduced use of fossil fuels for reasons similar to those of Possibility Alliance, and Rabbits are encouraged to consider how production has affected other humans, animals, and the earth when purchasing food and other goods.

When I participated in the Dancing Rabbit visitor program, we rotated through different eating co-ops so we could meet a variety of residents. Visitor sessions are held in the warmer months when more fresh produce is available for both residents and guests. While each co-op had its own food and cooking styles, the meals demonstrated considerable consistency, especially in contrast with the prevalent US diet, heavy in meat and processed foods. Overall, the meals resembled those served at Possibility Alliance and featured fresh vegetables or salad greens, legumes, and homemade breads. Meat, if it was served at all, was optional. Generally, Rabbits ate seasonally, rethinking what constitutes abundance, an anomaly in a country where many demand year-round strawberries. Tony Sirna explained,

> For us, seasonal does not mean scarcity. In the winter people want more of a certain thing, and getting our infrastructure in place will help. Now that Dan [a resident of Dancing Rabbit] has the hoop house and the greenhouse, we have more fresh vegetables. Just having salads throughout the winter feels different than eating preserved stuff. But this is salad season, and there's more than you could possibly eat. So, by the end of that season, I'm ready for the next season. It doesn't have to be scarcity as much as a series of abundances. There's always something abundant.

Like Possibility Alliance residents, Rabbits interpret voluntary simplicity in their food practices, but both groups view their choices in a positive context, such as appreciating seasonal shifts.

Dancing Rabbit has six ecological covenants, among them, no one may own an individual vehicle, all building materials must be of local origin or repurposed, and all agriculture on Dancing Rabbit property must be organic. These broad covenants provide for some lively discussions, but help avoid the imposition of a strict ideology. For example, while no herbicides or pesticides can be stored at Dancing Rabbit, no covenant or rule prohibits storing or eating conventionally produced foods. The system of multiple communities and co-ops suggests multiple approaches to a shared vision and makes Dancing Rabbit resilient. Each community and co-op makes its own decisions about critical issues such as food and shelter, so many potential conflicts are resolved within smaller groups and never involve the entire community.

The communities and co-ops of Dancing Rabbit and the entire Dancing Rabbit Ecovillage are intentional communities that residents join based on shared values. But even in an experimental community based on shared values, tensions form as the community seeks to balance flexibility with the maintenance of core values. Although most people I spoke with emphasized the importance of tolerance and multiple perspectives, I saw tensions develop over questions of long-range land use and the role of agricultural lands. While some residents preferred to have agricultural lands and animal operations on the outskirts of the village, others preferred to keep their gardens and animals close. This situation demonstrated the difficulty of translating abstract values into actual practice and adjudicating conflicts. It is hard to remain dispassionate, despite the best of intentions. Nonetheless, residents of these communities consciously attempt to live out ideals of nonviolence, self-sufficiency, equity, and voluntary simplicity through their methods of creating infrastructure, food production, and governance. Vision, rather than dogma, then becomes a potent force for moral persuasion and helps these communities avoid both orthodoxy and orthopraxy.

Tensions and Trade-offs

What we eat, how we prepare our food, and whom we eat with are intensely intimate and personal aspects of our lives, so, not surprisingly, food, cooking, and eating emerge as sources of conflict in communities. Anecdotally, and not surprisingly, cooking and eating seem to be some of the most conflict-ridden issues, along with cleanliness of the kitchen and food choices. It does seem ironic that food—as a means for bringing people together and in some ways a basis for community itself—is one of the greatest sources of tensions. Perhaps the emotional, cultural, and religious significance we place on food makes tensions inevitable.

Women, not surprisingly, can be either the biggest fans or biggest critics of shared eating arrangements, especially in regard to issues of cleanliness and labor. Even in communities like Dancing Rabbit that identify as feminist communities, women typically bring different standards and attitudes toward eating, kitchen cleanliness, and food preparation. Sandhill, a small income-sharing community three miles from Dancing Rabbit, for example, resolved community conflict over cleaning by creating highly detailed descriptions of specific cleaning tasks. In this egalitarian and feminist-aligned community, men and women share tasks that range from cleaning to processing food to tilling the soil, and men sweep as well as sow. Yet, what constituted "clean" differed among individuals. What does it mean to clean a floor, for example—a quick dab with a Swiffer or scrubbing on hands and knees? As a means of resolving this sort of continuing conflict, for each room, the community outlined exactly what constituted "clean" and the techniques for cleaning that room. Cofounder Laird Schaub marveled in a seminar on conflict resolution that they hadn't thought of that sooner.

In *The View from #410: When Home Is Cohousing*, author and cohousing resident Jean Mason writes that community kitchens in cohousing communities provoke the fantasies of two groups of women: those who love to cook and those who hate it. While some women appreciate the freedom of simply showing up to meals, women who enjoy cooking might not want to relinquish control over their food. She suggests that the chance to participate in cooking might be a draw for some, as opposed to the more institutionalized food practices of retirement communities. Mason notes that cooperative housekeeping is not new—women founded Boston's Cambridge Housekeeping Cooperative in 1870. (The enterprise eventually collapsed when the women's husbands withdrew their financial support.)[18] Although collective cooking and cleaning are efficient and save time, many people prefer to cook and clean to their individual specifications and might not desire the level of community that multiple shared meals entail.

These tensions raise questions: How much togetherness do we need to be considered a community? How much togetherness do we want? Egalitarian communities such as Twin Oaks and Sandhill pool all labor and income and eat all their meals together, and residents appreciate the freedom proffered by this communal sharing. More loosely bound communities, including cohousing communities such as Cobb Hill in Hartland, Vermont, or urban ecovillages such as LA Eco-village, have fewer requirements or organized opportunities for community socializing. Both communities have weekly potlucks, but family, work, and social obligations can make attendance sporadic. Attending a weekly potluck is one means of fulfilling monthly resident participation requirements, a seemingly minimal obligation for people who have chosen an intentional community. Nonetheless, as I mentioned in chapter 3, although participation levels vary, I heard multiple times that the figure of nonattendance hovers around 10 percent; in any group, inevitably 10 percent simply won't participate. While most residents join intentional communities *because* they seek tight social bonds, living that ideal constitutes a significant challenge to most communities.

6

Sustainability in Community

We call them Co-Ho moments, a moment of "This is why we're here." This is the functioning part of community.
—Peter Jessop, Pioneer Valley Cohousing

IT SEEMS OBVIOUS THAT living in a community that supports sustainable behaviors makes it easier to live sustainably. Not only do sustainability-oriented communities that share goods, labor, and land leave a smaller ecological footprint, but residing in such a community also reinforces and validates one's commitment to sustainable living in an iterative cycle. In these communities, although residents debate about how best to live out their values, few question their choices of practices, such as choosing cycling over driving. Intentional communities that are not deliberately organized around sustainability might yet boast a smaller ecological footprint due to shared infrastructure and facilities. In some retirement communities, for example, residents travel in vans or buses rather than cars and have scaled down to smaller apartments. Whether explicitly focused on sustainability or not, communities with shared resources and infrastructure offer physical and emotional advantages that make it easier for residents to move toward sustainable lifestyles.

Indeed, some people have argued that sustainability-focused intentional communities provide the best hope for reducing our environmental impact: first, because of their shared resources; and second, because their social systems—governance and communications—facilitate discussion and coordinated actions. Even though I vote and am active in local food and transportation issues, for example, I have little influence on the larger body politic, despite living in a small city. Individuals in most intentional communities, however, exert more influence on their governance systems both because the communities are smaller and, more important, the communities deliberately design their systems of governance to enfranchise their residents. While most people can pick and choose their levels of participation, residents of intentional communities are expected to serve on multiple committees and participate in all matters of governance, including community meetings.

Some communities make even stronger claims about the relationship between sustainability and social structures to assert that inequitable and violent social structures go hand in hand with environmental degradation. For example, storing hazardous waste near impoverished and vulnerable populations constitutes both social and environmental violence. Violent practices toward animals and the earth both reflect and result from violent and inequitable social relationships, including racial, gender, sociocultural, and economic. Changing our infrastructure and physical practices, such as cycling or eating organically, for example, is not sufficient in and of itself; instead, we must revise social structures that promote unsustainable practices such as continued use of fossil fuels. In response, communities are experimenting with social practices, from interpersonal relationships to gift economies to community governance, that mitigate the violence and inequities that permeate our social fabric. Their experiments and practices vary according to community, but they share several critical similarities: first, all communities have scrutinized their practices to root out hidden forms of violence, and all seek to develop nonviolent practices; second, these communities understand themselves as experimental demonstration sites where those interested can consider alternatives; and third, these communities have created forms of participatory governance and conflict resolution systems designed to balance the needs of the community with individual autonomy.

These communities practice Gandhi's bundled values—nonviolence, voluntary simplicity, self-sufficiency, and democracy—by integrating nonviolence and equity into their social as well as their ecological practices. Some communities, like Possibility Alliance and Sirius, focus on processes of personal transformation that help practitioners themselves become nonviolent, a process Gandhi considered the sine qua non for a nonviolent society. Further, the communities I visited—and this factor helped me select communities—tested forms of participatory governance to ensure that all voices would be heard, a critical aspect of social equity. Some communities that emphasized egalitarian, income-sharing, and/or feminist principles, took precautions to establish egalitarian gender relations. All communities had processes for conflict resolution, including nonviolent communication and restorative justice circles. In sum, these communities have made strong claims about the relationship between ecological and social sustainability, highlighting that nonviolence in all levels of social structures is necessary for sustainability. Possibility Alliance, for instance, frames its environmental and social practices around the concept of integral nonviolence.

Integral Nonviolence

Residents of the Possibility Alliance emphasize that nonviolence and social equity are necessary for sustainability because violence in any aspect of life seeps into other facets of life, and sustainability is not possible without addressing violence in all capacities, starting with any violence that we hold in ourselves. In chapter 5, I explored integral nonviolence in the context of food, but, for Possibility Alliance and many others, integral nonviolence structures all aspects of life, from food to governance. Ethan Hughes stated, "We are trying an American version of an integral nonviolent movement, doing inner work, rebuilding a society without violence, service to those in need, and standing up with love to institutions that are not allowing life to thrive."

The residents of Possibility Alliance aim to create an integral nonviolence movement, meaning that they hope to live all aspects of their lives in a nonviolent fashion—from food to interpersonal relationships to governance. In their dialogue and practice, they illustrate important links between sustainability and equity that are sometimes overlooked in efforts to achieve the environmental and physical dimensions of sustainability. Nonviolence, equitable social structures, and radical democracy, they argue, are not incidental but intrinsic to sustainability and reflect sets of integrated values that Gandhi and later Peter Maurin linked.

Gandhi integrated nonviolence in all aspects, from the individual to community to body politic, to participatory democracy. Self-rule, he thought, should extend to all people, rich and poor, male and female, so that all individuals could develop the capacity to participate in decision making. He highlighted the importance of the individual and encouraged a level of autonomy that had been beyond the reach of many groups, such as women and lower castes.[1] Gandhi's integration of nonviolence and radical democracy reflects understandings about nonviolence that had circulated in the United States from its early history, especially in the Christian peace churches such as Quakers and Mennonites. In the nineteenth century, much of the dialogue about nonviolence focused on the relationship between individuals and authority in accordance with the Anabaptists' (Anabaptists include the Amish, Hutterites, and the Mennonites) concept of radical individualism: any power over another individual can be construed as violent, which led to a rejection of hierarchical structures. Quaker styles of consensus governance embodied nonviolent egalitarian structures and served as models for some communities. Later, after the carnage of World War I, those discussing peace and nonviolence began to critique unjust and violent social structures and ask how we might enact more equitable societies, extending conversations about nonviolence from individuals to social structures.[2]

Gandhi's attention to nonviolence, democracy, and distribution of natural resources reflects a form of environmentalism that incorporates equity concerns. Ramachandra Guha has called Gandhi the "father of Indian environmentalism," and Arne Naess, the founder of "deep ecology," also cites Gandhi as an inspiration, particularly in the development of his "ecosophy" as he adopted Gandhi's linkage of "self-realization, nonviolence and . . . biological egalitarianism."[3] Environmental movements in the Global South tend to pair ecological and equity issues, yet the environmentalism of the poor has not always been recognized as environmental due to its emphasis on social concerns.

Although Gandhi's environmental thought addressed agrarian and environmental issues in the context of the social needs of village India, contemporary intentional communities reflect his concerns.[4] Freedom lies in democratic and broad access to the means of production and survival—for example, access to food, water, and healthy soils. Gandhi's environmental thought is inseparable from his social thought and has offered a paradigm to evaluate the intimate—and frequently overlooked—ties between the environmental degradation and social inequities that inform contemporary concerns about sustainability and the food we eat.[5] Gandhi's rhetoric about food and freedom influenced champions of food sovereignty, including the international peasants' rights group La Via Campesina (viacampesina.org/) and food activist and scientist Vandana Shiva, who articulates her food sovereignty campaign in Gandhian terms, such as Seed Swaraj (Seed Freedom) (http://www.navdanya.org/).[6]

In 1987 the UN World Commission on Environment and Development released *Our Common Future,* popularly known as the Brundtland Report, a statement that has become the benchmark for defining the term *sustainability*. The commission's definition of sustainability—often distilled to the "Triple Stool" of sustainability—emphasized the threefold bottom line: that ecology, economic growth, and equity comprise three necessary aspects of sustainability.[7] Social equity means both contemporary equity and intergenerational equity, meaning that humans today must not compromise the ability of future humans to meet their needs. More important for this discussion, the paired emphasis on ecology and equity reflects both Gandhian principles and the goals of contemporary communities to achieve all three legs of the sustainability triad.

Some individuals and groups have claimed that we need a benign dictator to enforce sustainable lifestyles upon an unwilling population, prompting John Lotherington of the Foundation for Democracy and Sustainable Development to critique this tendency he sees in green politics to gaze wistfully upon authoritarian regimes.[8] Communities such as Possibility Alliance, Twin Oaks, and Dancing Rabbit, though, embody a countervailing argument: that radical democracy is as necessary a component as nonviolence and equity for sustainability. These nonhierarchical societies and their bundled values of nonviolence, interdependence, voluntary simplicity, and radical democracy represent approaches to sustainability that are deeply tied to the quality of interpersonal and community relationships and recognize the necessary pairing of sustainability and social equity.

The linkage of sustainability, nonviolence, and human relations at Possibility Alliance drew J.R., an intern in 2011, to this community. J.R. said that the green movement "glosses over that aspect of human relations and relational intelligence. And that's a key component of what's going on here." For J.R., relational, or emotional, intelligence enables individuals to understand their own and others' emotions and so facilitates better communication and conflict resolution. Sustainability, he thought, is only possible in the context of a community that emphasizes personal and relational skills and nonviolent communication: "It would be difficult for people in Western society to find motivation to give up a lot of 'comfort' and live this way without a method or a tool such as nonviolent communication. Or without addressing relational intelligence and the need to express both positive and negative aspects of our experience in being accepted."

Residents of Possibility Alliance and other intentional communities reflect these views that nonviolence, participatory democracy, and social equity are critical for sustainability, and many act, either explicitly or implicitly, upon this concept of integral nonviolence.

Ethan Hughes and his friend Chris Moore-Backman, director of the Chico Peace and Justice Center, came up with the term *integral nonviolence* because they did not see Gandhian nonviolence lived out. Hughes commented that "it was being researched and discussed, and there were conferences all over the world. Gandhi said, 'Burn my writings and look at my life. The only way to propagate this wisdom is to live it.' Nonviolence is misunderstood. Modern nonviolence is making different consumer choices or going to the protests for the weekend."

Hughes echoes Gandhi's contention that being nonviolent means actively avoiding harm to other beings. It is not passive—it means intentionally seeking out and then acting, in thought, word, and deed, in ways that do not harm. Living nonviolently includes thoroughly scrutinizing our own ways of being to see how and when we inflict violence: for example, questioning the social and environmental harms that result from our food and transportation practices. For Hughes, integral nonviolence includes living primarily within the bioregion's resources to avoid financially supporting foods and goods made in oppressive conditions. Possibility Alliance demonstrates the lived practice of "Vote with Your Fork," the concept that we can act upon our values through our consumer choices or decisions not to consume.

Prior to founding Possibility Alliance, Ethan Hughes and Sarah Wilcox-Hughes lived at the Community of the Ark in France where they saw experiments in nonviolence in Europe. The founder, Lanza del Vasto, a disciple of Gandhi, founded this commune in 1948 to practice Gandhian nonviolence. Mark Shepard chronicles the community's history in his book *The Community of the Ark: A Visit with Lanza del Vasto, His Fellow Disciples of Mahatma Gandhi, and Their Utopian Community in France*. Hughes and Wilcox-Hughes decided to return to the United States and establish the Possibility Alliance as a living experiment in internal nonviolence. Groups in the United States and Europe excelled in different aspects of nonviolence, but few attempted to use nonviolence as a frame to evaluate all aspects of life. Hughes noted, "They may be going deep into simplicity but not doing the direct action. They may be doing peace witness but not growing their own food. Or they're doing inner work—meditation, prayer, self-purification—but shopping and living a pretty modern life. So each aspect is expressed in the United States, and individually groups do a better job than the Possibility Alliance in each aspect. But they do not understand that nonviolence means you bring love and the removal of violence in every single place: the heart, the mind, how you eat, and how you move around."

For Hughes and Moore-Backman, integral nonviolence addresses all facets of life, both horizontally and vertically. Horizontally, integral nonviolence includes a comprehensive approach to life from ecology to economics. Hughes said that the "integral pieces are inner work, radical simplicity, anti-oppression/solidarity work, service, activism, social engagement, and gratitude. Each project will have a strength. Right now our strength is the constructive program: building a new society without violence. We're developing our direct action and inner work, and most of our energy goes to rebuilding systems without structural violence. We get our heat mindfully, from wood on the land and energy from the sun."

Further, both Hughes and Moore-Backman reflect Gandhi's understanding that internal nonviolence, or personal transformation, necessarily precedes a nonviolent society; the latter is not possible without the first. Both, through their practices, talks, and workshops, are helping residents at Possibility Alliance and other like-minded communities develop techniques for living integral nonviolence. Moore-Backman has run a number of workshops on integral nonviolence, including one entitled Gandhi and the Call to Integral Nonviolence, and an invitation to a 2011 workshop was circulated widely to Catholic worker groups: "Could it be that Gandhi's holistic, comprehensive approach to nonviolent living—incorporating the personal, the social, and the political—represents the best antidote for the violence pervading our time? We will explore Gandhi's three-fold approach to social change: Inner Work, the Constructive Program, and Political Resistance."[9]

He ran this program at New Hope Catholic Worker Farm, a community near Dubuque, Iowa, that frequently dialogues and collaborates with Possibility Alliance. Moore-Backman's wheel of nonviolence, posted on the walls in several Catholic worker communities as well as at the Possibility Alliance, illustrates the practice of nonviolence. For both Moore-Backman and Hughes, integral nonviolence demands the deep discipline and commitment that develop from living practices over time and means radical transformations in personal lives and social structures.

In "Walking with Gandhi," Moore-Backman described his disillusionment at a 2003 peace walk in San Francisco when he realized that "we peace-minded folk were entirely unprepared for the battle at hand. Our so-called 'movement' lacked the depth necessary to sustain it. It came as no surprise, then, to see that after the bombs started dropping, we returned, with few exceptions, to our lives—to business, 'progressive' though it may have been—as usual."[10]

In contrast, Gandhi's 1930 Salt March succeeded, in part, because a core of seventy-eight people had undertaken "the training of spiritual discipline and constructive work of social uplift" and "submitted to its discipline and assimilated the spirit of its methods." In an act of civil disobedience, Gandhi and followers defied the British laws against making salt without paying a tax, and the Salt March, or Salt Satyagraha, became an important step toward Indian independence. According to Moore-Backman,

> Effective nonviolent political action does not spring from a vacuum; it grows out of daily living grounded in personal and communal spiritual practice, and in constructive service to one's immediate and surrounding communities. Nonviolence on the political stage is only as powerful as the personal and community-based nonviolence of those who engage in it. . . . This fundamental aspect of the Gandhian design almost entirely eludes us in our North American context. Here, we most often employ the reverse order of Gandhi's threefold approach, seeking a political response first, the building up of a constructive alternative second and the stuff of all-out personal transformation third. This reversal allows North American activists of faith to sidestep some of the most foundational aspects of Gandhi's nonviolent recipe: namely, radical simplicity, solidarity with the poor and disciplined spiritual practice.[11]

Hughes and Moore-Backman's integral nonviolence assimilates the corporal nature of Gandhi's activism and points to a critique of contemporary activism. For Gandhi, resistance meant placing your own body in harm's way, open to the possibility of injury, imprisonment, or perhaps even death. In 1963, years after Gandhi's Salt March, Americans watched in horror as Birmingham police set dogs upon African Americans during a civil rights protest. In both cases, the visceral horror of the events rapidly swung public opinion to support the Indian independence movement and the civil rights movement, but, in both cases, protestors paid a physical price. Today, Black Lives Matter protests are forcing North Americans to both recognize the structural injustices that plague African Americans and further to witness our militarized police force's violent response.

These cases, though extreme, and the lived nonviolence at Possibility Alliance point to the necessity of actually doing something in contrast to "slacktivism," defined as "the act of participating in obviously pointless activities as an expedient alternative to actually expending effort to fix a problem. Signing an email petition to stop rampant crime is slacktivism. Want to really make your community safer? Get off your ass and start a neighborhood watch!"[12]

I frequently receive and often sign Internet petitions, but I do wonder about their value. It does not cost me anything to sign a petition I support, but I do not know if it helps. The futility of Internet-based activism is satirized in Dave Eggars's 2013 novel *The Circle* when the protagonist protests terrorists by sending frowns, then later wonders if they might seek her out for retaliation among the hundreds of thousands of frown-senders. In establishing Possibility Alliance in 2007, the Hughes experimented with Moore-Backman's—and their own—acknowledgment of Gandhi's program of nonviolence: that no social transformation is possible without first living nonviolence and personal transformation.

Gandhi—and now Hughes, Moore-Backman, and others—emphasize the three-tiered vertical structure of nonviolence: personal transformation, a constructive program, and then, finally, political activism. Hughes described a fifteen-mile silent prayer walk to block entry to a nuclear plant in which he performed all three tiers of nonviolence.

> For a few hours we walked, and we were doing all three tiers simultaneously. We did the inner work, which was a prayerful walk for a few hours to prepare for the police and jail, silently. And then the second tier, we walked instead of drove, which has its own social and environmental implications. And then we walked to a place where we said, "We love you and we are willing to get arrested." That's the integral, similar to the Salt March. Gandhi did a prayer and the walk. He walked, using his own human power, to the ocean to show that you could get your own salt and broke a law. When you operate all three tiers at once, it has a bigger lever of transformation. So that's where we have some wisdom to share, in that second tier, rebuilding a society.

Imagine the three tiers as a pyramid: inner work is the broad foundation at the base; the constructive program, or practice (for example, creat-

Pyramid of integral nonviolence

ing sustainable economies) is the middle; and at the top is the political activism supported by these practices. A Possibility Alliance intern from California articulated the progression of practicing Gandhian nonviolence: "First it must be inside the self and with the people around you."

Karen, a multiyear resident at Possibility Alliance, echoed this vision of the progression of social change, with inner work providing the foundation for sociopolitical action.

> As I learn about Gandhi, what resonates the most for me is that piece about personal transformation, that nonviolence and peace is actually a spiritual path. To get to the root of violence means to get to the root of violence in ourselves. We're trying to constantly challenge ourselves to look at the violence in ourselves and in each other and come up with concrete ways to address that, and that means doing emotional work and spiritual practice. It means changing the ways in which we engage with the natural landscape, with the physical world. But it all stems from inner transformation. Any sociopolitical movement on peace can't be divorced from that personal spiritual transformation piece.

Karen, like many intentional community residents, understood inner work and personal transformation as a spiritual path. This spirituality was not necessarily linked to a particular religious or philosophical tradition, but emphasized working for the benefit of all beings.

Inner Work and Spirituality

Residents agreed that inner work is difficult because it demands deep changes in how we view and respond to others by, for example, calming long-held angry thoughts and reactions to others. Mark Becker stated that for him, "the most exciting thing is seeing how Gandhi said the most immediate, measurable and effective means of changing the world and reducing suffering is through self-discipline and self-mastery," but that "I see in my own life how that is really the hardest work of all. I see how my work in the past for reform has been coming from a place of violence within myself, and so my desire for change has constantly been frustrated because I've been acting from the seed of my inability to change myself."

Further, Becker stated, inner work instills a humility, a reduction of the ego, which facilitates the work of social justice. "Humility is a really important piece for social justice work," but difficult to achieve in part "because it can be really . . . boring." I understood the need for humility from my fieldwork and volunteering in these communities. Gardening for hours in the hot sun is difficult and often dull. Working with the group—talking and singing—can alleviate boredom, but the necessary work is long and requires self-discipline. Further, while gardening might hold some romantic appeal, tasks like laundry are rarely glamorous.

Inner work provides community residents the tools to practice nonviolence and to deeply connect to their personal religious or spiritual practices. J.R. practiced Vipassana meditation, a form of Buddhist meditation, and sought a community with like-minded others similarly engaged in the hard work of personal change.[13] But he admits, "There is a lot of internal kicking and screaming. My goal in finding a group is to let go of these conflicts and to become a better human being, to become an expression of love, or however you want to call it, in a higher state of being for the good of all. I mean in a practical manner—to not only understand sustainable forestry but also actually go out in the woods and practice it. I'm also interested in this being a lifestyle, not just a trial."

It is not enough to know something about nonviolence or sustainable forestry—you must practice it, and for J.R. and the others at Possibility Alliance, the point is discovering how to live and practice their values. The residents I spoke with view all aspects of life—from spirituality to nonviolence to sustainable agriculture—in a holistic context; a foundation of love and nonviolence toward other beings that stems from a personal transformation is connected to and translates into an ethic and practice of care in other dimensions of life. Karen, too, articulated a holistic view: "Nothing is separate in our lives, nothing is separate in this world. That's another piece of the inner transformation: to truly embody peace, you enact peace and love in every aspect of your life. So I hope that, as a community, we are just scratching the surface of what can be done and what's possible. Every little way we can be mindful is a step towards seeing the world that we want, or being the change that we wish to see."

Most residents agreed—and this seems fairly intuitive—that inner work is difficult, and much of the labor they performed was difficult as well. Despite the difficulties, I rarely heard laments or complaints. Instead, the prevailing mood was one of love and joy, words that emerged freely in conversation. Signs and posting around Possibility Alliance, for example, spoke of "joyful productivity" and "joyful abundance."

Joy, Love, and Motivation

Mark Becker's joy was infectious. No matter what he was doing, he usually sang, often making up tunes and songs. When I visited Possibility Alliance, I often sought him out simply because I always felt better being near him. Becker explained the joy he found in his work.

> In my own inner work, I see that any shift that I've been lucky enough to create has never come from a place of guilt. It's never lasted if it doesn't come from a place of real joyfulness and connection. I know that we are all microcosms of the larger whole, and we work in the exact same way that nature and society works. Because society just isn't this lifeless thing, it is individuals.
>
> But I hope that we can help to show through embodiment that the spirit of joy and the spirit of love is really what makes work fruitful. Even if we don't create anything, if the Peace and Permaculture Center and our projects flop, if we can create that spirit of being on the land and being joyful, then I think it would be a real success. But I get the sense that we're called to more than that. Cultivating excitement, enthusiasm, and joyfulness for this kind of work is going to help make it irresistible.

Becker illuminates two key points: first, guilt does not motivate lasting change. Guilt can and does motivate short-term, and sometime begrudged, actions, but those practices are not sustainable because few people respond well to guilt. In fact, guilt can be manipulative, provoking anger and frustration, the antitheses of nonviolence. In contrast, most volunteers—whether in community or not—find deep satisfaction in helping others, and that joy sustains their efforts. Second, their joy renders their work irresistible to others, and that joy is their leadership in the movement. They hope that their joy in their work will draw others to join them or try similar things elsewhere, recognizing that their experiments and alternatives will be sustainable only if they meet emotional needs. As Roger Gottlieb notes in *A Greener Faith,* the idea of motivating people to change out of love and hope rather than guilt is one of religious environmentalism's major contributions to environmentalism as a whole.[14]

One longtime resident of Sirius I spoke with echoed the Possibility Alliance's understanding that inner work and personal transformation will draw others and lead to larger transformations.

> I think the first and the most powerful way of bringing transformation is to transform yourself, so you've become an example of the kind of thing you want to practice. That has real power and has a real effect on people. You can change all the laws and the government and all the regulation you want, but if you aren't inwardly feeling this sense of the sacred and how we're connected, then it doesn't work. I think the transformation and the paradigm change we want is really coming from within people. People are waking up and having a different experience of themselves and the world around them. And once that happens, everything you do changes. You start changing how you relate to the world around you when you have an internal shift in consciousness.

Echoing Gandhi, cultivating nonviolence within ourselves provides the basis for nonviolence in our communities and social practices. For Becker and other community residents, the social transformations they seek in their own communities and beyond must first come from their own personal transformations.

Experiments, Not Ideology

Dan Truesdale, a Possibility Alliance intern turned resident, deemed the community an "experiment in creating an example of a different way to live that is in harmony with nature, that uplifts all life, and that is enjoyable and good." During my research, I identified, studied, and visited communities that emphasized their experimental nature rather than communities and individuals who assumed they had figured it all out. I value the spirit of experimentation because it encourages conversation rather than demagoguery. As demonstration communities, they engage in give-and-take with the broader public and other intentional communities. As experiments, they can both demonstrate their practices and benefit from experiments in other communities, whether intentional or mainstream. According to anthropologist Richard Fox, Gandhi understood "'experiment' to mean any confrontation with society or with oneself."[15] So, these communities are not experimental in a strict scientific sense; that is, they do not have controls, and desired results such as sustainability or equity are difficult to quantify. For Gandhi and these intentional communities, experiments provide cultural critique by evaluating alternative and innovative forms of social and material relations. Further, the sense of experimentation expresses another form of nonviolence: freedom from ideology and dogma.

Ethan Hughes tied Possibility Alliance's experimental nature to Gandhi, rightly warning of the dangers of ideology and righteousness. Like Mark Becker, he emphasized humility, the admission that they and their experiments are imperfect.

> We have to be an experiment because of the danger of righteousness, a false righteousness, where we think we have it figured out. And what I love about Gandhi is that he says, "Here's my imperfections." And we hope to emulate that and realize that we have so far to go, and we hope each year we'll have a little bit more to show in the experiment.
>
> We're not saying this is integral nonviolence. We're saying this is an experiment following the message of integral nonviolence as we interpret it. Help us interpret it. So we need the intellectual part. Help us live it. We need the physical part.

The challenge is to live and practice integral nonviolence and voluntary simplicity, for example, in all their intellectual, spiritual, and physical dimensions, not merely espouse them as philosophies. The Possibility Alliance experiment allows people to interpret and test the various dimensions, to "lean into it," as Hughes says.

Alyson Ewald of Red Earth echoed the spirit of humility and experimentation, believing that the community's openness attracts people and minimizes discord. Saying, "I'm right and you're wrong" is divisive and alienates people who might otherwise be interested. "And I think another thing appeals to people: at Red Earth we overtly say we have no idea what is a good way to live on the land. We are experimenting and humble about that. We're open to people trying different things and experimenting with different ways. We give people autonomy on their land to practice different ways of implementing what sustainability may look like. I think that taps into a deep human need to experiment and try things and not have other people tell you what needs to be done."

Ewald taps into the reality that few people like being to be told what to do. Most people dislike rules even when, as Alline Anderson of Dancing Rabbit stated, we have helped make those rules and believe they are indeed good rules. Red Earth provides autonomy because it is a homesteading community, meaning that individuals or families build and own their own home on the seventy-six-acre campus. In 2012, all but one of the six available homesteads had been filled. Unlike most communities, where people live in closer proximity, Red Earth's homesteading emphasis means that the homes are approximately one-quarter mile to a mile apart, separated by fields and small hills so that not all houses are visible to their neighbors. Red Earth's model resembles the American style of houses surrounded by farms and fields rather than the older style of grouped homes ringed by exterior farms that characterizes many ecovillages and cohousing communities.

Dancing Rabbit, Sandhill, and Red Earth support each other in part by creating a critical mass of like-minded people in the region, but each community demonstrates a different approach. Red Earth's emphasis on individual autonomy and homesteading provides a different community experience than the tightly knit, income-sharing Sandhill community or the larger, more community-focused Dancing Rabbit. Some residents have moved among the communities as their needs and interests have changed. Red Earth emphasizes agriculture and land practices, experimenting with a variety of soil-enriching techniques on the land. For example, several residents have tried *hugelkultur,* German for mound culture, a process of burying woody material in a pit or trench and covering it with more layers of nitrogen-rich material, such as grass, and soil, then planting on the mound. As the trenched and mounded materials break down, they release nutrients that feed the plants. At different households, I saw these experiments in various stages, in some cases, trenches filled with large slowly rotting logs. Ewald shared the results of her hugelkultur experiment in *Communities Magazine:* she placed her trench too far from a water source in a drought year, but community residents helped bring water to the surviving plants.[16]

Eco-Audit: Assessing Sustainability

As an experiment in sustainable living, Red Earth tests a number of environmental and social practices. Since this is a homesteading community focused on sustainable agriculture, residents hold themselves accountable for their practices, despite the relative autonomy within their small community. Although, as Ewald says, they recognize different ways of implementing sustainability, they assess their practices annually to see how their experiments are working. Throughout the year, residents keep track of practices and expenditures, on and off the property, and hand in a Red Earth ecological audit by April 1 of each year (http://new.redearthfarms.org/docs/REFCLT_eco_audit_form.pdf). In addition to physical practices, such as agriculture, they also answer questions regarding quality of life issues. The residents present the material to each other and discuss their progress to see how they might improve. The eco-audit highlights the importance of experimentation and feedback, and questions on the form point to the trade-offs residents have made in their sustainability efforts.

As Ewald notes, their audit format is still in progress.

> We haven't found an eco-audit that can do what we want it to do. Existing audits are for people in suburbia who want to see what the meter says each month or how many miles they drove on personal family vehicles. What if one family shares a vehicle with two other families, and how you do account for the repairs? We haven't got any kind of software that can figure out what is the climate impact of anything. Ultimately we would like to be able to do that, but for now it's just a measure of year-to-year progress compared to the last year.

They track money spent on food, but a food total does not parse where that money was spent, so does not account for values-based decisions about food purchases, such as trade-offs between expensive locally produced foods and cheaper imports. Says Ewald, "I would like there to be subcategories acknowledging, 'I did spend a lot more money on food because I bought my honey from Sandhill.' It costs twice as much as opposed to Zimmerman's, which comes from wherever."

The honey dilemma demonstrates trade-offs and decisions between values. Buying from Sandhill, a community only three miles away that produces and sells honey, keeps the money entirely within the local community. Buying from Zimmerman's, a local store, keeps costs down, but sends some money beyond the immediate community cluster. Keeping money within the communities helps ensure their financial and social stability.

The eco-audit also assesses quality of life, reflecting on the nature of the community and social ties as well as environmental factors. Residents are asked to rate their responses to a series of statements such as "I experience a healthy amount of stress" to "I am satisfied with my financial situation." The quality of life assessment is important; Red Earth is an intentional community, and its social and sustainability goals are linked. Residents' social and emotional health affects how the community as a whole works together. Ewald said that residents are trying to adapt the audit to account for their broader goals. "They suggested adding stories or photographs. We already have some photographs, but you could add more of species in decline on your land. And you could add stories about health. Are you happier here? How's your mental health? You could break down the food into organic, local, community-based."

The eco-audit indicates that not only is it difficult to be sustainable, but it is also difficult to assess sustainability. Even individuals within like-minded communities understand and practice sustainability differently.

Red Earth residents complete their annual eco-audit and then gather to assess their individual and community sustainability goals. According to Ewald, they chose this system of accountability rather than a series of rules and covenants, in part, because Dancing Rabbit's level of regulation was somewhat off-putting to the founders of this homesteading community. "From the beginning, Red Earth consciously set up the structure without 'Thou shall' and 'Thou shall not' rules. We don't have covenants like at Dancing Rabbit, and we don't have specific things that people have to do when they move onto the land."

Interestingly, one fellow guest who attended Dancing Rabbit's 2011 visitor session had the opposite reaction, perceiving the eco-audit as a violation of privacy. Although she ultimately did not join either community, she believed Dancing Rabbit's broad covenants and rules were much less intrusive than an audit of individual behavior. Yet, this informal system of accountability works well for Red Earth's small homesteading community and preserves the autonomy residents desire. Creating a sustainable community, no matter how small, requires governance and systems of conflict resolution. Even when residents agree on a goal, their modes of implementation can vastly differ, so communities have developed a variety of structures to ensure that residents participate in all matters of governance.

Civics 3.0: From Facebook to Face-to-Face

I focused on communities that tie their sustainability goals to radical democracy. Imposing practices from above, without the consent of those governed, represents a form of violence and force, so these communities have developed processes both to govern themselves democratically and to resolve nonviolently the conflicts that are bound to emerge in any group of people. In addition to learning about and adopting sustainable practices (for instance, composting toilets or water reclamation), new residents must also develop a set of interpersonal skills so they can participate in decisions about these practices. Living cooperatively and in community pushes residents to learn new skills of conflict resolution.

Individuals join communities because of deeply held values that they wish to practice, and their desire to live their values points to realities of life in community: conflict and personal growth. Inevitably, as values emerge in practice, conflicts arise as residents deliberate on how best to enact those values. Sarah Wilcox-Hughes of the Possibility Alliance commented that she appreciated the process of "pushing and stretching each other," concluding that "somehow, though that consensus process, we meet at this center place." Our tour guide at Sirius, a well-established intentional community based in Shutesbury, Massachusetts, stated: "We do work a lot with personal relationships. We have specific requirements and agreements about conflict when it arises. Notice I did not say if, but when, it arises. When people find themselves in conflict, it's usually a tremendous opportunity for growth."

Intentional communities recognize this potential for conflict perhaps more than in the mainstream because you cannot simply ignore your neighbors in community. Residents must learn new modes of social relationships, including conflict resolution skills, especially in communities that stress nonviolence and promote nonviolent communication.

Developing skills in listening and conflict resolution also proves valuable when communicating with outsiders or family members who are resistant to intentional communities and their values. Some parents, for example, are horrified when their children reject mainstream lifestyles to join an off-the-grid community. Sarah Wilcox-Hughes's mother, Victoria Albright, recounts what she experienced when she joined her daughter for two months at Lost Valley Educational Center near Eugene, Oregon. During this time, through learning to listen and be heard, she came to understand her daughter's choices and values, and their relationship improved and deepened. Like many communities, Lost Valley Educational Center gave workshops that taught skills of nonviolent (compassionate) communication and deep listening and also facilitated mediations to resolve conflicts among residents and others.

As a parent, Albright understands the conflicts that arise when children chose nontraditional paths: "I think it is pretty safe to say that most parents want what is 'best' for their children and for their children to be happy. But the rub is that parents can usually only offer what they know, which may include a steady job, benefits and health insurance, a traditional family lifestyle, and modern conveniences (cars/planes, computers, appliances) that all translate to them as a safe, secure life. Living in a community rarely fits into that picture, at least at first." Albright states that she has met "dozens of young communitarians who are truly devastated by the conflict they are experiencing with their parents over their decision to pull away from a mainstream lifestyle." Many of them have asked her to sit with their parents to help them work through their fears and concerns about their children's choices. Now, as a part-time resident at the Possibility Alliance, Albright sits with visiting parents and listens.[17]

Few people have learned the social skills needed to create, debate, and implement matters of policy—large or small—so communities typically have to teach new residents how to participate in these systems. Lara Morrison, manager of LA Eco-village, a consensus-based community, said, "Not only is it a place where we can support people in changing their lifestyles to be more sustainable but it's a place where we can support people in gaining the skills to operate cooperatively and to understand finances and legal structures. Most people don't get that opportunity at all."

LA Eco-village runs a facilitated consensus meeting each Monday and also occasionally runs facilitation and consensus trainings to educate residents and interested members of the public. The LA Eco-village tagline, "Reinventing how we live in the city," encompasses the community's social and governance practices as well as its environmental activities.

Intentional communities reintroduce social skills that some scholars, such as sociologist Robert Putnam, claim we have lost. Putnam maintains that North Americans are less and less likely to participate in civic organizations as we focus more and more on the individual and nuclear families.[18] Sociologist and psychologist Sherry Turkle writes that our reliance on devices and media such as Facebook has made us more engaged with the nebulous realm of cyberspace than with those sitting across from us at the table.[19] Watching four people seated together in a restaurant with each focused on his or her own smartphone makes her point difficult to refute. On the other hand, Mark Oppenheimer questioned both Putnam's and Turkle's assessments, citing research by communications scholar Keith Hampton suggesting that people connected by technology are often more responsive to emerging situations in their neighborhoods and more likely to participate in neighborhood events.[20]

Additionally, research based on comparisons of past and present photographs has demonstrated that public spaces, such as the steps of New York City's Metropolitan Museum of Art, not only attract more people than thirty years ago, but that a higher percentage of these people are women, a finding echoed in Philadelphia and Boston as well. "I mean, who would've thought that, in America, 30 years ago, women were not in public the same way they are now?" Hampton said. "We don't *think* about that."[21] Hampton's comment indicates that gender issues were less commonly researched thirty years ago. Also, perhaps, despite assumptions to the contrary, more people, including more diverse populations, seek out public spaces and possible interactions.

This body of research suggests several things. First, not surprisingly, technology is changing how we interact with each other and, as such, suggests new opportunities for communication and collaboration between communities and others. The Valhalla Movement's project (http://valhallamovement.com), which digitally tells the stories of sustainably focused intentional communities, draws on emerging skills and communication technologies to increase dialogue and exchange between distant groups. Hampton's work also brings up the issue of gender equity in social space, and as he noted, until recently no one had even questioned the relative lack of women in public space. So, while some lament the decline of older social patterns in which social relationships were supposedly stronger—and that might have been true among certain populations—I do not want to romanticize a past that was less than ideal for women and other populations.

Intentional communities that emphasize participatory democracy and nonviolence take care not to simply re-create older systems that institutionalize oppressive relations, such as sexism; they develop new systems of governance and conflict resolution. Founders and residents of the 1970s and 1980s lesbian separatist communities (for instance, OWL, the Oregon Women's Land Trust) created women-only communities based on radical democracy because they believed that withdrawal and separation were the only means for women to escape patriarchal systems.[22] Communities such as Dancing Rabbit and Twin Oaks developed inclusive communities that challenged existing gender roles and relationship structures, aiming to accommodate emerging and fluid gender identities, providing friendly and safe spaces for LGBTQ members. The FIC Wiki "Queer in Community" page offers support and lists communities that specifically address LGBTQ issues.[23] Dancing Rabbit, for example, cultivates a feminist sensibility, and its "Feminism, Empowerment, and Justice" statement highlights its commitment to be free to either work with or challenge traditional gender roles.[24] Dancing Rabbit and Twin Oaks use the pronoun *co* instead of *he* or *she* as a means to move beyond traditional gender labels. Dancing Rabbit and Twin Oaks are two of the five communities listed on the FIC website as feminist, and both stress participatory democracy even though, as its population increased, Dancing Rabbit moved to a village council model rather than full-group consensus meetings. These communities, although they are experimenting with different systems of governance, share a commitment to full enfranchisement of all residents.

Consensus and Nonviolence

Gandhi himself tied participatory governance to nonviolence and recognized the tensions inherent in balancing individual autonomy with the needs of the broader community. "I value individual freedom," Gandhi remarked, "but you must not forget that man is essentially a social being," and "unrestricted individualism must be curtailed by social conscience to strike the mean between individual freedom and social restraint."[25]

To ensure full participation, his disciple Vinobha Bhave established consensus-style governance in his ashrams, or devotional communities, because the one-person, one-vote system in democracy is inherently adversarial, and the majority could obscure the voices of the minority, a form of violence. Later, intentional communities in the United States reflected Gandhi's concerns about the tyranny of the majority, and communities such as Twin Oaks developed consensus-style governance systems to ensure that all voices would be heard. Paxus Calta, blogging about Twin Oaks' consensus system, wrote that the founders wanted a system that would improve on the dysfunctional majority-rule system.

> At its inception Twin Oaks wanted a decision model that was better than simple democratic voting. The founders thought that communards could make better decisions than what came from the "50% plus one" model which

dominated elections and government process. In the search for the elusive super majority, they did not want to set a threshold percentage, perhaps because they wanted something more subtle and dynamic than vote counting at the core of our process. They wanted to leave open the possibility that a small group with strongly held beliefs might be able to shift the group's outcome by carefully reasoned arguments and compelling logic. Twin Oaks started in 1967, before the feminists had borrowed and adapted the consensus process from Quakers—creating a decision tool which could be used in a secular environment. And since simple majority rule had created so many dysfunctional systems it seemed wise to try for something which was more representative, even if it was slower.[26]

The focus on process and experimentation practiced at these communities echoes the "quest for democracy," as described by sociologist Catriona Mortimer-Sandilands, in which we are obligated to continually consider what parties, human and nonhuman, might not yet be "at the table" or have a voice. Further, she argues, this quest is an ongoing process because the act of demarcating who or what is not at the table itself closes the door to unrecognized or emergent parties.[27] Many communities have borrowed and adapted consensus processes used in Quaker communities, and I have heard several times that a community's success is proportional to the number of residents familiar with Quaker processes.

Intentional communities have created a variety of processes to govern themselves and to resolve conflicts, and the goals of social equity and nonviolence provide the foundation for their efforts. One key point is that nonviolence and equity are bound up with sustainability. In agreeing to a certain model of governance, community residents must ask themselves how much they want to interweave their lives and what it means to share space and resources.

Interweaving Lives

Prior to buying the land that would become Dancing Rabbit, a group of students at Stanford deliberated for over four years about what sort of community they wanted to create. The long process created the foundation and mechanisms for the community to govern itself and resolve internal conflicts. Tony Sirna reflected on Dancing Rabbit's extensive visioning process: "Sometimes it felt slow, but we had a few years of just visioning and thinking before we ever got the land. It can be hard to do that once you already have land. A lot went on between 1993 and 1997, when we bought the land, to really shape Dancing Rabbit."

Merging lives and individuals into an intentional community requires serious thought and the ability to establish clear rules and guidelines for joining the community, resolving conflicts in community and, occasionally, removing residents from the community. People starting a community or considering joining a community need to determine the extent to which they wish to intertwine their lives. Sharing resources is an important component of voluntary simplicity, but sharing a car or house demands far more of co-owners than simply sharing a lawn mower does.

Dancing Rabbit, one of the larger communities I visited, developed a consensus-style governance system in which everyone participates in community-wide decisions. For example, the community has been debating different models for allocating lands between residential and agricultural uses. Dancing Rabbit's consensus style of governance—as opposed to a democracy in which 51 percent get what they want—means that everybody has a real voice and must be at least minimally satisfied with the measure. In practice, this means that most proposals are well discussed, vetted, and amended before being presented to the larger community. The founders of Dancing Rabbit envisioned a village inhabited by over five hundred people with sustainable economic, social, and physical systems, and when the number of residents exceeded seventy, they transitioned to a town hall–style of democracy that blended full-group consensus and empowered committees.[28]

For an intentional community, designing the process by which residents can live their values as a community is part of the creative process of being the change and reflects the integration of the three legs of sustainability: ecology, economy, and equity. According to Sirna,

> I really believe that the way we interact personally and interpersonally needs to reflect how we want the world to be politically or economically. I feel like we try to communicate here cooperatively. We try to have our economics be cooperative, and we try to have our decision making be cooperative. And that doesn't mean that it's always perfect, and it doesn't mean that there's not some people with more power. It's not utopian or anarchist. There are still leaders. Some people have more power, and I think that's okay. It's a matter of doing things with integrity and awareness.

That everyone has a voice and participates, which is one understanding of radical democracy, in decisions about food, transportation, and construction is critical to Dancing Rabbit's mission of sustainability. The rules and guidelines residents have developed are the tools that help them decide how best to implement their shared goals and values.

Dancing Rabbit's extensive visioning process seems to have paid off. The community has adapted to a larger population and passed a significant test—the departure of its founders. Cecil Scheib and, more recently, Tony Sirna, moved on to pursue other opportunities, but both remain involved with Dancing Rabbit. Although it was clear to me that Sirna was a respected leader and member, Dancing Rabbit had distributed its governance so that Sirna's departure was a sad event but not a catastrophic one. Some smaller communities with more fluid governance structures might not survive if their leaders moved on. While Possibility Alliance strives for shared governance, Ethan Hughes is a strong and engaging figure, and I wonder how the Possibility Alliance would adapt if the Hughes family left. Possibility Alliance has built strong relationships with neighboring communities and drawn like-minded individuals to the area, so although Possibility Alliance would certainly change if its founders left, its strong community support would likely ensure its survival in some form.

Nonviolent Communication

Residents of intentional communities join, for the most part, to live out sets of shared values that are explicitly documented in materials, such as by-laws, covenants, and rules. Nonetheless, communities inevitably experience conflict over the rules themselves or how best to implement values, such as, for example, deliberating what constitutes sustainable agriculture. Given their emphasis on nonviolence, they must establish processes to work through conflicts that engage participants in dialogue. *How* they resolve conflicts matters, and learning to do so peacefully and productively provides opportunities for personal and spiritual growth for residents. Our tour guide at Sirius, a community founder, explained, "As human beings, we're still not perfectly aligned pure beings, so conflict comes out. For me, who's been living in community for what seems like forever, I'm still challenged by living in community, and I think that's a good thing. I still find it challenging; it's pushing me to my edges. I need to smooth them out and work through it more and more. So I think community is a good place for spiritual growth."

Everyone acknowledges that living in community is personally challenging, especially given the combination of close proximity and community intention. While apartment dwellers in New York City do live in close proximity, neighbors can create material and psychological barriers to ensure their privacy. Residents of intentional communities, however, join for the community and have real social and governance obligations to their fellow residents that most neighbors do not.

For interpersonal conflicts, especially those that do not involve an entire community, small conflict resolution committees can work with residents to smooth over difficulties. For example, Cobb Hill has a conflict transformation policy for these situations. According to Judith Bush, "If two people are having a problem, they will quietly use it. It doesn't need to rise to the level of community observation." Similarly, Dancing Rabbit's conflict resolution committee facilitates communication between residents. Either the residents ask for help or, if others perceive that the conflict has escalated to affect the community at large, a third party will call in the resolution team.

Communities such as Dancing Rabbit require that all residents have some training in nonviolent communication (NVC); several sessions of Dancing Rabbit's visitor program emphasize NVC or a variant such as inner empathy, a technique for developing empathy for one's own self as well as others. Marshall Rosenberg's work has developed practices for nonviolence in personal relationships as well as in group dynamics.[29] The Center for Nonviolent Communication organizes training in nonviolent communication and nonviolent resistance that have provided the foundation for peaceful protests as well as group meetings (http://www.cnvc.org/). The Occupy Wall Street public meetings facilitated discussions using Rosenberg's NVC techniques, and the public witnessed—with confusion and sometimes frustration—the slow process of conflict and consensus.

Though conflict generally has a negative connotation, the process of deliberation using NVC consensus methods demonstrates the positive role of conflict in producing innovative solutions. In a consensus process, individuals and parties must respond to and incorporate the positions of others if they are to achieve broad agreement, whereas a majority-rule situation privileges winning votes and allies. One Dancing Rabbit resident told me that, in general, those backing a proposal generally shop it around and adapt it before presenting it at a general meeting, so proposals frequently achieve consensus because of widespread input. Conflict, though, plays an important role in helping individuals and groups think through various alternatives because dialogue—enhanced through understanding different perspectives—produces solutions that none had envisioned. Religion professor Mark Juergensmeyer describes how resolving conflict with NVC methods facilitates engagement with multiple perspectives and can create better ideas that benefit all parties. He elucidates two related points, both deriving from Gandhi: first, all parties must be at the table; and second, no parties should be demonized.[30]

No One Ever Said It Would Be Easy

Residents of intentional communities share challenges around questions such as participation, labor, and aging that all of us face. For example, although communities such as Sirius and Cobb Hill require a set amount of monthly labor, enforcing this requirement is virtually impossible. Intentional communities rely on volunteer labor, much like the shared governance of academic institutions, and some participants inevitably shoulder a disproportionate amount of the burden.

Governing residents who move to intentional communities to practice strongly held values can be especially difficult. As Lois Arkin of LA Eco-village notes,

> Intentional communities tend to be populated by people who are somewhat anarchistically oriented, so idealistic about democracy that they can be immobilized by their ideology. So was I in the very beginning. I was very inflexible on some things, for example, on consensus decision making. I had been on the board of the FIC for several years, and each year I attended meetings for five days with the best consensus facilitators in the country. They made it look easy.
>
> We go by consensus, but we didn't—I didn't—require that people be trained in at least a two-day workshop and that people be restricted from blocking until they had been well trained. I never made those requirements, so we had probably seven or eight years of hell, from my perspective, where people who didn't have a clue were controlling the community. And I don't know how I stuck that out.

Arkin expresses a tension that is especially apparent in LA Eco-village as it moves into its third decade: some members see policies determined through consensus as inviolate rules, while others see some policies in that light, but also feel strongly that many policies should be viewed as guidelines, and that flexibility should be exercised in certain situations. The spirit of the policy will be considered, but the individual situation must be evaluated according

Sustainability in Community   157

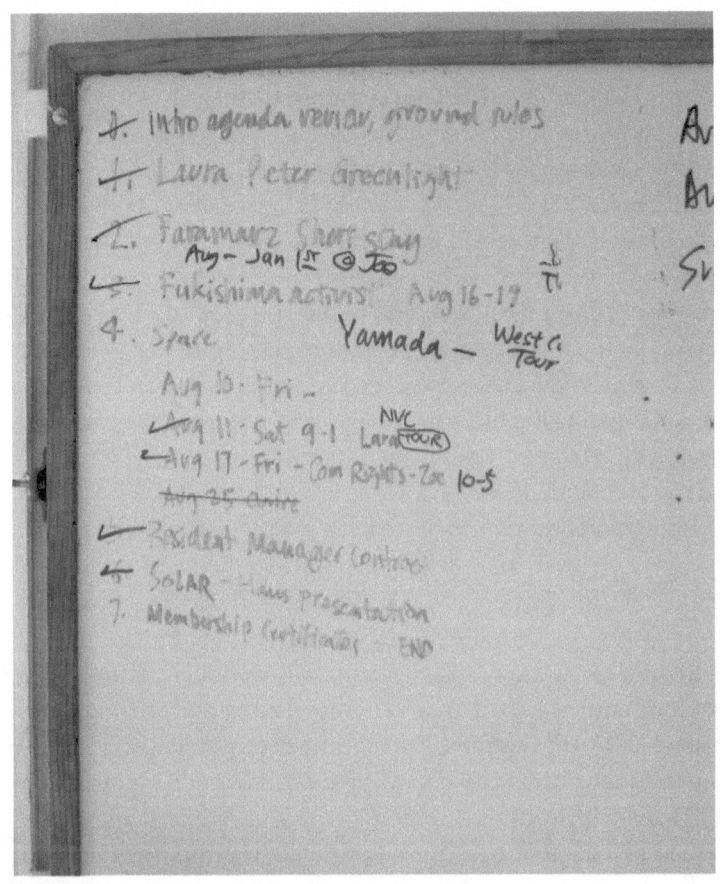

Community meeting agenda at LA Eco-village

to whether it enhances or detracts from the community and its purpose overall. If some members are committed to living out specific values in the context of community, such as democracy as manifested by consensus, with unanimity being the hard-and-fast rule by which decisions are made, they may grow increasingly inflexible as the community moves into maturity, depending on these hard-earned policies and rules for the final word on everything. And where there is no policy, they may spend countless additional plenary hours hammering out yet one more inflexible policy/rule. This becomes a recipe for conflict with those who prefer that some policies function as guidelines rather than rules or regulations.

Further, consensus-based governance, like anything, has a learning curve, and those not well versed in the systems can be disruptive, even if unintentionally. For example, in consensus decision making, a block should be used only if the proposal violates community integrity and values; it is not a simple opposition vote based on individual preference. Meetings can be bogged down in minutiae that waste valuable time and could be better solved by committee.

Silence might represent acquiescence to more forceful personalities or perceived leaders, subverting the consensus process. "We don't know how to interpret silence from most members on most issues," writes Paxus Calta of Twin Oaks. "It would appear that decision making power is tilted towards those who write on the O&I [Opinions and Ideas] board."[31] Tony Sirna commented that Dancing Rabbit is not utopia and that there will always be leaders and those with perceived power, yet community members are still moving forward to new solutions.

A number of communities have been experimenting with sociocracy, a dynamic form of governance developed in the Netherlands in the 1970s that, according to the Sociocracy Group (http://thesociocracygroup.com/), empowers circles, or committees, to make decisions for the group. Diana Leafe Christian, an acknowledged expert on intentional communities, wrote that her community, Earthhaven Ecovillage, a twenty-year-old community near Asheville, North Carolina, has recently incorporated sociocracy into its decision-making process and commented on the model's potential to mitigate problems with consensus-based governance.[32] Although sociocracy is still defined as a consent-based governance system, it is one that helps communities move beyond needing community-wide consensus for each and every decision.

Maintaining Balance

In addition to challenges regarding governance and conflict, residents of intentional communities struggle to maintain balance between their individual autonomy and their obligations to the community, especially when the communities understand themselves as demonstration sites. Dancing Rabbit, for example, holds about five three-week visitor sessions during the warmer months of the year. These visitor sessions are critical both for recruiting residents and for demonstrating the community's experiments to outsiders. Those who join Dancing Rabbit, Twin Oaks, or any demonstration community know that they are moving into a fishbowl, but the reality of strangers questioning your habits and peeping into your windows is a challenge nonetheless. High Wind co-founder Lisa Paulson stated, "Because High Wind had been receiving more and more publicity and was listed in community directories worldwide, increasing numbers of visitors and seekers were showing up on our doorstep and clamoring for programs on all sorts of topics. This put huge stress on our small residential community, which was already under strain. The simplified, peaceful life we had envisioned and were dedicated to creating and demonstrating had somehow slipped away from us."[33] These pressures, in part, influenced High Wind residents' decision to transition from an intentional community to an "ecological neighborhood."

Dan Truesdale, living at the Possibility Alliance, articulated residents' conflicting desires both to reach out and to focus on their own work. "There's a struggle because there's a desire to help other people out and also to continue to provide for our needs. It's easier to work on that balance when there are more people here because then people can be divided among different activities and still accomplish both tasks in a way that's not going to burn people out."

The Communities Conference at Twin Oaks that I attended in 2013 was held at a venue adjacent to the residential part of the community. Visitors were requested not to go into Twin Oaks proper unless on a guided tour or if specifically invited. Residents, we heard, appreciated the conference, but wanted to maintain privacy as well.

Social Sustainability

In their efforts to practice sustainability, intentional communities face a host of challenges around governance and conflict resolution. While they benefit from the presence of others with a shared commitment to sustainability, deciding how to live together and how to implement their values is a challenge few people in different kinds of communities face. Those of us living outside such communities choose our levels of civic obligations, and there are few, if any, penalties for avoiding civic duties. Residents of intentional communities owe significant committee and governance obligations to their communities, and although such participation draws them to community life, it is a significant time cost. Communities such as Twin Oaks count the emotional and interpersonal expenditure involved in governance and conflict resolution as labor, and the emotional burden of creating community stability is spread among residents, both men and women. This accounting of labor credits the time and emotional costs of community membership and also acknowledges that these tasks are, in fact, work. It takes a great deal of time and emotional work to live together, but this social cohesiveness is necessary to meet looming challenges such as climate change.

Community experiments in governance and integrated values—a commitment to weave nonviolence through all aspects of life—can teach us how to live cooperatively with shared resources. Community residents recognize that the larger community is watching them, as Belfast resident Coleen O'Connell writes, to see, among other things, how they conduct their lives and their governance. Can a small community learn together to share space and be "a gold standard for sustainability?"[34]

Everyone now faces a shared dilemma—how to preserve the commons, whether that is water, genetic resources, or air. Many claim that without private ownership or an environmental dictatorship, the commons will be consumed by a greedy landgrab of sorts. We will all suffer if we do not develop tools to share and allocate resources fairly. This is where coalition-building efforts among individuals and communities becomes critical because individuals and small communities cannot address global crises such as climate change on their own. The North American emphasis on individualism, the persistent belief that our individual efforts can solve large social problems, deflects criticism of corporate structures and places the burden of social change on the shoulders of individuals. This is one criticism of campaigns such as Vote with Your Fork, which suggests that better consumer choices can address the ills of industrial agriculture. Making better food choices is important on the individual scale, but we need change at the community and governmental scales to truly revise environmental policies. The "I" must become "we" to meet challenges such as climate change.

Political scientist Karen Litfin writes compellingly that ecovillages provide us with insight into how we might "scale it up" from small communities to coordinated global efforts. Ecovillages and other intentional communities combine a systemic approach to governance and policies, from architecture to food, with sharing and radical democracy, reflecting the idea that ecological sustainability requires social sustainability.[35] The shared governance and cooperative systems of intentional communities suggest both that democratic alternatives are possible and that nonviolence and equity are essential components of sustainability.

7
Rethinking Abundance

The challenge is breaking through the hold of consumerism. People are hypnotized, addicted and numb to what's happening among the poor and the disinherited.
—Victoria Albright, Possibility Alliance

LIKE MOST NORTH AMERICANS, I have too much stuff. Our garage is filled with old sporting equipment such as cross-country skis, which do me no good in Florida, and when I recently hauled off several bike- and carloads of clothes and gear to Hospice Attic, I felt liberated. I regained space to move around the garage, and I had no more responsibility for those items. Although I tend to be a packrat and Kevin prefers a minimalist approach, we would both like to downsize, both for our own sanity and to create a more sustainable lifestyle. I spent two years doing fieldwork in north India, where I lived in a small room in an ashram. Everything I needed—some books, clothes, and sandals—fit in that space. When I returned home after my fieldwork, I was overwhelmed by the amount of stuff that seemed necessary for life in the United States. For example, I have three bicycles—one for commuting, one for road riding, and one for mountain biking—and I use each of these bikes more than my car, so deciding whether having three bikes is sustainable is not easy or obvious. Many people struggle with the question of stuff—how much stuff do we need and where do we put it?—and our questions about stuff reflect related questions about time and busyness as crucial elements of our lifestyles. Everybody complains about how busy they are, but to the extent that these lifestyles are choices, perhaps we can choose another path.

Intentional communities around the United States, including ecovillages, Catholic worker communities, and cohousing communities, are experimenting with the concept of voluntary simplicity. For some communities, voluntary simplicity means sharing community resources, such as lawn mowers and cars, while for others it means attempting to live off the land or at least within the constraints of a bioregion, as in the hundred-mile diet (eating only food that is grown within one hundred miles of where you live). Most communities construct housing far smaller than the typical two-thousand-square-foot suburban house, an option that parallels the Tiny House Movement, which favors dwellings of one hundred to four hundred square feet.[1] In all cases, though, voluntary simplicity in these communities means asking hard questions about how much we really need to be happy and, on the flip side, rethinking what constitutes abundance. For example, residents of ecovillages and cohousing communities have willingly traded American "needs" such as individual cars and large lots for close neighbors and strong social bonds. And if we agree to share more of our goods, then perhaps we can reduce our workloads—and our busyness—while still having access to our bikes, kayaks, and lawn mowers. These communities are transforming the model of what it means to be middle class by demonstrating different paths to a middle-class lifestyle.

Freedom in Community

As I visited different communities, I heard a common theme again and again: most residents valued community and time over things. Elizabeth of Cherith Brook in Kansas City, Missouri, commented, "It's freeing to share." She lives in a "common purse" community in which almost all goods are considered community property. Dorothy Day recommended that Catholic workers live in voluntary poverty, and some Catholic worker communities have a common purse, pooling their income to strengthen their commitment to voluntary poverty and the Works of Mercy.[2]

Many communities, even some cohousing communities, have some version of a community clothes closet—commie clothes—where residents exchange clothes they have worn for clothes that are new to them, a process similar to freecycling, in which people give away used items to those who want them.[3] As part of community labor or service, community residents clean and mend the clothes so they are ready to wear. While not everyone would be willing to participate in such a clothing exchange, this process has benefits, such as reduced laundry labor for individuals because washing commie clothes is part of community labor. The commie closet also frees participants from the financial and consumeristic aspects of fashion. The clothing is free, and deciding what to wear is certainly simpler when choices are limited to what is available in the commie closet. For many, the benefits of commie clothes outweigh the lack of choice in style and size.

Similarly, Eric Anglada of New Hope saw community living and voluntary simplicity as "a way out of living busy lives. I actively cultivate not being busy, and I'm able to do that because of community. If you're just trying to meet all your needs yourself, there's no way. Community can help do that. The first time I saw community, it made so much sense to be reliant on others. If we share tools and gadgets, a washing machine or a refrigerator, then not every person needs one, and we don't need as much money to get by." Sharing and living in community are efficient because residents can share work as well as equipment.

Anglada's and Elizabeth's comments point to two contemporary dilemmas: the cult of busy and the treadmill of working to buy clothes, cars, and other goods so that we can continue working. Googling the phrase "cult of busy" generates thousands of links that discuss ways to escape the trap of constant busyness, much of which is self-imposed. Contemporary North American culture is one of action, not idleness, which reflects Puritan roots, echoing the admonition that "idle hands make for the devil's work." The cult of busy dominates the academic landscape, and the question "How are you?" often elicits the mixed boast-lament, "Crazy busy." Answering otherwise never seems appropriate and might doom you to not seeming serious about academia.

I did not realize how much the cult of busy permeated conversations with fellow academics until I began work as a kayaking instructor at the Nantahala Outdoor Center (NOC) in western North Carolina in 2006 and became immersed in a new culture. There the appropriate answer to "How are you?" was something to the effect of "I'm doing great," still a formulaic answer, but much more positive and energetic. Spending time at NOC gave me a fresh perspective on busyness, and I realized that I vastly preferred NOC's energetic culture. Later, as I spoke with residents of intentional communities, I recognized that they, too, had made cultural choices not to enshrine busyness as a lifestyle. Of course, NOC employees and residents of these communities work hard, and they are busy, but their conversational styles and culture reflect priorities of friendship and community over a rhetoric of obligations.

For some community dwellers, voluntary simplicity represented freedom from the growing demands of social media, such as Facebook and Twitter. At Sirius in Shutesbury, Massachusetts, few if any of the residents had TVs, and there were no TVs in any of the guest rooms or the community house. However, the community had Internet access, and I saw many of the younger residents and visitors using laptops, which demonstrates that technology does enable some forms of simplicity, such as working remotely. One older resident who had moved to Sirius a year ago commented, "Most people would come here and wouldn't like it. You don't have your own living room. I donated much of my furniture and my big-screen TV to the community. I don't watch TV now. I watch *Rachel Maddow* every day to keep up with the news and read the *New York Times* online, but I don't even do Facebook. For me, it's been a time of splendid isolation."

Class Matters

It is worth restating that residents of most intentional communities have chosen this lifestyle, which reflects the reality that they have had the means to make conscious and informed choices about their levels of consumption. Overwhelmingly, residents of these communities hail from white, suburban, middle-class backgrounds or had at least reached that status prior to rejecting middle-class levels of consumption, and not everyone appreciates romanticized stories about downsizing and cutting back to essentials. After the Great Recession of 2008, a spate of articles appeared in publications such as the *New York Times* that documented the (sometimes forced) trend of downsizing and moving to plan B. However, in many cases, these plan Bs were said to come with silver linings of stress-free lives or more fulfilling ways of life. But such portrayals did not accurately reflect the anger and stress of forced downsizing experienced by many Americans. Blogger Ron Byrnes wrote, "The high priests and priestesses of minimalism don't know it, but they have a problem. They're seriously disliked by the majority of people who are struggling to get by. Ordinary people deeply resent the 'voluntary' nature of most high-profile minimalists who write about the joys of downsizing on their numerous blogs, or for the *New York Times*, or *Sunset Magazine*."[4] Individuals and communities who choose voluntary simplicity—and boast about it—run the risk of incurring the resentment of those who do not have that choice, a problem for communities who understand themselves as educational or as coalition builders.

Cultural and religious traditions have embraced concepts of voluntary poverty and voluntary simplicity for millennia as foundations for monastic communities as well as charitable giving. The Buddha, for example, taught that craving ephemeral things would ensnare us in cycles of desires that could never be adequately fulfilled and would only leave us empty and wanting more. Many communities I visited echoed the idea, present in multiple religious traditions, that "joy can only come from within. Nothing external can bring it." Yet the idea that things will never make us happy runs counter to consumption-based economies and the advertising and marketing campaigns that try to sell us on how new products will enrich our lives. Today, the sheer amount and diversity of available goods distract us from being able to determine what we actually need. Moreover, our personal needs are conflated with what we are led to believe that our society needs, and the Great Recession has made it clear that when our consumer economy slows, we all suffer. The idea that North Americans ought to consume has a history that stretches back at least to the prosperous years after World War II when the United States began shifting from a military-industrial complex to a more consumer-focused one.[5] Consuming goods has almost become both an entitlement and an obligation for us in the United States, and gauging how much is too much is not an easy matter.

Activists and inspirational figures such as Dorothy Day and Mohandas Gandhi offer tools to help us distinguish need from greed. When I attended a permaculture workshop at New Hope in 2012, instructor Adam Campbell of the Possibility Alliance invoked both Day and Gandhi in a discussion about surplus and needs. Day believed that surplus goods should be distributed to the poor, but to do so, we must be able to identify what counts as surplus. Similarly, a quote widely attributed to Gandhi states that the earth has enough for everyone's need, but not greed, indicating that we must set limits on consumption, otherwise our desires will be endless. For Gandhi, as for the residents of the Possibility Alliance, New Hope, and other communities, bread labor helps distinguish between need and greed because bread labor teaches us what it takes to produce various goods (see chapter 4). When goods are easily available from stores, it becomes easier to inflate our need for these goods. However, when we have to do the work of producing goods, whether foods or clothes, ourselves, it might provide some focus to help evaluate whether we really need those goods.

In "Ethics and the Environment," environmental philosopher Kristin Shrader-Frechette proposes a tripartite schema to distinguish between necessities, enhancements, and luxuries: "Items in the first category include food, clothing, shelter, and medical care. Goods in the second class are more difficult to define but include such things as education and recreation, which allow people to express themselves and to determine their futures and thus go beyond mere survival. Luxury goods, on the other hand, are not essential to our well-being, although whether they are good or bad depends on the use to which they are put or the spirit in which they are enjoyed; they include items such as gourmet food and private automobiles."[6] While this framework is by no means definitive, Shrader-Frechette's concept of the three levels helps us evaluate our consumption.

In one of my early trips to Dancing Rabbit, I recognized how limits and bread labor shaped decisions about need. I first spent several days at Dancing Rabbit in the spring, when all the residents were appreciating the end of a long winter. I returned the following September for my first official visitor's session, where I learned more about the residents and their building and agricultural projects. During this period, the Rabbits I met graciously discussed their lives and projects with the guests although they were busy and focused on their preparations for winter. No one would survive a Missouri winter in a shoddily built house, so the Rabbits were working hard to finish their homes, collect wood for heating, and gather their harvest. Rabbits rely solely on the wood they collect to supply both their heating and cooking needs for the year so that they can avoid the use of fossil fuels for those purposes. This limited supply of firewood also means that they must make decisions and act intentionally regarding trade-offs between food and heat. For example, heating up the stove for late-night popcorn means there will be that much less wood for heat later in the winter.

Even more important in this context, Rabbits debate the benefits and consequences of tapping their silver maples to produce syrup. The silver maples offer approximately a fifty to one ratio of sap to syrup, not an especially good yield, but nonetheless, the silver maples are in their bioregion and available. Producing syrup is both laborious for humans and requires a significant expenditure of energy from wood burning, so Rabbits must balance the results with the time and energy necessary and must consider the possibility of running out of firewood by winter's end if they burn too much wood making syrup. A cord of wood (128 cubic feet) might yield between ten and twenty gallons of syrup, although the amount varies every year. The firewood or syrup dilemma is one more example of the time, expertise, and local resources necessary to live bioregionally. For most people, the consequences of using more resources are essentially invisible—a slightly higher electric bill, perhaps. For those living off the land, limited supplies require a strict appraisal of needs and desires because they perform, or at least understand, the necessary work and related consequences.

Experiments in Simplicity

Almost everyone living in the communities I visited thought that North Americans, including themselves, consume too much, but that did not mean they had concluded exactly what constitutes enough. Rather than providing definitive answers, residents considered their communities experiments in living simply and lightly on the land, and the nature of these experiments varied both among and within communities. I draw on anthropologist Richard Fox's understanding of "experiment" as a confrontation with either society or one's own views to explain how these communities demonstrate a range of experiments in opposition to the mainstream consumer culture.[7] Historian of American religion Rebecca Kneale Gould explores experiments in simplicity affiliated with the Nearings' homesteading movement and illustrates the spiritual and physical dimensions of these confrontations with mainstream society.[8] Intentional communities have added the complexity of conducting these experiments in community. Ecovillages and cohousing communities constitute experiments in sharing and efficiencies that appear closer to the mainstream, whereas communities like Possibility Alliance understand themselves as experimenters in radical simplicity, consuming no fossil fuels or electricity.

For Dan Truesdale, Possibility Alliance's radical simplicity, which he linked with nonviolence, was a draw: "What was special was the radical simplicity and no electricity, no use of petroleum directly on the property. That's what stood out to me. Living simply and trying to live a life with a more positive impact on the world necessitates a nonviolent approach. I look at how violence creates a negative impact, and I want to do something differently so there's a more positive impact."

Truesdale and others do not want to support the destruction of local cultures and ecosystems associated with producing fossil fuels, whether that means mountaintop removal in Appalachia or oil production in Nigeria. Similarly, J.R. saw the Possibility Alliance's radical simplicity as a way

Bicycle-powered washing machine at Lost Valley Educational Center

to live within the earth's means: "As much as we can be self-sufficient, with the idea of radical simplicity, we can live within the global means, whether that's food production or reclaimed building materials or materials harvested from the land in a sustainable manner."

J.R. echoed a common concern that most of us, including residents of intentional communities, are consuming resources beyond our fair share. We can visit websites such as the Global Footprint Network (http://www.footprintnetwork.org/en/index.php/GFN/) that allow us to test our ecological footprint to determine our personal consumption levels—such as, for example, learning how many earths are required to support our current lifestyles. Even after tweaking my travel and eating habits, my consumption levels are consistently sobering and, frankly, embarrassing.

Possibility Alliance residents probably have some of the smallest footprints in the United States, largely due to their abstinence from consuming most forms of fossil fuel. They wash their clothes in an old-fashioned hand-crank washer and dry them on lines, grow most of their own food, and travel by bicycle or, infrequently, by Amtrak. Many other communities are conducting experiments in drastically reducing their ecological footprint by adhering to the ecological maxim "reduce, reuse, and recycle." Lost Valley Educational Center designed a bicycle-powered washer.

Some practices, such as waiting longer to replace older appliances, might also be considered old-fashioned thrift. New Hope is also experimenting with alternative laundry methods and reducing their needs for electricity-powered technology. Anglada noted, "Half the community goes to the laundromat, and the other half does this soaking method that we read about in *The Plain Reader*. The people who wrote it opted out of technology, and one woman wrote an essay about how she doesn't use a washing machine or soap. Wind and the sun on the line really clean them. When something breaks, we're able to meet this need ourselves. At each step we're trying to analyze, do we need this? Now that it's broken, can we do without it or not?"[9] Residents are evaluating which items they need to maintain a comfortable lifestyle. For some, soaking and wind-drying clothes is adequate, but for others, especially larger families, trips to the laundromat are necessary.

Residents of New Hope, like those in many communities, also have attempted to reduce their transportation needs, but their decisions must respond to their geographical context as well as their income. New Hope lies in a rural valley outside Dubuque, Iowa, and getting there involves traveling up and over the long, steep hills of the Mississippi River Valley. Despite Iowa's reputation of being pancake flat, the river bluff regions on the state's east and west edges are steep and hilly, with winding roads that are not conducive to walking or cycling. While bicycling is a viable option for urban communities and rural communities such as Red Earth, Dancing Rabbit, and Mustard Seed, bicycling would be difficult and dangerous for residents of New Hope, especially after dark. Anglada reflected on the difficulty of choices, wanting to walk or cycle but faced with the economic and safety necessity of driving: "We need our car for our jobs to get in and out of town. Biking is too brutal with the hills. So we're keeping the car."

I remarked to Anglada that this process of considering, "Do I really need this?" is not typical in the United States, or at least is not often done voluntarily. Of course, the poor go through this process on a daily basis, but most of us have become conditioned to consume more as our incomes grow rather than constantly reevaluate our consumption and needs. He responded, "More and more of our lives becomes just meeting our basic needs. It seems like people living in suburbia go to a job to pay to have those needs met elsewhere. Instead you can simplify that process and meet your own needs as much as you can."

For some, voluntary simplicity is a means to step off, or at least slow down, the treadmill of jobs and needs, but simplicity or voluntary poverty will never appeal to everyone. Alice McGary of Mustard Seed in Ames, Iowa, stated that while she is drawn to voluntary poverty, she understands that not all residents feel that way. She recalled a conversation with one who said, "I realized I didn't have the charism [the spiritual aspect of personality] for poverty and that made me happy because I didn't want to be poor anymore." Not everyone needs to live this lifestyle, McGary continued: "This member had lived at a different Catholic worker [house] before that, and now she is part of our team. She is not living as poor, but she is living a modest lifestyle. There are certain things we're drawn to, and I don't think we should give up on something that seems like a good value. But not that many people are into poverty or simplicity. And then there's us compared to Gandhi." This conversation reminded me that McGary and most of the residents of communities whom I met did not necessarily urge their lifestyles on others, nor did they view their own work as finished. Although McGary lived a frugal and modest life on the farm, she noted that Gandhi's poverty and asceticism set a high bar to attain.

LA Eco-village also intertwines its simplicity message with one of social justice, but does so in an urban context. Unlike some of its rural counterparts, LA Eco-village's three building, fifty-unit complex is tied into the electrical grid, and many residents work to make the city's power, food, and transportation infrastructures both more sustainable and more available for low-income Angelenos. While rural communities often have options to generate their own power (for example, wind power at Dancing Rabbit), few city regulations grant communities or individuals those freedoms.

In August 2012, I attended an LA Eco-village monthly meeting at which residents discussed a proposal to install solar hot-water heaters. The discussion made it clear that the community wanted to pursue additional efficiency measures (such as insulating pipes) and that the Management

Committee would look at costs and bring a proposal back to the group. LA Eco-village founder Lois Arkin later told me that the community "has made a substantial investment in solar hot water, and we expect to have a solar hot-water system within the next six months. Half the smaller building is on solar, and we are working with a solar consultant about putting both buildings on solar in the coming year."

She also said that, although Los Angeles winters can get relatively cold, about one-third to half the residents never turn their heaters on: "Some of us don't like the quality of that heat, and I never use mine. A lot of people don't. Our gas bill is about—depending on the season—between $600 and $1,300 a month. Our water and electricity and sewage are usually around $2,000 a month too. There will be an enormous savings in going solar in hot water and going solar on the rest of the structure." She amended, "Well, I don't know if there will be that much savings, but we'll feel better about it."

The bills, Arkin said, are high because the buildings are old and have significant air leakage. LA Eco-village has gas heating, and residents make their own decisions about their levels of heating and cooling. The community pays the electric and heating bills, so individual practices affect the entire community. Arkin commented, "No one needs air-conditioning, at least in the dry heat of Los Angeles, but certainly many LA Eco-village residents and the general public would disagree." While she and some others have acclimated enough to live without heating and cooling, this level of hardship would be unacceptable to many others.

Acclimating your body to outdoor temperatures—within reason—is one simple way to move toward voluntary simplicity, and is, perhaps, the energy equivalent of eating locally and shopping from farmers' markets. When I moved into my house in Ames, I discovered that all the windows had been painted shut, depriving the previous residents of fresh air during the temperate spring and fall. Now, in Florida, we use our heat and cooling as little as possible, bundling up in the damp winter and acclimating to our summer heat. Most of our friends follow similar practices, but I realize that many Florida residents live in climate-controlled houses year-round, and for them, the summer's heat must seem even more oppressive, given the larger temperature differential between inside and outside. Many old Florida homes, though unfortunately not ours, were built to take advantage of summer breezes, and simple architectural changes such as siting for passive solar would reduce energy costs and consumption.[10] Kevin's and my experiments in energy-related voluntary simplicity are minimal compared to those of the communities I visited. Whatever gains are created by our solar water heater and conservative heating and cooling practices are offset by our pool, which I am loathe to give up, so I am willing to make great trade-offs in other areas to offset the water use of our pool.

My dilemma, though trivial, hints at the choices and trade-offs we make when we consider reducing consumption. Most people do not downsize across the board but pick and choose among options and areas of specific concern, and I wonder if my cafeteria-style voluntary simplicity is really significant or just a means for me to feel better about my choices. Food and agriculture are particular concerns of mine, while Kevin is especially focused on energy efficiency. Voluntary simplicity is a process or a series of choices along a continuum, and practices such as cycling to work that seem fairly easy to some might, in fact, be unreasonable or impossible for others.

Pioneer Valley in Amherst, Massachusetts includes shared lawns, the Take It or Leave It clothes room, and a community laundry that is an enormous time-saving choice for those who opt in. However, one resident I spoke with stated, "Not everybody uses it. I can guarantee that my nurse-trained wife isn't doing her laundry with fifteen other households. She's not going to come down here and put her laundry in with everybody else's dirty stuff." Even within communities, what constitutes simplicity varies considerably.

In some ways, Pioneer Valley, like many cohousing communities, most closely resembles mainstream society in terms of personal property ownership, but debates about what constitutes simplicity have greater consequences in common purse or communal societies. One resident of Cherith Brook commented that individuals must seek a balance between meeting their own needs and desires and asking too much. "We don't want to abuse the common purse, but it helps that we are similar. We all want to strive to live simply. I guess that can mean different things for different people, too." Residents must agree on both what constitutes appropriate levels of consumption of food and material goods, for instance, and what levels of work are necessary to sustain their chosen lifestyles. In one Catholic worker community, the question of beer arose: whether community money should be used to purchase alcohol when not all residents drank it. Finding agreement on issues such as consumption demonstrates the importance of shared governance. Even when a community accepts broad goals of voluntary simplicity, defining what this means in practice presents a challenge.

"Cradle-to-Cradle Sandwich"

Growing food and eating locally or bioregionally help individuals in and outside of intentional communities achieve goals of sustainable and simple living. Despite the prevalent narrative about the superior productivity of industrial agriculture, small diversified farms produce large amounts of food and are remarkably efficient. For example, entomologist Miguel Altieri, whose work demonstrates the productivity of small-scale farms, helped develop agroecology, a theory and practice that "seeks the diversification and revitalization of medium and small farms and the reshaping of the entire agricultural policy and food system in ways that are economically viable to farmers and the general public."[11] Despite attempts to portray organic and alternative methods of food production as inadequate, or worse, unscientific and New Agey, a University of Michigan study demonstrated that such methods produce three times more food per acre than industrial agriculture.[12]

New York Times columnist Mark Bittman writes that small-scale diversified farms "produce more food (and more kinds of food) with fewer resources and lower transportation costs (which means a lower carbon footprint), while providing greater food security, maintaining greater biodiversity, and even better withstanding the effects of climate change." He also notes that small farms achieve all this without the benefit of the enormous subsidies and incentives given to large-scale agriculture.[13] For example, the 2014 Farm Bill allocated $134 million over ten years in crop insurance and supports to commodity crops, a substantial benefit for large-scale agriculture.[14]

Rather than importing externalities into their local systems, these small communities conduct experiments in building fertility that draw on their own biophysical processes. In this way, these communities reverse what Karl Marx called the "metabolic rift," wherein soil nutrients are exported to urban areas, then released into streams and rivers rather than being returned to the soil through human (night soil) and animal waste. Alyson Ewald of Red Earth explained her goal of the "cradle-to-cradle sandwich" as opposed to the cradle-to-grave paradigm that governs most industrial production. Ewald's concept reflects how, in their book *Cradle to Cradle: Remaking the Way We Make Things,* William McDonough and Michael Braungart envision manufacturing processes that reuse and recycle all component parts. Ewald states, "One of my ideas is the cradle-to-cradle sandwich because we have a composting toilet. We can grow the grain. We're going to have an earth- and wood-fired bread oven. Local culture, wild culture in the dough, and then we bake it here, grow the vegetables, and use the compost on the field."

As at Dancing Rabbit, Red Earth's homes have humanure systems that compost human waste products and return them to the soil.[15] Because northeast Missouri's terrain is one of steep rolling hills, the area is not appropriate for large-scale agriculture. Each of Red Earth's homes is built into a hill so that gravity adds efficiency to the humanure system. The toilet is located at the level of a second story, so the waste drops down into a compartment below and composts. Users toss in a handful of sawdust after each use, which neutralizes odor, and the heat of the composting process kills disease-causing organisms. Many people have used the composting toilets in America's national parks, and well-designed composting toilets do not smell. Once a pile is complete, it sits untouched and cures for about a year before it can be used. Doors allow easy access to the pile so that Red Earth residents need to tend the systems only once every several months rather than constantly carry buckets of waste. Rabbits, on the other hand, do not have the two-story advantage because their land is less hilly, so they must carry buckets of night soil to be composted.

Ewald and other Red Earth residents experiment with agricultural techniques so that they can meet many of their own food needs: "I'd like to experiment with growing small grains here. Sandhill grows their own oats and wheat. You can have bread and grain and beans. So it's possible that Scotland County can grow everything it needs." Red Earth, Dancing Rabbit, and Sandhill are all situated in Scotland County, a fertile agricultural region that supports a wide range of crops, from grains to vegetables to fruits like apples and peaches. The region's potential for localized production and bioregional living is part of what drew the communities to locate here.

Scotland County could certainly fulfill most basic needs of its residents as small communities in the United States did prior to innovations in globalized retailing, transportation, and food storage such as flash freezing.[16] Year-round strawberries and aisles of coffee, chocolate, and bananas have accustomed us to constant supplies of foods that were once deemed exotic. Cacao, for example, is a Central American food whose production damages human populations as well as the environment, but it has become routinized to the point where Hershey marketed the Hershey bar as the "great American chocolate bar."[17] I personally cannot imagine a morning without coffee, an indulgence that has plagued me with caffeine headaches in several caffeine-free intentional communities.

When I mention voluntary simplicity and bioregional living, bananas, coffee, and chocolate are often the first foods people claim they could not live without, and I tend to agree. However, voluntary simplicity and reducing our food needs are processes that take place on a continuum, and individuals and communities choose their own emphases. Kevin and I eat chocolate and drink coffee, but we eat little meat and grow fruits and vegetables, choices made possible, in part, because we live in Florida where the climate allows us to produce a large part of what we eat.

Eating locally and seasonally also confers some real culinary and taste benefits, and while the constant availability of most foods is convenient, it can also make us blasé. When I visited the Possibility Alliance one spring, one of the residents received a package with two large lemons. Since Possibility Alliance residents eat primarily bioregionally except for gifts, the lemons were a real treat, and they infused several meals with a well-appreciated citrus flavor. I recalled the story of Laura Ingalls Wilder and her siblings receiving oranges in their Christmas stockings in *Little House on the Prairie*, and I imagined how good that then-rare orange must have tasted in the cold, snowy midwestern winter.

Eating seasonally and locally brings our lives and eating patterns in tune with our ecosystems and helps us appreciate foods as they become available. Rather than viewing seasonal eating as deprivation or hardship, residents of Dancing Rabbit and Red Earth focus on seasonal abundance, an intentional process of rethinking what constitutes abundance.

Less Is the New Normal

Living in intentional communities like Dancing Rabbit requires significant physical efforts to meet basic needs, like carrying buckets of night soil. Also, most Rabbits bike or walk for transportation. In the years since Dancing Rabbit's founding, life has become somewhat easier as residents have completed many of their buildings, and new members can buy or rent existing houses. Tony Sirna reflected on their labor, stating, "Early on we were in the pioneering aspect of creating our infrastructure, and it was hard work, chopping wood and carrying water. The enjoyable part was working together for this goal. The lifestyle here is so much more fulfilling, so many more connections and more resources. So it's really not about sacrificing—it's about choosing happiness and connection over consumption and acquisition." For Sirna and many other residents, the strong social bonds more than compensate for the physical demands and ethic of reduced consumption, and residents privilege the abundance of connection and seasonal foods, for example, over the goods and services that define abundance for many Americans.

For residents of communities who have chosen these alternative lifestyles, less is the new normal. However, adapting to this lifestyle is not possible for everyone, even those for whom voluntary simplicity resonates emotionally and intellectually. This is one reason why intentional communities hold extensive visitor sessions followed by probationary periods of up to two years for provisional residents. This cooling-off period gives potential residents time and space to consider the pros and cons of life in community. Attending a visitor session is a bit like summer camp, meeting new friends and participating in activities, and this honeymoon period makes it difficult to assess realistically how one might fit with that particular community. I fell in love with the people and communities I visited, and while I was there I could see living in any one of them. But in retrospect, not all the communities would have been a good fit for me.

Some guests, on the other hand, know immediately that a particular community is not appropriate for them. One guest at Dancing Rabbit later told me that she realized this community was not right for her the instant she stepped out of the car. Dancing Rabbit is still building its buildings, roads, and paths, and to this visitor, the construction materials lying around made the community feel incomplete and messy. She stayed for the whole of her visiting week but no longer considered Dancing Rabbit as a potential home.

Conversely, Alline Anderson describes her and Kurt Kessner's first visit to Dancing Rabbit thus:

> We got to Dancing Rabbit and pulled up in front of this double-wide trailer, and the front door was peeling. There was no landscaping, and the yard was all weeds. It was bleak and probably should have been depressing. It had never been my life's ambition to live in a beat-up trailer in the rural Midwest. But we found we loved it. We stayed for a week—there were eight people there, and it was incredible. There was so much work to be done, and we felt that the founders had a lot of integrity and a great plan. After we were there for three days we looked at each other and thought, "Let's move here." We asked for membership, and we went into the soundproof booth, which was actually Cecil's [one of Dancing Rabbit's founders] bedroom, and came back, and we were Rabbits. We felt like it was a real way to walk our talk. I don't

think we thought we would still be here twelve years later; it's become our life, not just a spur-of-the-moment adventure.

Ethan Hughes of the Possibility Alliance has witnessed many visitors adapt to the community's radical simplicity and then experience culture shock when they return home:

> When people are here for a few weeks, they get into the rhythm, and they don't really miss the industrial paradigm. They may be a little edgy when they have to light the stove to have a bath. But for the most part, life feels so full: the dynamics of visitors and community service. I think it hits them once they leave. They lived in a place with the fruits of the garden, a spoon someone carved, and a composting toilet. When they go home, they see that everything [they] touched for a few weeks made sense, like it had some level of mindfulness, imperfect but moving in a direction.
>
> When people go home, the profound letters come. They realize that everything they touch is turned on. Where's that electricity coming from? They flush the toilet. That's when it hits home in a positive way. "I can live where everything I touch doesn't have the same costs."

Neither community residents nor the visitors themselves can predict how guests will respond to the varying levels of voluntary simplicity practiced in these communities. Based on my observations and discussions with community residents, though, visitors of all ages and backgrounds can adapt to these alternative lifeways. The social capital of like-minded individuals helps enormously because visitors both see a supportive community of many individuals who are living more simply and realize that these lifeways are not as difficult as they might appear at first. For example, when visitors observe an entire community discussing and using alternative energy sources, they begin to understand that logistics for implementing alternatives like these are feasible.

Demonstrating Simplicity

Intentional communities that understand themselves as experiments in voluntary simplicity offer their experiences as demonstrations and education for the general public. Rather than preaching about what others should do, these communities practice voluntary simplicity in multiple capacities and model alternatives to our default modes of consumption. Kessner and Anderson built and now run the Milkweed Mercantile Eco-Inn and Cafe at Dancing

Rabbit. The Merc, as Rabbits call it, combines a bed and breakfast with a store and bar. Facing Dancing Rabbit's common square, it is one of the first things visitors see upon arrival. The general store and bar occupy the first floor, and four guest rooms, each named after a prominent environmentalist, take up the second floor. I have stayed in the Rachel Carson room several times, and Anderson now refers to it as "my" room. The light-colored walls are offset by dark wood trim on doorways, and the building feels calm and tranquil.

Kessner and Anderson built the straw-bale Milkweed Mercantile to code so that it could be approved as a commercial enterprise, but guests might not otherwise recognize this building as an example of alternative building techniques unless it is pointed out to them.[18] Kessner and Anderson's building demonstrates to their guests that sustainability, beauty, and comfort are not mutually exclusive. Kessner said:

> I just want everybody to see that this is one way to go. Even as hard as we're working, I'm quite sure we're using something like three planets, so we still have a long way to go. With our outreach work, Alline and I hope to appeal to the more mainstream society who can stay in a comfortable bed and breakfast and see that composting toilets aren't that weird. The lights are still on, and it's all off the grid. We tell them the power has been low lately, so please conserve, and they say, "Well, I guess we can do that." And hopefully they'll take some ideas home with them.

The Milkweed Mercantile functions as a liaison between Dancing Rabbit and the world. Guests and visitors are often the "choir"—they have already embraced a sustainable lifestyle. For those who are not yet convinced or are apprehensive about what a "sustainable home" might look like, the Merc provides an easy entry point, where guests experience sustainable living in a fairly luxurious manner. The Merc shows guests that composting toilets do not smell and how the interior of a straw-bale structure remains cool throughout Missouri's hot summer days. Appliances like composting toilets that might otherwise seem scary and weird emerge in the context of normal life. (After five days of camping at Possibility Alliance, I thought I had died and gone to heaven—even without coffee.) The Merc also demonstrates that being green occupies a broad spectrum and that Rabbits and the Mercantile hold a range of views on food, energy, and construction styles.

Moreover, guests learn that running a sustainable business, like all other aspects of living in an intentional community, requires compromises and trade-offs between commerce and an ecovillage ethos that rejects consumerism. For example, Anderson and Kessner must be mindful in their selection of foods and products for sale, balancing residents' and guests' desire for coffee and chocolate with the social and ecological impacts of those products. Similarly, Twin Oaks, supported in part by its tofu and hammock businesses, must balance the need for income with community values around labor.

Nicholas Leete from Mustard Seed discussed how demonstrating and performing an activity such as bicycling to work can change peoples' attitudes and behavior. Leete commented that his friends thought he was crazy for riding to the farm—a response that many of us who commute by bicycle experience:

> I got a ride out in a car to the farm, and people were saying, "Oh Nicholas, he's so crazy, he rides his bike onto the farm." Then Andrew biked to the farm for National Bike to Work Day, and I think he's planning on doing that most times. That doesn't actually reduce the amount of cars coming to the farm, because people still drive. But people realize it's not a big deal to live more simply, use fewer resources, be involved with food production, and think about spirituality or social justice. People change their behaviors sometimes.
>
> One of our work shares joined to get vegetables, and now he is a part of our farm team. He is thinking about what economic system is beneficial and how you treat workers. I think we affect some people.

Changing behavioral patterns is a notoriously difficult process, and many people perceive sustainable practices like cycling, composting, or eating locally as frightening, strange, and difficult. When intentional communities or—even better—friends translate these practices into the realm of fun and possibility without being perceived as preaching, others are more likely to consider trying and adopting these practices.

LA Eco-village's Arkin explained the distinction between demonstrating and dictating, recognizing that if communards impose their views on others, they alienate those they hope to reach. This distinction is especially important because the environment, sustainability, and social justice are values embraced by increasing numbers of people as more and more individuals fear the impacts of climate change on the earth and on vulnerable human populations. The ways intentional communities present alternatives to predominant patterns of consumption determine, in part, how the public will respond to these ideas. According to Arkin,

> We have to stick to demonstrating how we walk our talk without imposing on other people. Someday that may not matter, because we may need some

kind of eco-benevolent dictatorship. We're not regulating nearly as fast as we need to, and perhaps we never will, and so as resources become slimmer and more degraded, we may be inching closer to a kind of eco-fascism. As long as we are able, we need to do as much as we can to demonstrate with a lot of goodwill and good cheer.

For me, and some of the other people that share the ecovillage vision, this business of social justice taking precedence over the ecological work that we're doing is frustrating, because ecological degradation is at the base of social injustice. Social sustainability, economic sustainability, ecological—it's all connected. Fortunately, the eco-justice movement is rapidly recognizing and more effectively integrating these connections.

Arkin's comments echo statements by thinkers such as Fred Kirschenmann of Iowa State University's Leopold Center for Sustainable Agriculture. Kirschenmann argues that the repercussions of climate change, including water and energy shortages, will—and are—changing life on earth and will require drastic transitions in existing lifestyles.[19] The changes are coming, he says, but how we transition through them remains to be seen. For example, will reductions in consumption be peaceful or violent? To meet these challenges, Kirschenmann draws on Aldo Leopold's concept of land health—that is, the "capacity of the land for self-renewal"—and, like Leopold, recognizes that human health and land health are bound together.[20] Leopold's concepts of land health and the biotic community provide an important touchstone and measure for rethinking abundance and questions of sustainability.

Julianne Newton and Eric Freyfogle critique the slipperiness of the word *sustainability*.[21] What are we sustaining? they ask. Couldn't the ubiquitous term include sustaining contemporary lifestyles and industrial agriculture? Sustaining land health, on the other hand, offers criteria directly related to biological and human health. Intentional communities that experiment with voluntary simplicity demonstrate pathways to sustainability that incorporate both social justice and participatory democracy.

Sharing and the New Middle Class

Our tour guide at Twin Oaks told us that addressing climate change demands that we—mainstream North Americans—reduce our impact on the environment by 80 percent. Although we can reduce our footprint by approximately 40 percent through efficiency and lifestyle changes, the remaining 40 percent will require major systemic shifts. Communities like Twin Oaks that share virtually everything illustrate not only that we can reduce our footprint significantly, but also that this reduction can be both fun and beneficial in ways that might not be immediately apparent.

Twin Oaks residents live communally, meaning that they pool their income (but not their assets), and the community provides health care, jobs, food, and housing for residents. Our guide claimed that residents of Twin Oaks enjoy a middle-class lifestyle on approximately $5,000 annually per capita, well below the official US poverty line, a claim that raised a few eyebrows on the tour. He cited most of the hallmarks of a middle-class existence as he ticked off some benefits of Twin Oaks: he walks to work and has access to multiple cars, a sauna and pool, and clean clothes, among other things. Residents have access to a swimming hole in the river that runs through their property. Children at Twin Oaks receive an education and music lessons, and seniors receive medical and palliative care. The practice of pooling income, or shared finances, radically departs from the norm in the United States in which salaries and benefits accrue to individuals. In this communal and largely cashless society, residents do not have immediate access to their "earned" income, but instead enjoy access to housing, health care, and shared cars, for example, and a small allowance of $100 per month for incidentals.

Sharing items such as cars, bicycles, large appliances, and sports equipment also distinguishes Twin Oaks from a typical middle-class lifestyle. Most people in the middle class individually own and control these things. Yet, many of these items sit unused for much of the time, even cars, which might remain parked in office lots for eight or more hours each day. Living more simply reduces material needs, so that less income is necessary to live well.

At a workshop at the 2014 Communities Conference, Laird Schaub of the Federation of Egalitarian Communities distinguished between ownership and access, noting that most people really need only the latter. If cars are always available for use, for example, is individual ownership necessary? This question has popularized services such as ZipCar (zipcar.com) that offer convenient short-term car usage. ZipCar is available on the University of Florida campus, and I have found it convenient for running quick errands. In any car-sharing system, the test is the car's availability for last-minute use. At Twin Oaks, bikes and cars are almost always available for a last-minute request, so the system is not overstressed.

Twin Oaks does not prohibit residents from owning their own bicycles, but the sharing system gently pushes residents toward the collective and away from private ownership or hoarding. For example, the bike shop maintains all bicycles in the shared system, so that you can always use a bicycle in good condition. On the other hand, bicycle owners who ask the shop to repair their bicycles have the time taken from their labor credits. Similarly, the community's commie clothes system offers clean clothes. In response to a question about hoarding clothes, our guide noted the advantages of the shared clothes system. First, there are always clean clothes, and residents continually find new and interesting stuff, so there is little incentive to hoard. Moreover, hoarders have to do their own laundry.

Purchasing items in bulk and even performing labor such as laundry in bulk result in efficiencies of both time and money, as illustrated in the co-op movements of the 1970s. Sharing items like cars and lawn mowers seems a step that might be palatable to many, but sharing labor and income is typically one step farther than even many intentional communities are willing to go, despite the benefits and efficiencies. Sharing labor and tasks ranging from collective laundry to cooking and shopping makes it much easier to live on drastically reduced income. Schaub noted that it is easier to divide tasks efficiently in larger households or communities, with at least twenty individuals, so that some individuals might focus on producing income for the community while others serve household or community needs. With these numbers and task sharing, each person can do more of what he or she enjoys.

Dancing Rabbit is not a communal society like Twin Oaks and Sandhill, but the community emphasizes sharing items, space, and labor. Rabbits use cars from Dancing Rabbit's pool of well-maintained vehicles rather than owning them individually. Tony Sirna emphasized the importance of efficiency and sharing: "It's all about efficiency, as in efficient lightbulbs. That gives you essentially the same product, just much more efficient. But then there's the other level—do we need so much stuff? Do we need such big cars? There's both efficiency and scaling back, downsizing, rightsizing, simple living, or whatever you want to call it. And if we can do those things and reduce the demands that we're putting on the ecological system by 90 percent, then we can talk about how to meet those needs."

The original residents of Dancing Rabbit chose Missouri in part because existing building codes enabled them to test building techniques, and the community's status as a land trust has enabled residents to share common buildings. In many circumstances, sharing homes and cars with unrelated individuals and groups creates legal challenges. Sirna commented,

"It's easy to talk about straw-bale buildings and biodiesel or electric cars or solar panels, but here are the key things we are doing: we live in small houses, we don't consume a lot, we use 90 percent less electricity and 90 percent less water. We drive 90 percent fewer miles. Cooperation can be a very powerful way to reduce your dependence. Sharing vehicles, having a common house, sharing equipment, and living more closely together allows us to consume less by sharing. But building codes don't always allow eco-things, and legal codes make sharing difficult."

Zoning and building codes, for example, can make the density demanded by ecovillages problematic in suburban regions, and some practices such as graywater systems are illegal in many areas. Further, the US legal system does not accommodate shared structures well, which is why egalitarian communities, or communes, must use the tax structure set up for monasteries and religious orders and develop resources for dealing with legal issues. For example, the fall 2015 issue of *Communities Magazine* was themed "Community and the Law" and featured a collection of articles on dealing with codes and laws that thwart communal living.

Living the Triple Bottom Line

Intentional communities that focus on voluntary simplicity have rethought the concept of abundance to incorporate ecology, economy, and equity, otherwise known as the triple bottom line. While abundance often indicates quantity—consider the horn of plenty, or cornucopia—residents of these communities have reframed abundance to include social connections and the excitement of seasonal tastes. Arkin most strongly ties LA Eco-village's simplicity with goals of social equity, recognizing that environmental degradation disproportionately affects vulnerable populations. Perhaps the most challenging aspect of the triple bottom line is social equity; for example, proponents of organic food typically express more concern about the quality of the food (for instance, is it pesticide-free?) than about the effects of pesticides on the often-exploited workers who produce food. Pressure from the larger organic producers led those writing the USDA Organic Food Production Act of 1990 to drop provisions that protected farmworkers.[22]

Intentional communities, with their integrated systems of governance, social concerns, and sustainability, offer models that can be adapted to the mainstream through entities such as cooperatives. Many food co-ops, including Citizen's Co-op in Gainesville and Wheatsfield Cooperative in Ames, incorporate a range of equity, economic, and environmental concerns in deciding what products to carry. They continue the tradition of the co-op movement of the 1970s, which linked values of equality, social justice, and natural foods. Intentional communities that are committed to radical democracy also provide pathways to social equity through their deliberations about sustainability.

Establishing social equity as a leg of sustainability also addresses the perceived "whiteness" of the sustainability movement and the relative privilege of both residents of intentional communities and sustainability advocates. Adult residents of most intentional communities have chosen this lifestyle and consciously decided to rethink what constitutes abundance. Yet many individuals in the United States and around the world have no choice but to live simply and, if given the opportunity, would happily upscale. Thomas Friedman argued that much of the world's population underconsumes (for example, many villages in India and Africa do not have electricity), while most North Americans and elite populations around the globe consume a disproportionate amount of resources.[23] Affirming that marginalized populations should be allowed to consume more and that privileged populations should rethink their consumption levels could reframe sustainability efforts as pathways to social justice. Urban intentional communities, such as LA Eco-village and the Emma Goldman Finishing School in Seattle, Washington (http://egfs.org), that highlight links between equity and ecology showcase individuals and communities that create alternatives in more challenging urban environments.

8

Extreme DIY for Interdependence

The most important thing is to demonstrate, demonstrate, demonstrate and not preach and not be self-righteous and not be judgmental.
—Lois Arkin, LA Eco-village

Do-it-yourself—DIY—has captured the imagination of the post-recession United States, and the prevalence of DIY programs on cable TV and videos on YouTube reflects a growing interest in taking on, or at least watching, shows about how to repair our homes, cook gourmet meals, and pimp our cars. I own several DIY books on gardening and cooking and have learned how to make my own mustard and can my garden produce. For me, these projects function more like hobbies, and Kevin has often wondered if simply purchasing all of our food would be less expensive than my gardening. The answer to that question is debatable, but nonetheless, pursuing these projects has taught me valuable skills about cooking, processing, and gardening, and cooking with my homegrown foods frees me from the added sugars, pesticides, and preservatives that come with most commercially processed foods. My garden projects are on a family scale—that is, I share some foods with my friends, but generally, these foods are for Kevin and me.

Intentional communities that focus on voluntary simplicity, bread labor, and self-sufficiency experiment with DIY on the individual, family, and community scale, which we might call extreme DIY. Communities such as LA Eco-village, the Possibility Alliance, and Baltimore Free Farm collaborate with their own neighborhoods and with other intentional communities to enhance competencies in growing and construction, for example, so that the newly skilled can gain autonomy over their food, shelter, and transportation. For instance, the Possibility Alliance's fledgling Peace and Permaculture Center teaches skills such as grafting, canning, and permaculture, and LA Eco-village's Bicycle Kitchen teaches bicycle repair, providing LA residents with low-cost transportation options. In most cases, this education is free or low cost, and the instructors aim to democratize their knowledge, so that the know-how and skills circulate among the public. Developing these skills frees communities and individuals from big oil and big food, to some extent, and the circulation of goods and skills reflects ideals of interdependence and regional self-sufficiency.

While many people have taken small steps, like my family's kitchen garden and solar water heater, many communities and individuals have made more comprehensive changes in meeting basic needs. I have termed these projects "extreme DIY" because many of these communities are partially or completely off the grid in some capacity. For example, Cobb Hill in Hartland, Vermont, and Sirius in Shutesbury, Massachusetts, fulfill their heating needs solely from gathered wood; in that capacity, they are off the grid. So while Kevin and I supplement our food supply through my gardening, we purchase our grains, wine, and fish, while the Possibility Alliance, Sirius, and Lost Valley Educational Center in Dexter, Oregon, produce a much higher portion of their own food needs. The communities I visited demonstrated a wide range of self-sufficiency, and this range, to some extent, depended on location and available resources. Rural communities had more opportunities to farm and rely on alternate power sources, while urban communities could work with existing infrastructure and, like Cherith Brook in Kansas City, Missouri, and Baltimore Free Farm, obtain food through their food-rescue efforts, that is, gathering food that might otherwise be thrown out.

Interdependence or Self-Sufficiency

Dan Greenberg, a resident of Hearthstone, the community that surrounds and supports Sirius, commented that *interdependent*, a Buddhist term, is more accurate than *self-sufficiency* because the word captures the fact that fundamentally our biological, financial, and social lives are interdependent. (It has also become a key term for scholars of disability and aging because it acknowledges the reality that everyone is dependent on others to some extent.) While we walked through the woods around Sirius, Greenberg said that community life offers interdependence, and many of our lives have become so atomized that we have lost the awareness and ability to live in community. Greenberg developed a program called Living Routes, a study-abroad program that placed students in communities around the world. That project later evolved into Earth Deeds, a set of online tools that facilitates tracking and measuring environmental impact. When he asked students what they most desire, most listed house, job, and car, but few mentioned community life. Interdependence and community ties alleviate the hyper-individualism and loneliness of contemporary society, but many seem unaware of the loss.

That anomie prompted Danish architect Jan Gudmand-Hoyer to develop the concept of cohousing in 1964.[1] Coleen O'Connell of Belfast noted that cohousing communities originated in response to human social needs for interdependence, not for ecological reasons. "It wasn't designed to be ecological. It was a human need and a social science experiment about how humans could support each other." While cohousing communities tend to be environmentally friendly due to their smaller footprint and shared goods, fulfilling the human need and desire for community interdependence is the real reason they exist.

One sixty-something resident of Sirius echoed Greenberg, noting that Sirius "was not trying for self-sufficiency but interdependence," meaning that residents take care of some of their own needs but also rely on neighbors. Further, single self-sufficient households would be less efficient, added another Sirius resident, while small- or human-scale systems make much more sense. Human-scale systems, interdependence, and village self-reliance better reflect both Gandhi's Constructive Program and Maurin's Green Revolution, which emphasize regional economies rather than individual self-sufficiency, an emphasis reflected in the locavore movement. Human-scale economies, technologies, and systems allow these projects to be created, maintained, and enhanced at the regional level, rather than requiring specialized and expensive technologies and personnel, so that the benefits, expertise, and thus the autonomy remain with the community rather than going to external corporate or governmental entities. These communities recognize the reality that we are all interdependent, that economically, ecologically, and socially, the entire biotic community is interdependent, and they are consciously choosing how—on a regional and community level—to be interdependent.

In this vein, Dancing Rabbit aspires for regional sustainability rather than self-sufficiency and partners with residents and farmers in Scotland County in Missouri in ventures such as a local farmers' market. Kurt Kessner stated, "Our thrust here at Dancing Rabbit is not so much self sufficiency, but self reliance. It is bridge building for communities, shopping locally and developing relationships with local farmers." Dancing Rabbit neighbor Red Earth aims to create intersufficiencies, or trust sufficiency, to strengthen its own community as well as to create bonds within the region. According to Alyson Ewald,

> We wanted to set up a community where people had land to experiment with sustainability and trust sufficiency or intersufficiency. All of us want to do what we can either by ourselves or with our neighbors. We share childcare. We share gardening. We have work parties. We have potlucks. We play ultimate frisbee together. We help each other build our houses and our homesteads, and it is empowering to set up your life using mostly things that we can manage and fix ourselves. We don't need the Internet or electricity to live out here, or even the phone. If we're low power, we unplug all of those things and we're fine.

Red Earth's residents gain a measure of autonomy by relying on human-scale technologies such as energy systems that they can manage and maintain themselves.

Nonetheless, creating and maintaining these systems is time-consuming and difficult, even at the small community or village scale. Alline Anderson of Dancing Rabbit acknowledged that small systems take their toll on residents. "There's real burnout here; I've never worked harder in my life. We're doing it all ourselves. Everything. I don't really believe that there is any such thing as the simple country life. We heat with wood. We use composting toilets, and those buckets have to be hauled. We cook with whole foods. We grow our own vegetables and preserve them. We do all of our own governance; we build our own houses and roads. It's time-consuming, and often difficult. But it is how we choose to live."

Village self-sufficiency and interdependence offer individuals and communities a level of autonomy, creativity, and freedom that most of us do not enjoy. While they are still subject to the whims of a global economy, communities like Sirius and Dancing Rabbit meet far more of their food, energy, and social needs within their own community networks than most of us do. Their residents recognize that although the work can be laborious and difficult, they also reap the benefits of the social connections that emerge from collaboration and community building.

The New Economy

Communities and groups that retrieve and develop new technologies work within what has been termed the New Economy, and sometimes the New

New Economy, to distinguish it from the post-NAFTA economy that has ground down the American middle class. The 2013 Communities Conference at Twin Oaks held a one-day symposium on the New Economics on the Monday following the conference, offering workshops such as Beyond Conventional Financing, Multi-stakeholder Co-ops, and Mapping and Networking. While de-skilling, outsourcing, and layoffs plague our existing global economy, cooperation, open-source technologies, and small-scale innovations distinguish the New Economy. The New Economy incorporates practices such as alternative currencies, time and labor banks, open education, and emphases on gifting and sharing as means to move beyond the mainstream monetary economy. Instead of living within the economic system they inherited, New Economy enterprises are creating the system they want.

Interest in the New Economy exists well beyond intentional communities and includes people from all sectors of the political, social, and economic spectrum. The New Economy Coalition, formerly the New Economics Institute, which grew out of the E. F. Schumacher Society, focuses on creating an economy that considers the needs of people and the planet. The New Economy Coalition coordinates efforts among different entities working for economic change; its website lists over one hundred organizations, including Equal Exchange, Slow Money, and the Donella Meadows Institute, which is associated with Cobb Hill.[2]

Social media connect people and projects in ways unimaginable even ten years ago, and communities such as the Valhalla Project work to enhance these connections. During the New Economics symposium, representatives of Solidarity Piedmont and SolidarityNYC described their mapping projects to identify existing small, local solutions around the United States and to build new capacity.[3] SolidarityNYC defines a solidarity economy as one that "meets human needs through economic activities—like the production and exchange of goods and services—that reinforce values of justice, ecological sustainability, cooperation, and democracy."

Drawing upon the model of the Creative Commons (http://us.creativecommons.org), these groups emphasize sharing, cooperation, and the end of corporatism by extending "open source" beyond software to technologies such as machines and seeds, with the provision that they be continually modified and improved. The ongoing evaluation and modification of open-source technologies enable the public and developers to learn from success and failures alike and can lead to more robust solutions than the licensed alternatives.

Intentional communities intersect with the New New Economy through educational workshops, social media, and small-business incubation, and acquiring skills and technologies enable communities to attain more autonomy from mainstream economies. For example, Open Source Ecology (http://opensourceecology.org/) has developed a line of fifty low-cost DIY machines such as tractors and backhoes that can be constructed for a fraction of the cost of commercial machines. "The Global Village Construction Set (GVCS) is a modular, DIY, low-cost, high-performance platform that allows for the easy fabrication of the 50 different Industrial Machines that it takes to build a small, sustainable civilization with modern comforts. We're developing open source industrial machines that can be made at a fraction of commercial costs, and sharing our designs online for free."[4]

Similarly, plant breeders have recently begun to release open-source seeds so that farmers can trade and modify seeds freely.[5] Seed-sharing networks have been sprouting among community gardeners and others in recent years, including the national Seed Savers Exchange (http://www.seedsavers.org/) and our Grow Gainesville's local seed-sharing collective (growgainesville.wordpress.com).

At the same time as they develop new technologies, communities such as Red Earth have revived older practices such as hugelkultur, which uses logs to increase soil fertility. These communities are consciously blending traditional skills with innovations to help them meet contemporary challenges in food, shelter, and transportation. For example, 3-D printers enable communities to inexpensively experiment with reviving traditional tools as well as more complex machinery such as tractors. Interestingly, though, I saw few DIY experiments regarding clothing other than at several craft-oriented Catholic worker houses. Many communities exchanged clothes and had commie clothes closets, but most emphasize shelter and food over clothing, which makes sense given the availability of inexpensive or free clothing options.

These attitudes toward technology reflect what we now think of as *appropriate technology*, a term coined by E. F. Schumacher.[6] Gandhi emphasized the development of human-scale, village-based technologies that enhanced agricultural productivity and returned the benefits to village populations.[7] To evaluate appropriate technologies, he asked the simple question "Who benefits?" His question was rooted in neither an anti-science nor an anti-technology view, but reflected the point that appropriate technologies diffuse knowledge, fit local conditions, and benefit local economies rather than, say, externally owned corporations.

Appropriate technology includes innovative technologies such as solar power as well as revived technologies such as scythes and functional Amish farm tools. Amish farm tools are powered by humans or animals, do not require fossil fuels, and are generally easy to repair. A fellow guest at Sirius asked me how intentional communities felt about technology, and while I responded that I have seen a broad range of approaches, I recognized that she, like many, considered only high-tech machines such as computers or tractors as "technology," not simple tools such as hoes and scythes. In some cases, using the appropriate technology means retrieving the skills needed to use Amish farm implements.

Both Alyson Ewald of Red Earth and Alice McGary of Mustard Seed noted that using these older tools involved educating residents as well as volunteers on how to use them properly. Alice taught me how to hoe the right way, using the weight of the tool rather than brute force, when we were preparing the ground for carrots. When I said that while I needed instruction with the hoe, I was able to easily help with the laundry at Cherith Brook, Alice replied that I would need instruction in the older style of doing laundry at Mustard Seed. Clearly, like many who wish to help, I have much to learn. Ewald said, "We found that we teach people to cook and to mow. We have scythes because we don't have a tractor. It's slow and meditative, like Tai Chi, and you can do it all day. We're relearning those basic skills." The Amish use simple tools such as the scythe because it helps them slow down, enjoy God's creation, and appreciate their work as a spiritual practice. Ewald's description of the "slow and meditative" aspect of scything—likened to Tai Chi—similarly views this work a spiritual practice of sorts.

Ewald and other Red Earth residents hand-mow with the scythe and use the fallen grass as a mulch to restore soil fertility. Much of the hand-mowed area is hilly or near trees or their pond, so this human-powered technology is appropriate for their needs. Ewald, McGary, and other community residents educate themselves and visitors like me on how to use older forms of technology, and such demonstration and education form an important part of their missions. Nonetheless, teaching takes time, and they must balance between teaching and completing their work.

Open-Source Education

One strength of appropriate technologies is that they can be adapted and taught to a variety of people, so communities or regions do not need to rely on highly specialized knowledge. Kurt Kessner came to Dancing Rabbit with existing building skills, and the community has attracted others with practical skills that have enabled them to create their physical structures and teach these skills to other Rabbits and visitors. Kessner commented, "Some people bring skills, and some people learn them here. Sirna and the others were computer techies and built a two-and-a-half story straw building, learning as they went." Designing houses and buildings still requires specialized knowledge and skills—no one wants to live in a building on the verge of collapse—but residents design systems and structures that can be maintained at the community or sometimes family level. The skills and systems are such that most motivated learners can master them through practice. Most intentional community visitor programs include several "work parties" in which the guests help residents with some tasks. The parties help residents and visitors get to know each other, but more important, they show guests the skills and labor necessary to thrive in these communities.

At Dancing Rabbit, I spent several mornings plastering walls at different houses.[8] Since many Rabbits build their own houses, exposure to rudimentary building skills offered me a taste of what residency at Dancing Rabbit might be like. One afternoon, my fellow visitors and I helped mix and apply a second internal coat of plaster. Mixing it was easy and fun. We piled a mixture of sand, straw, and clay on a tarp, and then danced around in our bare feet to mix it up. Next we sprayed the walls with water to keep the plaster moist and smoothed it on by hand, which was painstaking and difficult work. Since the homeowner would have to live with the results of our labor, we all wanted to do it well. In the process, I learned more about plastering, but more important, we learned to work together as a team, which would be crucial if we sought residency.

Many intentional communities actively transmit skills through demonstrations and workshops, programs that also showcase the communities to potential residents. Sirius, for example, is an educational center and incorporated as a 501(c)3, the tax code for a nonprofit. In addition to its visitors' program, the community offers a Permaculture Design Certificate class and an organic farming internship. Internships and work-exchange

Mixing plaster

programs draw visitors and guests who seek to gain new skills. Alyson Ewald of Red Earth noted, "One of our goals at Gooseberry, our homestead, is learning from other people and teaching other people. So for two summers now, I've had homesteading interns with me. We walk around every week and write down what needs to be done, and over the course of the week, we talk to each other. We always have two to three times the applications we can accept, and they're from Pittsburgh, Florida, Vermont, Oregon, and California."

While some interns and work-exchange students request permanent residency, most students and temporary residents carry their new skills beyond those communities, thus spreading them even more broadly.

Diffusing basic life skills among diverse populations comprises an important element of democracy or self-rule. Growing food or building shelter offers security and autonomy and creates an empowered citizenry. Possibility Alliance is creating a Peace and Permaculture Center on eighty acres of its property that is modeled on Peter Maurin's agronomic university. Ethan Hughes said the community plans to "start a full gift economy and Peace and Permaculture Center. Activists can come there, and people can learn hard skills. Eventually, with our urban contacts, like in the Gandhian movement, we will take homeless people, send them through the school, give them the skills and hand them three acres of land for free. Here is your freedom, self-rule."

The fact that this center is free and open source reflects Possibility Alliance's social justice mission. My first visit coincided with that of a visitor from Oregon who taught a workshop on grafting fruit trees that was free and available to anyone who was interested. Ethan Hughes later commented that learning to "propagate our own trees is not only good for us but then we can teach that to people in the inner city."

For Hughes, teaching skills for free is part of the gift economy, a nonmonetary economy of exchange in which goods and services are given freely. Unlike a monetary economy or even a barter economy, in which goods and services are provided quid pro quo, the gift economy relies on the trust that needs will be fulfilled, something like "what goes around, comes around." To better understand this concept, Hughes directed me to Lewis Hyde's *The Gift*, a book popular among artists, which suggests we should understand art as a gift and not a commodity. The point, he said, was that we should offer what we can rather than being bound by rates, monetary or not, dictated by the market. The models of exchange described in *The Gift* structure both patterns of exchange and reciprocity among many Catholic worker houses and groups such as Possibility Alliance and reflect quasi-mainstream practices such as freeganism, gleaning, and freecycling.

Alternate Currencies and Time Banks

As communities strive to insulate themselves from the globalized economy, many of them have developed systems such as time banks and alternative currencies. These systems enable communities to decide for themselves the value of goods and services, and local currencies such as BerkShares, created in the Berkshires region of Massachusetts, keep the money within the local economy.[9] Such alternatives differ from a gift economy in which no values are predetermined, instead reflecting community decisions about worth. Dancing Rabbit created the ELM, or exchange local money system, which functions like an online banking system except the balance is reinvested in the community (http://www.dancingrabbit.org/about-dancing-rabbit-ecovillage/social-change/economy/local-currency/). All Rabbits have an ELM account and use this currency for most of their daily transactions within the community. According to Dancing Rabbit's webpage, "The ELM system is a modified version of a LETS (Local Exchange Trading System), a general term for locally-initiated, democratically-organized, not-for-profit community enterprises that provide a community information service and record transactions of residents exchanging goods and services." Since most individuals and micro-industries at Dancing Rabbit accept the ELM, Rabbits are encouraged to shop locally, thus benefiting their friends and neighbors. The Milkweed Mercantile accepts ELMs, and some local businesses are beginning to accept them as well.

Time banks are another mode of trading and rethinking how services are valued. In the mainstream economy, service values are dictated by their worth on the market, and services that are equivalent in time might have vastly different dollar values—for example, what you pay for an hour of babysitting versus an hour of plumbing. Twin Oaks in Louisa, Virginia, developed one of the more extensive time and labor systems and had to decide how to allocate labor credits for different tasks. As Twin Oaks is a communal society, all residents participate in the labor system as a condition of membership and in lieu of jobs outside the community. Since the community was founded initially as an experiment in applied behaviorism, it gave more credits for jobs deemed unpleasant. This original system failed because residents flocked to the so-called bad jobs, and the hours did not work out evenly. The residents then revised the system to make all work equal, so that one hour of making hammocks equaled one hour of childcare. In this system, Twin Oaks redefines what counts as labor; for example, shopping, providing entertainment for the community, and dishwashing all count toward residents' labor credits, so this system eliminates the second and third shift many Americans, especially women, experience in addition to their normal forty-hour week. At Twin Oaks, labor that is typically not compensated, such as childcare and housekeeping, counts as actual work.

Unlike Twin Oaks, LA Eco-village is not a communal society and, as at Dancing Rabbit, its residents support themselves, generally through either outside work or a community micro-industry. Lois Arkin encourages residents to participate in the Arroyo Seco Network of Time Banks, the time bank created under the Cooperative Resources and Services Project (CRSP) fiscal umbrella (http://laecovillage.org/time-bank/). Arkin stated that she envisions "a time when some people would pay a portion of their rent in Time dollars or another type of local currency. Then we can have a decent quality of life without too many US dollars." Like the Twin Oaks system, this time bank is egalitarian, meaning each hour banked equals one hour earned. The Arroyo Seco Network is expanding the time bank to larger networks so that participants have a large array of available services, ranging from computer programming to legal counsel.

Aspects of the New Economy, such as time banks and alternative currencies that circulate within local economies, have been adopted by nonresidential intentional communities and groups and have vast potential to attract a broad range of participants. Alternative currencies, for example, help local and small businesses because they encourage people to shop locally, a practice that has bipartisan appeal. Exchanging alternative gifts for the holidays—a home-cooked meal or an hour of childcare instead of a tie—is another way to avoid a consumerist mindset. Further, both time banks and alternative currencies remove transactions from governmental scrutiny and taxation, which appeals to libertarians as well as groups such as Catholic workers who do not want their taxes to fund war.

Similarly, nonresidential communities such as the Neighbors have formed around members' needs for community support and interdependence. In Greenfield, Massachusetts, Sandra Boston began the Neighbors in response to her concerns about ecology and economy. The group of twenty-eight "spends time learning together, engaging in mutual aid, and inspiring one another to learn new habits in order to live in a new economy with ecological limits." The Neighbors focus on "gifting and sharing. We admire the time bank and time dollars approach, but don't want to spend all the time keeping score."[10] Gifting, sharing, and creating time or labor banks help these neighbors develop resilient community economies, and their efforts are mirrored by Common Security Clubs and Resilience Circles that provide social and financial aid to their members.[11]

Micro-industry and Innovation

Residents of intentional communities have developed a range of microindustries to support themselves and their communities, and in general, their businesses and innovations support social and environmental goals. LA Eco-village, for example, has incubated several micro-industries, including the Bicycle Kitchen, "a nonprofit bicycle repair educational organization," and the Food Lobby, a food co-op and buyers club located in the lobby of LA Eco-village's main building.[12] These micro-industries both foster self-sufficiency and keep profits circulating within the community, which is known as the multiplier effect. The Bicycle Kitchen's mission statement reads, "Our mission is to promote the bicycle as a fun, safe, and accessible form of transportation, to foster healthy urban communities, and to provide a welcoming space to learn about building, maintaining, and riding bicycles." The Bicycle Kitchen later outgrew its space at LA Eco-village, bought its own building, and defines itself as a DIY "bike shop, workshop, and education space" (http://www.bicyclekitchen.com/).

The Bicycle Kitchen dovetails with LA Eco-village's goal of making LA amenable to bike and pedestrian transit in addition to public transportation. While most media portrayals focus on the city's car culture, I found Los Angeles fairly easy to navigate by bus, train, walking, or cycling. When I first went to Los Angeles in 1994, I had to get a duffel bag, a backpack, and myself from Santa Monica to Encino on the bus. The trip took much of the morning and three bus changes, but what struck me was that when I went to the kiosks near bus stands, no one could really tell me how to make the trip. Arkin and LA Eco-village residents are partially responsible for improved public transportation and bike/pedestrian facilities. One resident invited me on a bike tour of LA on a sunny Sunday afternoon. After my initial terror, I thought, "Why not?" and joined him on a safe and pleasant ride through downtown LA. We saw a street festival, LA's beautiful historic library, a convention center, and the recently opened Grand Park, and riding rather than driving around LA gave me a much better sense of the city and its residents.

On the East Coast, the Baltimore Free Farm incubated ReCycle (http://www.baltimorefreefarm.org/2010/09/09/recycle/), a collective that repaired and recycled bicycles. Although the initiative lasted only a year, ReCycle members taught about bike repair once a week and distributed bicycles to local residents. For both of these urban communities, bicycle transportation fulfills ecological and social goals; bicycle transit is both environmentally friendly and an inexpensive transportation option for low-income residents. Like many urban regions, Baltimore has become more bike friendly over the past five years, according to Reagan Hooton, my twenty-something tour guide, although she admitted that the potholes of Baltimore's roads make cycling difficult.

Communal societies such as Twin Oaks and Sandhill Farms have developed small industries that help support the entire community, not just individual business owners. Twin Oaks' hammock business (http://www.twinoakshammocks.com/) constitutes a significant portion of the community's income, and until recently, annual sales to Pier One amounted to approximately $10,000 annually. A single rope hammock now retails for approximately $109 on Twin Oaks' online retail site. Weaving hammocks fulfills residents' labor credits, and our guide described the production as "perfect hippie work." The hammock racks are designed so that workers face each other and can socialize, and weavers can stop and start at will, reflecting a noncorporate attitude toward work that emphasizes fun and sociality over efficiency and profit.

Sandhill in Rutledge, Missouri, sells mustard, honey, and other vegetables, but sorghum provides its greatest agricultural income. Sandhill produces and sells sorghum syrup to customers as far away as Minneapolis, and workers travel from neighboring communities—and sometimes farther—to help during the sorghum harvest in September and October.[13] For midwesterners who are attempting to eat bioregionally, sorghum is a local sweetener that can be produced in mass quantities, and I ate the syrup produced from it for breakfast at both Possibility Alliance and Dancing Rabbit.

Intentional communities create micro-industries and develop innovative technologies in agriculture, energy, and transportation and for building homes and other structures. These developments emerge organically out of local geographies, community needs, and local capacities. However, developers must consider local regulations because state and local regulations shape the extent to which communities can create and use alternative technologies.

Food and Agriculture

Most communities have developed some businesses around food and agriculture, in part because for many people—in and out of intentional communities—choosing to eat more sustainably is one of the easier and least invasive behavioral changes. People often seek out local and organic foods well before they adjust their building and transportation habits. Shopping at the farmers' market or joining a CSA has become mainstream practice that for many does not represent anything out of the ordinary. (Joining a CSA supports a farm, and the consumer receives a share of the farm's produce.) Cobb Hill in Hartland, Vermont, has incubated several small agricultural businesses out of the community, and members' efforts are aided by Vermont's history of small farming. Additionally, Hartland is home to the Sustainable Food Laboratory, a group that initiates projects and partnerships designed to create sustainable food systems.

I arrived at Cobb Hill on a crisp morning in October, enjoying one of the last days of New England's spectacular fall colors—heavy rains blew in the following day, denuding the trees. On that day, though, seeing the panoramic view from the ridge above Cobb Hill's residential area, I knew why people love New England. After I contacted Judith Bush, Cobb Hill's visitor coordinator, residents Alan and Ruth Keitt, who had previously lived in Gainesville, kindly invited me to stay with them overnight. A group of students from nearby Green Mountain College joined me that day as we ate lunch on the common house porch, discussed Cobb Hill, and later toured the campus. To get to Cobb Hill's common house and residential area from the agricultural areas at the bottom of the hills usually means walking up a steep hill, which keeps residents active and fit. The community's website describes Cobb Hill as

> a community of people who want to explore the challenge of living in ways that are materially sufficient, socially and ecologically responsible, and satisfying to the soul.
>
> Situated in rural Hartland, Vermont, we try to practice sustainable land management—ecological farming and forestry, energy efficiency, and minimization of waste. We are also developing the skills of community: sharing, responsibility, compassion, communication, consensus building, conflict resolution, appreciation of diversity and love. We believe that these skills are necessary to bring the larger society to sustainability and sufficiency, and we want to learn them to the best of our ability. (cobbhill.org)

The community's enterprises include, among others, Cedar Mountain Farm (http://cedarmountainfarm.org), a commercial farm that produces milk, vegetables, and flowers; Cobb Hill Maple Syrup; Cobb Hill Cheese, which sells cheese and frozen yogurt; the on-site Farm Store; and Cobb Hill Mushroom Enterprise. Cobb Hill also has laying chickens, Icelandic sheep, and Jersey cows for milk.

Cobb Hill's Farm Store is one of the first buildings visitors encounter, making the community's products easily available to consumers. The Farm Store, the barn, and most of the agricultural enterprises sit close to the road, and this section of Cobb Hill looks like a working farm—which it is. According to resident Judith Bush, Cobb Hill's businesses range from "livelihood businesses to what might be called, not disparagingly, hobby activities. It's

Award-winning maple syrup at Cobb Hill

not so much to make money, but just to do it, like maple syrup. And honeybees, which are essential for a farm but more or less at a hobby level here."

Stephen Leslie and Kerry Gawalt, owners and managers of Cedar Mountain Farm at Cobb Hill, have gained regional fame for their experiments with using horse power, and they conduct educational programs about draft horse power. Leslie plows with two Norwegian fjords, Cassima and Tristan, fourteen hands high (about fifty-six inches) and 950 pounds each, and has forged a bond of trust working with this team for over ten years.[14] He uses the horse team for much of his plowing, but employs a tractor for plowing heavy ground and hauling manure, an example of mixing and using technologies as appropriate for the task, geography, and energy output. "I envision a day when live horse power will be joined in tandem on farms with new and cleaner technologies that will include tractors and delivery vans that will run on alternatives to diesel such as recycled vegetable oil, locally and sustainably produced biofuels, and solar-powered batteries, just as the glory days of horse power in North America and Britain coupled advances in horse-drawn implements with stationary steam-powered engines."[15]

Leslie's book, *The New Horse-Powered Farm: Tools and Systems for the Small-Scale, Sustainable Market Grower,* illustrates the growing role of the horse in contemporary small-scale agriculture, a practice I also saw at Possibility Alliance. Farmers are drawn to horses as a means of "being back in touch with nature, of regaining a kind of rhythmic elegance to our lives."[16] Additionally, integrating animal traction both makes small-scale farms energy efficient and creates a closed loop system in which the horses' manure enriches the soil.

Cobb Hill Cheese has successfully become part of Vermont's artisanal cheese resurgence. One resident became an apprentice to a farmer forty miles away in 2000, and by 2005, their Ascutney Mountain Cheese variety had won first place in the Farmstead Cow's Milk category at the American Cheese Society Competition, the first of a string of awards. They sell their cheese on-site at the community as well as locally and online (cobbhillcheese.com). Subsequently, they began making frozen yogurt out of the surplus milk, enabling them to gain a higher price point for the milk.

Cobb Hill Cheese functions as a private enterprise, run by three women, but Judith Bush also discussed Cobb Hill's community-wide enterprises, including forestry and chickens. Residents do not pay additional costs for these ventures—the enterprises cost them little or nothing, because they already own the land, in the case of forestry. However, the community would pay expenses and receive profits, if those arose. Bush described the community's enterprises, private and public, as creative visions in cooperation. She traced the community's origin and priorities to Donella "Dana" Meadows, now deceased. Meadows, lead author of *Limits to Growth,* lived across the river at Foundation Farm, and her systems thinking has influenced the social, economic, and ecological aspects of Cobb Hill. According to Bush, the founders of Cobb Hill envisioned "a residential community that would experiment with all kinds of technological and social things. We would have a think-do tank called the Sustainability Institute, where people would work on all these projects."

Despite Cobb Hill's enthusiasm for new industry, setting up an enterprise on cooperatively owned land presents a challenge. Each enterprise reports every other year to the Land Use Committee, documenting its successes as well as upcoming challenges. Resident Alan Keitt recalled his term as chair of the Land Use Committee; members debated and developed the enterprise proposals and periodic report formats: "What does the community deserve and need to know about various enterprises, and how do they impact on our community?"

A new enterprise, Bush said, requires a proposal detailing its anticipated effects on the land and the community: "How will it impact? What will it need from the community, and what will it give? What are the good reasons to do it?" Like cohousing communities everywhere, Cobb Hill established a set of bylaws, as required by law. Although, as Bush says, the community would like to be creative with its enterprises, the bylaws were developed to govern how residents share the land and they do not want to continually revisit these bylaws. While some residents of intentional communities join or establish communities to avoid what they see as oppressive state and local regulations, the shared and cooperative nature of these communities itself requires regulations and bylaws to preserve the social and environmental lifeways they have built.

Feeding Scotland County

Dancing Rabbit, Sandhill, and Red Earth are situated within Scotland County, a rural agricultural region in northeast Missouri. The land is fertile but hilly, so this region is suited to small-scale growers, unlike the flat corn-growing belt across Iowa and Illinois. Residents in all three communities have started agricultural micro-industries either as individuals or in partnerships (or the community as a whole, in the case of Sandhill's sorghum business) that serve their own residents as well as outside individuals and communities. Residents also patronize local businesses such as Weiler Dairy in Rutledge, which offers on-site pickup of raw, organic milk from its Dutch belted Holsteins. The presence of small-scale businesses and producers provides communities with social capital that helps the communities themselves and their micro-industries survive.

Because Dancing Rabbit is neither a communal society like Sandhill nor a homesteading community like Red Earth, Rabbits must be especially entrepreneurial to support themselves, and many have developed micro-industries around food and growing. Dan Durica, for example, received a USDA grant for a hoop house and now provides the community with fresh vegetables throughout most of the year. He also produces the feta and mozzarella cheeses that many Rabbits eat at the Milkweed Mercantile's much-loved Thursday Pizza Nights. The Mercantile provides a showcase and point of sale for locally produced goods and foods, and its coffee, food, and beer attract both community members and local residents to this combination restaurant and store.

Residents of the Rutledge communities have also worked to develop local food markets in Scotland County, both to bolster their own sales and to increase the demand and supply of locally grown foods. They helped establish a farmers' market in Memphis, approximately ten miles north of Rutledge and the largest town in the area. Red Earth resident Alyson Ewald said, "Our goal of the farmers' market is to say, 'Scotland County can feed itself. We don't need to just grow commodities.'" The aim is not to eliminate all commodity production in the area because those crops support most of the agriculture in the region. However, historically, successful small, diversified farms meant that residents possessed and maintained a broad range of skills, from mending to growing, that were essentially survival skills and provided community resilience. Ewald discussed how the farmers' market and regional networks can draw upon the benefits of small, diversified farms and provide income through traditional means such as selling eggs and vegetables, including broccoli and cabbage, that are considered specialty crops because they don't have sufficient mass-market appeal or their shelf lives are limited. In the past, "every family had a pig, a cow, some chickens, a small kitchen garden, sold eggs, did mending. They had a diversified economy and knew how to work with different animals and plants."

Like Maurin's and Gandhi's regional self-sufficiency—or interdependence—plans, the point is not for communities to withdraw from broader society, but to enhance their own skills and resilience while developing interdependence with neighbors and within the bioregion. The three communities are fortunate in that Mennonites constitute a significant percentage of the farming population in the region, so their neighbors are receptive to local markets and community interdependence.

Despite this welcoming local community, developing a local food system remains a challenge. Relatively few growers in the region have been willing to set up stalls at the market to sell their goods and produce. Further, Scotland County has a high percentage of low-income residents who are not likely to seek out a diet of local, organic foods. At this point, the market does not accept SNAP or WIC, another disincentive for low-income residents to shop there. While many communities aspire to live bioregionally, in reality, most still rely for financial security on broader networks of sales, trade, and gifts.

Acorn's Mail Order Seeds

Acorn Community Farm in Mineral, Virginia, runs the Southern Exposure Seed Exchange (https://www.southernexposure.com/), a thriving mail order seed business that sells seeds throughout the United States. It sells over seven hundred varieties of plants. Most are best suited to the mid-Atlantic and Southeast, but farmers and gardeners across the country grow these seeds. Acorn describes itself as a "farm based, anarchist, secular, egalitarian community," and is thus a communal society like Twin Oaks and Sandhill Farms. Acorn "budded" off from its parent community Twin Oaks in 1993, and today meets its limit of thirty residents. While Acorn's labor, consensus, and financial systems are similar to Twin Oaks, both Acorn and Twin Oaks residents noted that Acorn's small size allowed it to be more laid-back about issues such as labor hours. Our tour guide noted, "At Twin Oaks, everybody is expected to do at least forty-two hours of work per week, and all work is counted equally. Twin Oaks asks everybody to keep labor sheets, and Acorn does not. Acorn lets people choose their own work much more than Twin Oaks does. Here it's much more face-to-face communication, which largely goes along with having a smaller population." Most Acorn residents and some Twin Oaks residents work in some capacity for the Southern Exposure Seed Exchange, which provides the bulk of Acorn's income and represents the "right livelihood" sought by residents.

The heart of Acorn is an old sprawling farmhouse surrounded by fields, seed-storage units, and farm buildings. Residents built additional housing as the community grew, and, as at Twin Oaks, each resident was allocated one room. I visited in late summer and saw fields of flowers grown for seed as well as what our guide called long-keeper tomatoes, a variety that has been bred to keep for a long time after harvest. Residents had recently planted their fall garden with carrots and greens. While Acorn does not produce all its residents' food, it does grow a significant portion. During my visit to Acorn during the 2013 Communities Conference, Acorn and Twin Oaks residents laid out a buffet that included fresh foods as well as many varieties of pickled or otherwise preserved foods. I tested several kinds of pickled green beans, and the labels on the jars made it clear that the cooks were proud of their efforts.

Several of the smaller, farm-based communities served varieties of pickled vegetables, which makes sense because pickling is one of the safer methods of preserving vegetables.

Acorn residents sort, clean, and dry their seeds in a three-year-old barn built for drying and agricultural storage and store their unpacked seeds in a large, cooled trailer. We took turns walking through the trailer to see how they stored their seeds. Shelves holding bags of wholesale seeds and buckets of seeds lined the trailer, and at the back were five freezers full of seeds in smaller containers. In 2011, Acorn received a government grant to build a high tunnel (an unheated greenhouse) that both extended its growing season and helped residents grow seeds that need protection from rain.

Acorn's Southern Exposure Seed Exchange emphasizes agricultural sustainability and the rights of all farmers to save seed. Residents grow and save many of their own seeds and also work with small farmers to procure seed. Our guide said, "We try to get as much organic as we can, and we collaborate with small farmers who grow seed for us and offer more heirloom and organic varieties." They grow over fifty-five varieties of tomatoes on their property, some patches for seed and others for tasting events and marketing photos. The farm has been certified organic, and more than 60 percent of the seed residents sell is organic, a percentage they hope to increase over time. Southern Exposure Seed Exchange lists its seed as free of genetically modified organisms (GMOs) and has signed the Safe Seed Pledge promising to abstain from using GMO seed (http://www.southernexposure.com/our-nongmo-policy-ezp-15.html#pledge). For small farmers living in intentional communities, genetically modified seeds and the necessary technological packets they entail, such as herbicides and pesticides, are far too expensive to consider, so the issue of GMOs is largely irrelevant to them. Even if GMO seeds were affordable, most farmers and gardeners in sustainability-focused intentional communities would reject them, in part because they are embedded in industrial agricultural systems.

For farmers and gardeners living in communities that aspire to live bioregionally, saving, developing, and trading locally adapted seeds are paramount concerns. Southern Exposure Seed Exchange and similar seed companies tie the exchange of seed to increased biodiversity and attempt to broaden the skill base and practice of seed saving among large numbers of farmers. This practice of diversifying the knowledge base echoes Gandhi's and Maurin's emphasis on appropriate technologies, that is, technologies that can be maintained and adapted at regional levels. Our guide reflected that counter-intuitive as it may seem, "We encourage people to save seed, and if people end up buying less seed from us, then okay. As some people have put it, we're trying to slowly put ourselves out of business." Acorn, Southern Exposure Seed Exchange, and all micro-industries in these communities must ultimately balance their books or they cannot survive. However, their bottom line includes ecological and social considerations in addition to economic gains, so profit is not the sole gauge of success. So, for Acorn and the Southern Exposure Seed Exchange, contributing to the diversity of both knowledge and seed fulfills their mission.

Biofuels, Energy, and Building

While food and agriculture often serve as the entry point for sustainability, intentional communities, whether cohousing or ecovillages that construct and design their communities also focus on construction and energy. Rural, urban, and suburban communities have experimented with energy-efficient natural building techniques and alternative modes of energy production such as solar and wind power. These experiments enable them to design and adapt systems for their specific climates and geographies. Builders in these communities account for the features of their specific locations when designing their homes—for example, they think about creating courtyards and social spaces adjacent to buildings and orienting houses to maximize solar power and passive cooling/heating. Unlike most conventional real estate developments, these communities adapt their buildings to the surrounding environment, both built and natural.

The Milkweed Mercantile's straw-bale building, for example, stays pleasantly cool throughout Missouri's hot summers without air-conditioning. Photographs from the Valhalla 101 blog "10 Reasons Why EarthShips Are F!#%ing Awesome" illustrate how inexpensive and sustainable earthship homes provide beauty and comfort that match, or perhaps even surpass, most American homes.[17] Most natural buildings and alternative energy sources rely on locally available materials and require fewer specialized skills to build and maintain. Sirius built its community house with interns, for example, and small-scale wind-, water-, and solar-power structures do not require the same vast infrastructure and expertise as industrial-sized power facilities.

Energy and Biofuels

While urban communities such as LA Eco-village and Baltimore Free Farm rely on bicycles or public transportation, rural and suburban communities still need vehicles. Rural communities like Dancing Rabbit, Twin Oaks, and Red Earth maintain car co-ops, but these cars need alternative energy sources such as biodiesel or solar- or wind-generated electricity to be "off the grid." Today many cars at Sirius (which are individually owned) run on waste vegetable oil that would otherwise be discarded but has been recycled by the community's biodiesel micro-industry. The pumping station, which is adjacent to the community building, filters and de-waters the oil. However, selling waste vegetable oil is illegal, so members pay a fee and join Club Recycled, which distributes, but does not sell, the oil.

Collecting and reusing vegetable oil illustrates a win-win situation on efficiency and sustainability. When Sirius first began Club Recycled, restaurants that had been paying to have someone haul away the oil as waste gave Sirius the oil for free. Sirius contracted with different restaurants to take their oil that for several years, they filtered at Sirius. Even after the community began to pay restaurants for the oil, Sirius saved about $30,000 in fuel costs. Later, when a resident wanted to start a business, Sirius lent him money and turned over its contacts, and Re-Energizer was born (http://localvegoil.com/). Re-Energizer provides used cooking oil and food by-product recycling to commercial food service and agricultural industries in the five-state region around western Massachusetts. Managing member Pete McAvoy cites multiple advantages of biofuels, including weaning the United States from foreign fuels, clean energy, and the growth of local economies.[18] Sirius still maintains a biodiesel co-op, but Re-Energizer and the Sirius community participate in Co-op Power, a regional energy nonprofit that supported the development of Northeast Biodiesel, a biofuel manufacturing plant in Greenfield, Massachusetts, with an annual production of 3.5 million gallons of recycled vegetable oil (http://www.cooppower.coop/).

Solar, Wind, and Energy Efficiency

Sirius also integrated passive and active solar systems into its buildings to reduce its energy needs. The community building, for example, uses passive solar energy from south-facing windows and a greenhouse for heating, and because of the ways the residents insulated the walls and roof, that thermal mass retains heat through much of the night. The wall between the dining room and greenhouse is not insulated because the greenhouse generates heat that warms the dining room on sunny days. Sirius residents use firewood they have stacked and stored to heat with wood stoves and a radiant floor-heating

Garden pond in Sirius ecovillage community building

system. Sirius installed active solar systems, including photovoltaic panels and a windmill power generator; our tour guide told us that this system, "between the solar and wind power, provides all the electricity we need from green sources." Sirius remains connected to the grid in case its power supply runs low, but its efficient buildings and solar- and wind-power generation ensure it mostly puts power back into the grid.

The greenhouse on the south side of the community building generates enough heat for heat-loving summer crops such as eggplant and stays warm enough during the winter to grow cold-weather crops. Except during the coldest days, the greenhouse stays above freezing, so residents do not have to use the wood stove much. The greenhouse—warm enough for a fig tree—includes a frog pond, and the frogs eat some of the insects and pests.

Water from the roof cistern irrigates the greenhouse. When the cistern is full, the water flows into the frog pond, and when the frog pond is full, the water flows outside. Our tour guide described the permaculture principles behind the greenhouse: "In permaculture teaching, you always build something that has at least three functions. So, it's food production, it helps heat the building, it collects water, and it's also a dining room. So there are actually four functions for the greenhouse." In addition to heating the community dining room, the greenhouse serves as a social space. The weekend I visited in early October was cold and rainy, but the greenhouse and dining room created a warm and green space that felt like being outside.

When I first visited Dancing Rabbit, the community generated all its own power. Residents relied on solar panels and wind, and a bulletin board displayed monthly power usage and weather conditions. A color-coded system tracked current battery capacity and allowable usage. One chart used five colors ranging from green (90–100 percent) to black (0–49 percent) to illustrate capacity and allowable uses. For example, yellow capacity (75–90 percent), defined as the normal operating range, allowed for virtually all activities with the exception of external power outlets and high-power-draw appliances and tools. During the summer, when they were building and when the panels were actively generating current, Rabbits could plug power tools into external outlets. Red (50–59 percent), defined as a period of serious cutbacks, restricted usage to only lights and floor heating for warmth. Current capacity color codes were posted, and the system worked, but it required a community ethos of "We're all in this together." Without such spirit, if someone developed a "lifeboat ethos," replicating biologist Garret Hardin's tragedy of the commons theory, a situation wherein users of shared resources act only in their own interests to the detriment of the group, no energy would have been left for basic needs.[19]

In addition to the community energy production, many individual homes had either solar panels or wind turbines to take advantage of the Midwest's strong winds. Milkweed Mercantile's wind turbine provided its power, and I was asked to limit my energy use on days when the wind was low. The community also erected a wind turbine to power residents' electric cars.

In 2011, after much discussion and deliberation, Dancing Rabbit connected to the grid, with the proviso that the community would export twice as much renewable power as it consumed, but Milkweed Mercantile and some

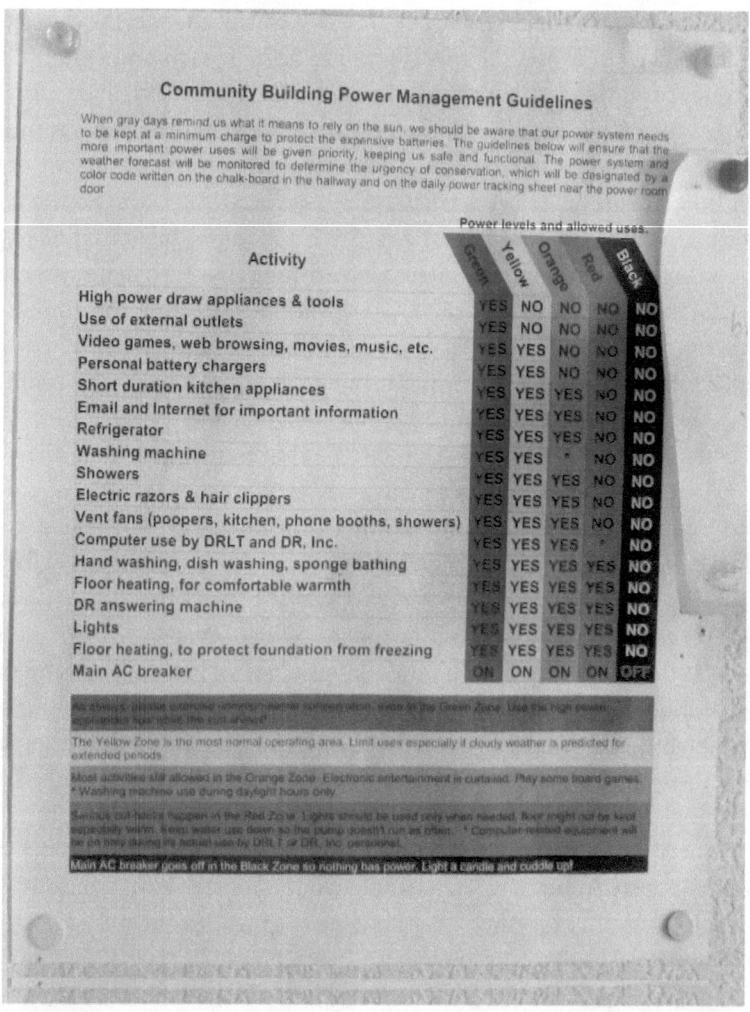

Dancing Rabbit's electricity color chart

smaller communities within Dancing Rabbit chose to remain off grid. While Dancing Rabbit still practices energy conservation and focuses on renewable energy, connecting to the grid represented a significant change for the community because the natural limits are gone. Prior to connecting, heating and energy use was constrained by the amount of firewood cut or solar or wind power harnessed, and some worried that removing these natural limits would lead to a slippery slope of increased energy usage. The controversial decision to plug into the grid reflects the delicate dance between testing new ideas and remaining true to core values. The founders created broad covenants so the community could experiment, adapt, and grow, but the lack of clear rules on issues such as connecting to the grid also led to controversy and conflict. Tony Sirna stated, "We recently connected to the grid, and we're exporting solar energy. I want to diversify so that we have wind- and some type of biomass-powered generator. We will show that we can produce all of our energy renewably because, one, we reduced by 90 percent and, two, because we find a balance of solar, wind, a little bit of battery from storage, and some sort of biofuel." Regardless of whether Dancing Rabbit is tied to the grid, its community-wide use of renewable energy demonstrates that, as Sirna says, such options are viable on a larger scale.

Natural Building

Sirius and Dancing Rabbit, like many other communities, have experimented with natural building techniques that emphasize local and/or renewable materials. Dancing Rabbit has defined natural building as including "a variety of building techniques that focus on creating sustainable buildings which minimize their negative ecological impact. Natural Buildings often rely on non-industrial, minimally processed, locally available, and renewable materials and can also utilize recycled or salvaged materials. Natural Building ideally incorporates sustainable design practices to integrate the building into its environment. It may also integrate electricity production, water catchment, passive heating and cooling, and alternative waste-treatment."[20]

Natural building employs a range of technologies, including earth bags (bags filled with earth or sand), cob (a mixture of clay, sand, and straw), rammed earth (suited to a desert climate), and cordwood (short pieces of wood and mortar).[21] Builders must determine what kinds of buildings and which construction technologies fit their geographic region and microclimate. Although few universities have integrated natural building into their curricula, many ecovillages provide trainings, internships, and workshops in natural building.

Residents of both Sirius and Dancing Rabbit constructed homes and other buildings out of repurposed wood, straw bale, and cob. These materials are cheap and locally available, which allows communities to build inexpensive but comfortable and durable buildings. Builders, though, must use materials that are appropriate for their environment; for example, a straw-bale house constructed in a humid environment will rot. Dancing Rabbit and Sirius also encourage the use of repurposed materials. Rabbits term materials gleaned from other sites "urbanite"; often people who are demolishing a building will call the Rabbits to quickly retrieve materials that can later be integrated into building projects. Nonetheless, the term *repurposed* is broad, and Rabbits have debated whether materials auctioned off can be considered "used" simply because they are leftovers or inexpensive.

Sirius constructed a number of cob and straw-bale buildings in addition to its wooden community house. The community's eight residential buildings vary to provide a range of living situations, including shared residences and private apartments. Our guide explained that residents have preserved much of the ninety acres of land because it is sacred to them and to the Native Americans who once lived there. "We decided to build only on certain parts of the land that are less beautiful or less sacred. We beautify the land with our buildings."

Their buildings are well insulated, solar powered, and energy efficient, and they use the most local, ecologically sound materials in all their building processes. Our guide continued, "Most of the wood in the building comes from trees that we cut ourselves. We always meditate on the trees before we cut them. It is gratitude. Trees don't like being cut. Cutting them wreaks ecological havoc on them. It is possible to communicate with the trees. Under the right state of consciousness, you can connect with that consciousness and communicate directly with the trees and plants and animals."

One of Sirius's "Four Pillars" is spirituality, and this consciousness permeates all activities, including siting and building. Sirius recently completed a stone sanctuary for meditation in the forest that took about four years to build. Residents used ropes, levels, and pulleys to roll the eight-foot-tall stones up the hill to the site and cut the stones by hand. The stones are aligned with the four directions, and all stones have significance, such as marking the rising movement of the star Sirius in the east.

The use of local materials and natural building techniques enabled Sirius to build the community for a fraction of the normal cost. Mostly inexperienced people built the community building over a ten-year span. Building it themselves using local materials and expertise let residents avoid bank loans and a mortgage, and this financial freedom provides the community with a great deal of security. Since no money leaves the community for housing costs, and residents produce much of their own energy and food needs, they can live a middle-class lifestyle, although somewhat austere, with far less income than is usually necessary.

Dancing Rabbit has also built its community from the ground up, includ-

Sirius community building

ing buildings, roads, and energy systems. Ziggy, or Brian Liloia, and his wife, April, built their home, called Gobcobatron, which is shown on the cover of a 2010 issue of *Yes! Magazine,* in 2008 and 2009, and documented their work in a book.[22] The house has a living roof, and they use no propane or electricity, which is austere even by Rabbit standards. They named their cooking cooperative Wabi-Sabi to reflect a Japanese aesthetic of incompleteness and simple elegance. In an interview with Avi Solomon, Ziggy discussed why he chose cob materials.

> There is something very primal about building with cob. You take your shoes off, pile up a bunch of sand and wet clay, and stomp it together with your bare feet to make a sticky, pliable, sculptural building material. It takes no heavy machinery, and the ingredients are completely natural, local. It's been practiced all over the world (in slightly different forms) for thousands of years.
>
> I have spent less than $4000 on building materials for my house and improvements. I spent another $1000 on labor. The walls for my 200 square foot home cost less than $500 in materials. The clay came straight from our

land. Straw came from the fields of local farmers. Really, though, cob building is just a lot of fun, especially with the help of other people.[23]

Ziggy and April also completed a larger timber-frame and straw-bale house, Strawtron, and made their plans available on the Tiny House blog.[24]

While visiting Dancing Rabbit, I spent several afternoons helping Sharon Bagetell and Dennis Hofarth, a retired couple, plaster what would be their two-story home complete with ramps to accommodate future needs. A group of work exchangers (aka wexers) provided labor for the house in exchange for learning the building techniques.[25] Building primarily by hand was their guiding paradigm so that the work could be replicated if materials became scarce or the United States experienced another economic crash. Bagetell and Hofarth used black locust, a local invasive species, little electricity, and repurposed materials, which means that their house holds less embedded energy than many structures. Removing the invasive black locust trees also helped with prairie restoration. Nonetheless, they acknowledged some trade-offs; the carpet and their vapor barrier (a plastic sheet to stop water vapor going through walls and roofs) represent embedded energy. Also, although they tried to avoid using fossil fuels, they needed a truck to deliver loads of gravel, something that is nearly impossible by bicycle.

As we worked on a hot summer day, Bagetell and Hofarth discussed concerns about quantifying their energy savings. For example, like most ecovillage residents, they live a lifestyle designed to reduce their ecological footprint, and they assume they are doing so. From my own observations, Rabbits seem to consume far less water, energy, and goods than most North Americans. Quantifying these assumptions is notoriously difficult, though; for example, how do Rabbits account for existing embedded energy, time, and labor in measuring their footprint? For this reason, Dancing Rabbit welcomed scholars Sarah Fredericks, Joshua Lockyer, and James Veteto to the community to develop assessment tools for sustainability. University of North Texas student Kayla Brooke Jones conducted ethnographic research for her master's thesis that confirmed that Dancing Rabbit's carbon footprint is significantly below that of most North American communities and also that they have developed a culture of sustainability.[26] Indices such as those developed by these scholars can help communities gather data to assess their sustainability efforts. Even so, Rabbits chide themselves that "life is too easy here" and that they should be doing more to reduce their carbon footprint.[27]

Since most individuals and families build their own residences, Dancing

Rabbit's homes demonstrate a range of creativity and innovation, including a repurposed school bus and grain bins and a house with a reciprocal roof. (A reciprocal roof is a self-supporting structure in which each log rests upon another in a spiral without requiring a single center support.) The school bus residence, named Aubergine, incorporates an insulating berm on the north with south-facing windows and a solar panel, and several houses have green roofs that both insulate and provide growing space. A 2012 blog post shared 2002 intern Betsy Merbitz's reflections on Dancing Rabbit's progress.

> Of all the incredible growth and change that occurred, buildings are by far the most visible. I remember meetings in the rented trailer to discuss winter housing and who would be sleeping in the not-yet-converted grain bin or the outdoor kitchen with straw bales piled up to hold in meager heat. Now, with about 70 residents, there are more houses than I could count! During a tour, I saw an eclectic-looking yurt made of brightly colored recycled awning material, the textured brown earth on Gobcobatron, and the vibrant yellow and red washes on the lime plaster of another house, to name just a few of the many new homes (and new styles of homes) that weren't there ten years ago.
>
> In addition to all the beautiful successes I saw, I learned of the mistakes and failed experiments. There were earth berms causing mold problems and reclaimed lumber that couldn't withstand harsh weather conditions. I heard about layers of cob being stripped off a woodstove that had been covered in too much thermal mass and many other tales of arduous efforts that ultimately had to be undone.
>
> But other projects thrived. Peach trees that were young saplings are taller and bearing fruit. There's a gravel road going through a village of homes in what was formerly all grass and dirt. In addition to the common house that was built in 2004, there are now community social spaces. The spacious La Casa Cultura with its shiny finished dance floor and the cozy dining room of The Milkweed Mercantile where there's pizza served every Thursday night are a long way from the carpeted living room of the double wide trailer.[28]

As Dancing Rabbit grows, residents continue to learn and enhance their construction skills, including learning from their mistakes. I saw some of these mistakes, including a sagging living roof, and heard stories of others. Kurt Kessner commented, "Most of what we've learned is how not to do some things, and that's important, too. It's frustrating that people come to Dancing Rabbit and do not take advantage of the brain bank that's here. They make some of the same mistakes that we've already made, but I guess that's part of learning, too." Perhaps learning, repeating mistakes, and relearning are all part of the process because intentional community members learn from all their projects, whether mistakes or successes.

Codes and Regulations

Creating lifeways and communities continually requires trade-offs and compromises both between the communities and broader society and within the communities themselves. Their innovations raise questions about regulations. For example, how do their more sustainable solutions (for example, graywater systems and straw-bale buildings) meet code (they can), and at what point do communities impose their own regulations? While Dancing Rabbit encourages alternative building techniques and experiments, existing mistakes have caused some to wonder whether they might need to create their own building codes. Tony Sirna noted, "We've always talked about needing building codes at some point. We still want to experiment, but we're ready to say that we want things to meet standards. It has to be at least energy efficient, or you have to justify why you want to do something different. We try and make sure people don't make some of the same mistakes we made in some of the earlier buildings." Sirna continued that giving people freedom within certain key constraints has been extremely successful. But "we are in a stage now where we have to clarify things where, in the past, it was pretty obvious what the spirit of things was. We have case law that says, 'No, you can't do this' and 'Yes, we really did mean that that.'" As Dancing Rabbit grew, the community experienced the tensions between freedom for experimentation and ensuring safety while maintaining its core values.

Communities such as Dancing Rabbit and Sirius attract freedom-seeking people who wish to experiment with a range of sustainability—and other—alternatives. Sustainability-focused cohousing communities allow for alternative foods and building, for example, but operate under bylaws and codes that are equivalent to those of homeowners' associations. The strictures ensure that, for the most part, buildings and projects maintain the community's core values, but they can also stifle innovation and creativity. Peter Jessop, a resident and general contractor at Pioneer Valley in Amherst, Massachusetts, spoke about the process of making changes to existing housing. "Here, we tend to goodwill towards each other, and that makes a big difference. It isn't a neighborhood where people say, 'Over my dead body.' Instead, people discuss potential problems—'That's hard for me because I'm going to have a view of that.' In a regular neighborhood, you can hide behind a law. Even so, solutions do not always come easily."

The desire for community life and participation differentiates cohousing communities such as Two Echo, Pioneer Valley, and Belfast from most homeowners' associations because residents move to these communities in part since they seek close community bonds. Conflicts inevitably arise over design and other issues, but these communities have developed processes such as conflict resolution committees that facilitate conversations, mutual agreement, and compromise.

Complying with state and local codes represents an even greater challenge, and experimental communities, especially those in suburban and urban areas that seek innovative solutions to building, water, and sanitation infrastructure, face significant hurdles. Straw-bale structures can easily comply with some existing codes. For example, the Milkweed Mercantile complies with Missouri's commercial building code. The building's strength relies on its wooden frame structure while the straw bale provides insulation and temperature control. Designing straw-bale buildings to code is not difficult because of the wood structure, but few codes exist that regulate—and thus enable—natural building techniques such as rammed earth, cob, and earth bags. Perhaps this trend will change as more trained architects build code-compliant—or demand codes for—natural building methods. A conventionally trained architect came to Possibility Alliance specifically to learn natural building techniques that she hoped to make compliant with existing codes. Companies such as Down to Earth Design (http://www.buildnaturally.com/EDucate/Workshops/WO-current.htm) include instruction on complying with code, while others discuss code compliance as well as "outlaw" methods.

The Quest for Composting Toilets

Composting toilets—and the ability to use them—represent a sort of bellwether for public attitudes on alternative structures. Composting toilets are not smelly or unclean, but many people have a visceral response to the concept—or a fascination with it. One Cobb Hill resident recalled, "The most amusing time I had here, in terms of dealing with the media and the outside, was when we had a New Hampshire public TV crew in our house taking pictures of our toilets. I never expected that to ever happen but they were so interested in these composting toilets."

While northeast Missouri is relatively free of restrictive building codes, rural Vermont's codes have dictated Cobb Hill's composting toilets. Cobb Hill's internal regulations call for composting toilets, so, to take advantage of gravity, all toilets are on the second floor. Vermont code requires burying humanure for thirty-eight months, and the community had to work closely with the Vermont Department of Environmental Conservation to receive their permits.[29] In any case, the community's horses and cows provide enough manure for fertilizer so the humanure might not even be necessary.

Sirius installed composting toilets because flush toilets waste both water and good fertilizer. Composting toilets preserve both. "It takes two years and two chambers. You seal it off, move to the other chamber, and then two years later you empty out the other chamber that's been sitting there with no fresh input for two years. To be super safe, because many people have fecal phobia, we put it in black plastic barrels in the sun for another year so it actually heats up. So everything is baked and cooked."

The State of Massachusetts requires burying the manure under six inches of dirt after removing it from the composting toilet, but the Massachusetts General Law (chapter 176, acts of 2002, sec. 3) allows "self-contained, zero discharge, stand-alone composting toilets."[30] Sirius does not add the humanure compost to vegetables, assuming that many people would object. On the other hand, our guide continued, "Urine is a great resource, very high in nitrogen, so we add it to wood chips, sawdust, leaf piles. It breaks it down quickly. You can dump tons of urine on a wood chip pile, and in two years, you have this black, rich soil that is great for the gardens and the orchards."

Sirius built its own composting toilets for about $500 in materials, but commercial ones retail for $5,000 to $6,000. The toilets are clean and do not smell, and the wooden seats are more elegant than those on the porcelain toilets in our house.

Lois Arkin hopes to integrate a Living Machine (http://www.livingmachines.com/About-Living-Machine.aspx) into LA Eco-village that deals with both graywater and blackwater. Graywater refers to water used for dishwashing or laundry, while blackwater is water used to carry away human waste. A Living Machine cleans water without chemicals, using plants and microorganisms, and, Arkin stated, "turns it over in twenty-four hours to a potable quality." While California might not be ready for a Living Machine, the state's extended drought has prompted discussion of different water systems, including gray water. In 2014, the State of California requested that residents reduce their water use by 20 percent and allowed homeowners to install their own recycled water capture systems from showers, sinks, and washing machines.

In April 2014, Laura Allen, founder of Greywater Action (http://greywateraction.org/), demonstrated how a graywater irrigation system works at LA Ecovillage. Although the parts for the system cost only a few hundred dollars, the permits and inspections represent hurdles that block many from adopting the system.

One Angeleno who went through the process is Mark Vallianatos. He got permits and installed a system that captures all the graywater in his house. But there were a few speed bumps in the inspection process. Health departments worry do-it-yourselfers will accidentally cross the streams, mixing drinking water with the dirty stuff. A health inspector made Vallianatos's contractor redo part of his installation.[31] Despite the hassle, Vallianatos was glad he made the change, and he can now irrigate his fruit trees with graywater. In view of California's continuing drought and the ever-expanding threat of volatile weather patterns, the state's legislators may begin to take more progressive views about water conserving and reclamation efforts.

Building Gender Equity

Most of the communities worked to address gender equity, and several, including Dancing Rabbit and Twin Oaks, specifically identify as feminist communities. Creating gender equity on jobs and tasks traditionally gendered male or female remains a challenge, although the numbers of women building and men cooking represent a significant departure from the mainstream. In 1999, Dancing Rabbit held a women's building workshop and hired two contractors from the Southwest. Sixteen women from Dancing Rabbit and the wider community attended, and they built Belle Ciao, a one-room straw-bale cabin. Alline Anderson reflected on her experience: "We learned a lot and made a lot of mistakes with that building, but it was cool to use power tools and not be 'little ladied.' This is a feminist ecovillage, and we're trying to stay away from gendered stereotypes. It's more difficult now that we're getting older. It seems like most of the builders are men. There currently are a lot of women construction interns, and many of them have gone on to be builders."[32]

In subsequent conversations, Anderson and I discussed some challenges around gender and building that had arisen in our own lives. Anderson and I had bonded almost immediately, being about the same age and having had many similar experiences. While both of us would like to have the option of building and working with machinery such as chainsaws, we naturally gravitate toward activities like growing and cooking. However, both of us resent assumptions that we *can't* take on these traditionally male tasks.

Geographer Jenny Pickerill studied gender and building in eco-communities, exploring the subtle sexism that characterizes the lack of female builders as a matter of personal choice. "Gender exclusion today is rarely blatant; it tends to rely on often quite subtle assumptions made about women's minds, bodies, and roles in society, which are then reinforced by both men and women repeating and performing those roles."[33] Most women have experienced these subtle assumptions when being given unwanted advice or help—to the extent of having tools or boards removed from our hands.

A group of us experienced this at Dancing Rabbit when we were helping raise a reciprocal roof in a work party. Raising a reciprocal roof requires multiple individuals to lift heavy logs one at a time and then drill nails that bind the logs. Each subsequent pole is heavier because it supports the weight of the others. We six visitor-volunteers (five women and one man) had raised two poles, and the process was difficult because nobody knew who was holding the weight of the poles. None of us had a good grip, and it would be dangerous if anyone let go or slipped. One female visitor suggested that she hold the end of the log so we knew who had the grip. The idea was a good one, but the male visitor, standing behind the woman, simply removed the logs from her hands without asking if she needed help. She resented his assumption that she was weak. Ultimately the job was too difficult for the existing crew, and the builder hired an experienced crew the next day, but the incident elicited discussion about capacity, competence, and gender roles. It is important that communities like Dancing Rabbit have robust internal processes, such as conflict resolution mechanisms, to provide forums for discussing difficult situations. Mechanisms to handle structural problems such as sexism or personal conflicts help these communities maintain community stability.

In a 2014 Federation of Intentional Community blog post, Dancing Rabbit resident Sam Makita reflected on the complexities surrounding gender roles and building.

> In addition to the offensiveness of the implication that a woman in a man's world must need our help to succeed, I have concern about how giving such advantages affects the resulting workplace. Imagine, for example, that you're hiring a work crew of six carpenters and want to have 50/50 gender balance. If you get applications from qualified candidates in a ratio proportional to the ratio of carpenters in the U.S. as a whole, which according to the Bureau of Labor Statistics was 1.4 percent women in 2010, you have to turn down about 194 qualified men even if you hire all of the female applicants. If the three men you hire are the best three for the job, then those men are almost

certainly going to be better at the job than the women, not because men are necessarily better carpenters than women overall, but because you had to hire the best, middle, and worst woman candidates available, but only the top 3 percent of the men. On the worksite, then, those guys, and those gals, are certainly going to see more evidence to back up the very stereotype we were trying to counteract.[34]

Hiring less competent builders, she notes, only reinforces existing stereotypes, as the tokenism of the 1970s illustrated. Instead, providing educational opportunities and building capacity will generate a larger population of skilled female builders. Pickerill's article suggests some next steps, including education about gender bias, women-only building workshops, and eco-build support groups to share expertise and experiences.[35]

Dancing Rabbit and many other intentional communities have worked hard to eliminate barriers to jobs and tasks, but as new residents bring entrenched gender stereotypes with them, existing residents work to maintain feminist sensibilities within the community. As Makita argues, Dancing Rabbit has made great strides in gender equity:

> We're . . . doing well insofar as sharing chores across established gender lines. Most people here take a cook shift, most people clean public and private spaces, all parents (and many others) participate in childrearing. There're men and women in leadership roles here, and on physically, technically, and socially strenuous tasks. More importantly, there's not the expectation or requirement that people of a certain gender are the ones who perform a certain task. We're free to choose how to contribute based on our interests and talent—one reason I am proud to be a part of this community.
>
> We're far beyond most of the country in terms of accepting people for who they are and the contributions they bring, regardless of their gender. Part of that's thanks to Dancing Rabbit's foundation in feminism, for which I'm grateful. I think there's room for us to be more open-minded and objective around gender, and I look forward to watching that unfold at Dancing Rabbit and beyond.[36]

Intentional communities such as Dancing Rabbit, LA Eco-village, and Sirius integrate social and gender equity into their micro-industries and innovations. First, these communities are actively rethinking gender relations and strive to separate particular tasks from gender. For example, our tour guide boasted that Twin Oaks had an all-female mechanic shop at one point. Residents choose their labor weekly, so they can both change jobs and allocate their time among multiple tasks. Second, these communities actively count as labor tasks such as cooking and, at Twin Oaks, the emotional work of processing and governance, recognizing that typically female-gendered tasks have often been rendered invisible. These strategies alleviate one of my concerns about the new food movement—that the emphasis on homegrown foods and canning will become yet another burden on women.

DIY to the Mainstream

In December 2014, an article in the *Gainesville Sun,* "At This Workshop, They Teach 'Skills of Resilience,'" highlighted a local workshop on processing chickens. Joni Ellis, owner of Crazy Woman Farm, demonstrated how to process a live chicken, from slaughter to cooking, during "Don't Ask, Don't Tell."[37] Attendees learned, among other things, how to use all parts of the chicken, thereby reducing food waste. Ellis, who lives on her farm on the outskirts of Gainesville, frequently demonstrates skills of urban resilience and homesteading, and this event tied in with the annual Florida Earthskills gathering, which typically draws over one hundred attendees (floridaearthskills.org). By choosing Don't Ask, Don't Tell as her workshop title, Ellis reflects—or perhaps co-opts—LGBTQ struggles even as she acknowledges the reality that many people simply do not know, or do not want to know, the sources of their food, especially meat. Similarly, composting toilets force us to acknowledge the reality of human waste and perhaps question the wisdom of flushing our waste with clean drinking water.

So much of our food and other products appears neatly packaged, and our heating, cooling, and cooking energy arrives with the flip of a switch. However, composting toilets, food-processing workshops, and construction practicums pull back the curtain to reveal the human and environmental costs of our food, housing, and transportation. Lee Walker Warren of Earthhaven Ecovillage argues that our American lifestyles rely on unacknowledged wage labor and energy slaves, the latter being "the human labor we'd need to support our modern lifestyle if we weren't relying on oil-based technologies (i.e. energy)."[38] Learning how to provide for our needs, or at least what our needs demand from others and the earth, opens dialogue about how to scale back those needs.

The ubiquity and popularity of workshops such as Don't Ask, Don't Tell in Gainesville and around the United States suggest that the general public is increasingly interested in learning basic resilience skills. People attend skills workshops for a variety of reasons, including financial necessity and a desire for autonomy, but increasingly people seek to understand how to meet their own basic needs and what that entails. The popularity of workshops that teach basic homesteading and resilience skills illustrates that the goals and experiments of the intentional communities I visited are also reflected in mainstream populations.

9

Bringing It Home

People who have interned with us have gone on to do amazing things. They visit and call, saying that "my family gave up our car after we took your tour." It's not necessarily anything that we're doing, but we trigger a reaction in them that already was there. We're just living what's in our hearts, and I think that's the best thing we can do: live what's in our hearts and hope that it will encourage other people to live what's in their hearts.
—Sarah Wilcox-Hughes, the Possibility Alliance

INTENTIONAL COMMUNITIES that are founded on bundled values of nonviolence, self-sufficiency or interdependence, participatory democracy, and voluntary simplicity serve as experiments that others can observe and learn from to help imagine and consider as societal alternatives for their own lives. I would like to see this cluster of values lived out in a more systematic way, at multiple levels throughout all our communities. Living more simply helps resist the consumerism that bothers many North Americans, and stronger community ties can remedy the isolation experienced by many, particularly aging women. This final chapter explores some ways that we can bring these lessons home to our own communities and how we can rethink existing urban and suburban neighborhoods to build stronger communities and sustainable food systems. Nonetheless, significant hurdles remain. How do these lessons translate beyond the white middle class to the urban poor? And how do we overcome roadblocks such as entrenched opposition to bike-sharing and energy-saving programs? Community residents and those hoping to transplant the seeds of change must negotiate a balance between their aspirations and trying to live in the realm of the possible.

Many community residents told me that creating community and learning to handle conflict productively were the most difficult tasks they have undertaken, far outweighing physical hardships. Watching them struggle with conflict resolution and nonviolent communication has pushed me to evaluate my own relationships and question what sort of person I want to be. Visiting these communities profoundly changed me and has made me reconsider not only what kind of community I want, but also how I contribute—or not—to my own community. I still wonder where we go from here and how those of us who are intrigued by the kinds of experiments being lived out in intentional communities can help bring these ideas into our own lives and communities.

Although I am not likely to move to an intentional community, I know that I can be more intentional about how I live my life and how I treat others. I like living in Gainesville, and rather than moving to a new community, I prefer to strengthen my bonds in my existing one. I do not need to live in an intentional community to live out core values of nonviolence and voluntary simplicity but, because intentional communities have applied these concepts in varying situations, their tests teach me how to bring these values into my own life. Focusing on the source of my food by joining a CSA—supporting a local farmer—and choosing to eat seasonally are simple ways to eat more intentionally and enact what I value.

I wonder, then, what it would mean to extend these ideas beyond myself into my neighborhood, for example, or even further. Kevin and I started talking with our friends and neighbors about possibilities for mutual support as we age. Creating a mutual support network will not necessarily fulfill all our needs as we age, but doing so might help us be proactive rather than reactive. Cooking occasionally with our friends or sharing tools rather than all buying our own could make it easier for us to be intentional about enacting our shared values of voluntary simplicity and interdependence. Perhaps others might see our experiments and be prompted to try out these ideas themselves. Most people belong to multiple communities, including neighborhood associations, recreational clubs, civic groups, and religious organizations, and some of these communities already are or might be amenable to enacting values of nonviolence, voluntary simplicity, and self-sufficiency.

Intentional communities promote the testing and circulation of new ideas, sharing feedback with one another and with others outside their communities. Residents of intentional communities tend to be mobile, what Possibility Alliance calls "beautiful migrants, beautiful souls who are adventurous and seeking different experiences." This tendency toward transitoriness, although widely perceived as a failure of intentional communities, might in fact be a strength because it allows their ideas to circulate far beyond any individual community.[1] For example, Mark Becker left the Possibility Alliance in 2014 in response to events in Ferguson, Missouri, and he now draws upon skills he learned in the community in his work for racial justice and Black Lives Matter. Similarly, one past resident of the Miccosukee Land Cooperative noted that her residence prepared her for her current community-building efforts—strengthening neighborhood bonds to provide mutual support as the neighbors age. Sharing ideas and practices creates networks beyond our immediate neighborhoods. Experimenting with new ideas and adapting them as necessary help intentional communities—or any small community—develop flexibility and resilience. Without change and flexibility, communities risk becoming ossified and resistant to change, which is one reason many people flee small communities in the first place.

I have frequently heard the criticism that "we can't all move to farms and rural areas." At one level, this is true—we can't all move to the country and create new communities, and no one argues that we should. Nonetheless, communities like Dancing Rabbit and Possibility Alliance have benefited from locating in rural areas. For example, their relative isolation has forced them to rely on each other for social and economic needs and has allowed them to experiment without the distractions of urban life. Watching Dancing Rabbit's experiments and adaptation of lessons learned demonstrates the tension between knowledge that might be applied broadly and knowledge that is specific to place and context. Techniques for nonviolent conflict resolution, for instance, can easily be applied in diverse contexts, whereas natural building and farming must be adapted to local conditions. However, lessons from those experiments can be translated or upscaled into our own lives and into our communities, wherever we live.

Rethinking Our Systems

"People in the wider world say it's impossible to provide for all your needs with renewable energy, or it's just too expensive. I think it is possible, and demonstrating it on the scale of a small village shows that we can do it here. Then you can do it for a larger region, then a larger region, and then the whole grid." Tony Sirna's words express the hope and potential that intentional communities embody.

Residents of intentional communities design their physical spaces to meet multiple community needs, and lessons gleaned from their experiences can help us rethink how our public spaces could enhance community interactions. Open grassy spaces could be transformed into suburban farms, and public buildings such as libraries or schools could serve numerous community functions after hours. These transitions are already happening—Prairie Crossing, a wealthy suburb near Chicago, has preserved open space for prairie conservation and set land aside for a suburban farm (prairiecrossing.com). Furthermore, Darrin Nordahl's work illustrates how local governments and agencies have transformed public spaces into places for urban and suburban agriculture, providing examples of scaling up from the individual to the social.[2] Rethinking suburban spaces could help alleviate problems such as food miles and at the same time address the anomie and isolation of these spaces. A psychiatrist living in Sirius in Shutesbury, a town adjacent to Amherst, Massachusetts, observes, "When I drive around or just see suburban America, I see isolation and houses. The nuclear family is insular, and I see a great deal of sadness and isolation. Living in community offers a sense of being with other people who care for each other. Car-centric suburbs with few porches, sidewalks, or bicycle-friendly roads make it harder to have spontaneous encounters with neighbors."

Redesigning streets to increase the possibility of encounters and interactions could help build stronger community ties, a goal of the National Complete Streets Coalition, which strives to make streets safer for people bicycling and walking.[3] In creating Pioneer Valley, resident and general contractor Peter Jessop said they designed for "interaction with each other and to not cover more of the land with parking and paving." Sidewalks and bike paths encourage face-to-face encounters, and even nooks and crannies between yards offer spaces for community building between neighbors. These efforts reflect the larger movement toward a New Urbanism that has emphasized planning compact, walkable cities for the last several decades (newurbanism.org).

Writer David Leach became interested in communal living after a visit to a kibbutz in Israel.

> I became conscious of how architecture brings people together or keeps us apart—and how that sense of community impacts the environment, too. I'd grown up in a sprawling Wonder Bread subdivision with the carbon footprint of Godzilla. I later worked for Greenpeace, and my late-blooming ecological awareness nagged at my imagination. Wasn't there a better way to live? Could we design a community to be friendly both to its neighbors and to its environment? Could we replicate such eco-'hoods on a large scale, as we'd done with suburbia?

I stumbled across clues to this puzzle in surprising places. My wife and I bought a house in Toronto, Canada's biggest city. It was situated in an odd parallelogram of older duplexes, hemmed in by two busy roads, a subway yard, and a train track. Eco-paradise it was not.

And yet neighbors had turned the geographical constraints to their advantage. They had christened this forgotten corner "The Pocket"—a micro-neighborhood that didn't exist on any official map. One family opened their doors every Saturday to sell fresh-baked bread. Other residents published a regular newsletter to broadcast the history, culture, personalities, and urgent issues of The Pocket. (It evolved into a lively online social network.) A sense of community developed around what had been just another postal code. This common purpose was built, like the kibbutz movement, on a foundation of shared myth. We weren't isolated strangers, powerless and alone; we were the people of The Pocket.[4]

Most suburban and urban regions have naturally existing pocket neighborhoods that create small-scale communities amid large population centers. Pocket neighborhoods, also a design category, attract baby boomers hoping for "smaller neighborhoods with a bigger sense of community."

This increasingly popular housing option generally consists of a dozen or so compact houses or apartments that share common or green space. That might be a pedestrian walkway, garden, courtyard or shared backyard or alley. Central mailboxes give neighbors even more opportunities to interact.[5]

These smaller, self-consciously created neighborhoods offer opportunities not only to socialize but also to help neighbors take care of each other as they age.

Cohousing Communities

Cohousing communities are growing in popularity, in part because they best replicate existing patterns of individual ownership that few are willing to abandon. Described by one resident as the 1970s commune grown up, cohousing offers individual autonomy in a cooperative community setting. Coleen O'Connell of Belfast stated, "People come together, share land, and share resources, but they have their own jobs, they have respectable houses, they're not hauling wood and hauling water. They're not roughing it. They're having a typical American, middle-class life but they're doing it intentionally and more communally. The cohousing model offers community and shared resources, but also replicates most patterns of middle-class life."

Cohousing communities have several drawbacks, however. First, most are formed as homeowners' associations and are legally obligated to sell to any buyer, regardless of that buyer's interest in sustainability or community. Ideally, people will join the community *because* of these goals, but enforcing rules and participation can be difficult. Like most intentional communities, Pioneer Valley has requirements for participation. According to resident Peter Jessop,

> We have a group called the Hub that organizes all the work, and they ask people once a year: How much are you doing? What are you doing? Do you want to change tasks? Do you want to do something else? We require six hours a month per person, and even this is probably not quite enough to get all the work done that needs to be done in the community, but we make it work. I mow lawns, plow snow, and wash dishes, and I'm on several committees. You get out of it what you put into it. When I mow the lawns, I get a lot out of it. Ironically, my payback is that I get some alone time.

Few communities want to expend energy policing their friends and neighbors so, especially in cohousing communities, residents rely on the goodwill of the fellow residents. Further, as Jessop notes, "You get out of it what you put into it"; many benefits of community participation are subtle and not easily quantified.

Second, on the housing costs spectrum, cohousing communities tend to be expensive, so they are primarily open to the well-established upper middle class. Chuck Durrett argues that the cohousing model is not intrinsically expensive due to shared resources, and many cohousing communities are populated with lower-income residents, but the middle-class stereotype persists.[6] Some cohousing communities reserve space for lower-income residents, but most lower-income Americans cannot afford them. Peter Jessop of Pioneer Valley stated, "When we built these units, the original sale price was $75,000 to 135,000. We worked hard to get the construction price down. We have bylaws, and you have to pay your condo fees. Our condo fees cover our operating expenses and long-term capital expenses for the community. We are fiscally responsible, and we are financially stable. It's not necessarily cheaper to live in cohousing than it would be to live out in the world, but it's better."

For Jessop and others who have chosen cohousing communities, community bonds and the social relationships fostered by these tight-knit communities provide an antidote to the looser social bonds and potential loneliness of mainstream neighborhoods.

Unintentional Sustainability

Residents of cohousing communities are attracted by the social cohesion, but—intentionally or not—cohousing communities become more sustainable in the process. Some cohousing communities, such as Belfast, specifically identify environmental sustainability as a core community value and mandate sustainability measures such as car-free zones or composting toilets in the community's bylaws. In many communities, including Pioneer Valley, the shared resources and smaller house sizes are sustainable—whether intentionally or not—relative to North American norms. Peter Jessop explained,

> We don't call ourselves an ecovillage in that way. We did build slightly smaller houses here than the standard American house, but I've been to Central America five times, working with Habitat for Humanity, and we live in mansions here. Our house is only about fifteen hundred square feet, smaller than the house we used to have, but huge, so we didn't really scale down here if you look at our footprint. My daughter lives in Brooklyn. Her carbon footprint is significantly less than mine. She doesn't have a car. Her living space is small, and it's bounded on six sides by other people's heating. She uses public transportation. Maybe we should all be living in big urban areas.
>
> On the other hand, we are building a social connectivity here that doesn't exist in many other situations in America. It's hard to get this level of community where we talk to our neighbors. I can think of as many things that we don't do. But when I think of what we do, I'm moved by how much social connection there is here and how available we are when there's a problem. You've got a lot of friends here.

Whether or not sustainability is a core value of a particular cohousing community, some residents perceive it as such, in part because of their community's reduced footprint.

When I participated in Pioneer Valley's weekly community dinner,

Dining room at Pioneer Valley Cohousing

our dinner table conversation turned to sustainability. Jessop had invited me to the dinner and asked people who might be interested in my research to join our table. About sixty people came to dinner that night, and we sat down to soup, salad, and homemade bread. Some groups like ours reserved a table, but others chose tables randomly. Since almost everyone else lived at Pioneer Valley, they all knew each other fairly well.

Our discussion revealed that even among those at my self-selected table, residents held differing views on whether sustainability actually constituted a core value of Pioneer Valley (although not whether sustainability *should* be a goal). For example, Jessop argued that Pioneer Valley was not especially focused on sustainability or residents would have built more multiunit structures with shared walls. But several others at the table argued that sustainability, or living lightly on the earth, as they put it, and nonviolence constituted two core values of the community.

While some residents like Jessop believed that Pioneer Valley focuses too little on sustainability, he maintained that what has become the community's norm differs significantly from the mainstream. "We forget how unusual this looks when you walk in from the outside. First visually, the parking, and you have to walk up the hill every time to get to your house from your parking space. I think it is good to remember how unusual it is and not judge ourselves too harshly." Residents park their cars on the perimeter of the community and walk to their homes. The pedestrian loop that reaches all units allows for major deliveries and emergency vehicles, but walking is the norm at Pioneer Valley as opposed to driving straight into the garage.

I also found this pedestrian and communal space at Two Echo in Brunswick, Maine. The central part of the community is car-free so that children can ride their bikes freely and safely. Residents emphasized the social benefits of their community (such as relationships and close neighbors) in addition to sustainability. The smaller house size, reduced number of car trips for socializing, and shared common space gives this community a smaller footprint than many American suburbs have.

Perhaps benefits such as increased social cohesion and walkable neighborhoods render sustainability more palatable when the unintended benefits outweigh the perceived obstacles. Making neighborhoods friendlier to bicyclists and pedestrians has become a goal for reasons of safety and health, not simply sustainability. For example, the Safe Routes to School program illustrates the growing popularity of "walking school buses" around the United States. As with conventional school buses, the children are chaperoned by adults and join and leave the bus along a planned route. Walking school buses are catching on in school districts nationwide because they are seen as a way to fight childhood obesity, improve attendance rates, and ensure that kids get to school safely.[7] Although the article about walking school buses never mentions sustainability, reducing car and bus traffic lessens our carbon footprint while demonstrating the social pleasures of walking with friends.

Challenges to Change

Innovative communities face multiple challenges and roadblocks, especially when they attempt to demonstrate and mainstream their experiments. Many people are simply indifferent to their ideas, while others actively resist these changes. Some urban residents, especially minorities or low-income populations, perceive environmental and sustainability issues as white middle-class concerns, and sociologists such as Julie Guthman have questioned the efficacy of fresh-food programs directed toward

African Americans. CSAs and farmers' markets, she argued, tend to be "white spaces" and not necessarily accessible or friendly to minorities.[8] Gary Younge echoed Guthman's concern that progressives speak for, rather than to, the populations they aim to serve.[9] Similarly, Antonio Roman-Alcala offers strategies and methods for white activists aiming to "change the norm of a white-dominated food sustainability scene," starting with "Go to where people are at, not where you want them to be."[10] Such concerns prompted the 2010 A Place for Us: The Black Farmers and Urban Gardeners Conference, which was "attended by over 500 black-identified people, representing urban and rural farming networks, food justice organizations, government officials, policy makers, and good foodies."[11]

Although the perceived whiteness of CSAs and urban farming has overshadowed the contributions to those movements made by African Americans, Natasha Bowens writes that African American farmer Booker T. Whatley pioneered the concept behind CSAs in rural Alabama in the 1960s and 1970s, well before the term *CSA* was coined (by Robyn Van En of Indian Line Farm in Massachusetts in 1985), to help African American farmers remain solvent.[12] Leah Penniman describes the role of food and farming in the civil rights movement, noting that "without black farmers, there would have been no freedom summer." She adds that farms like Soul Fire Farm, "a family farm committed to the dismantling of oppressive structures that misguide our food system," are crucial for the success of movements like Black Lives Matter because they bring local self-determination and the power over food back to the people.[13] Writing about influential African American food system leaders such as Rashid Nuri of downtown Atlanta's Truly Living Well Farm, food activist Mark Winne acknowledges that food justice will not be attained solely through the efforts of well-intentioned white people.[14]

The stereotype of the urban hipster farmer has become mainstream enough to be satirized in a Grist comic called *My Intentional Life* (http://grist.org/my-intentional-life/). This comic, though, did provoke discussion among urban homesteaders. "And I feel kind of weird about that! I know it wasn't their intent, but 'My Intentional Life' made me feel like this is all just some kind of scene."[15]

Representatives from two urban collectives, Baltimore Free Farm and the Midden, discussed their concerns about gentrification and imposing their values on potentially unwilling neighbors at the 2013 Twin Oaks conference. Alex, who spoke for the Midden, an urban homesteading community in Columbus, Ohio, pointed out that, despite good intentions, many actions aimed at helping lower-income neighborhoods might harm the neighbors. For example, upgrading property can change the neighborhood dynamic, and up-and-coming neighborhoods invite developers who ultimately make the neighborhood unaffordable for the original inhabitants. Neighbors have very real concerns about their ability to remain in their homes when others nearby are upgraded.

Over the past few decades, LA Eco-village residents in particular have successfully worked on public policy changes that aid efforts in both social justice and sustainability, including issues of affordable housing, climate justice, and transportation. In urban and suburban communities, attitudes and policies emphasizing individual and family property ownership have hindered efforts to create structures for community ownership.

Urban sustainability represents some of the greatest challenges and greatest opportunities. More than 50 percent of the US population now lives in urban regions, and population density facilitates public transit as well as walking and cycling. Further, the row houses and apartment buildings that already exist in the built environment provide efficiencies in heating and cooling. Ethan Hughes argued that simply creating communities in rural regions is not adequate and that work in urban communities must include social justice. Integral nonviolence includes addressing urban crises, and the Possibility Alliance has trained people to work in urban areas, including the Being the Change urban homestead project in Reno, Nevada. Urban outreach helps the Possibility Alliance extend its arms far beyond La Plata, Missouri, and Hughes notes that the community's network of over seven hundred allies can respond to disasters such as Hurricane Katrina.

> Half the planet is urban, and so our eighty acres must benefit half the population, but we can't pretend that this is realistic for the whole planet. That's why we need to vision and experiment with the urban connection. How do we do this in a country where there's a whole history of oppression of Native Americans and African Americans? How do we create atonement where we are actually humbling ourselves to the embedded experience of existing in America?
>
> I come into the inner city not to say, "This is what you should do," but "What do you need?" We hear, "I need a house because I haven't been able to own a house my whole life, my grandmother couldn't own a house. We can't rent because we're black." Help them buy a house. Don't go down

there and tell them, "You should take a vow of holy poverty" after hundreds of years of oppression. How do we become servants to these oppressed groups because we can't fathom their situation?

If we [Possibility Alliance] don't develop that in the next year or two, we are a place of privilege, not integral nonviolence. And the structural abuse is still happening—in the prison systems, in the Ninth Ward after Hurricane Katrina. It was astounding to go down to Hurricane Katrina. The rich areas were already repaired after three months.

Hughes's words, spoken in 2011, seem prescient in 2016 as current events have renewed debate over racial injustice and structural inequities, and Possibility Alliance's emphasis on integral nonviolence illustrates one approach to enacting the three legs of sustainability—equity, ecology, and economy.

Catholic worker communities also illustrate integral nonviolence. Hughes's concerns about not imposing his views on others were echoed by other communards I spoke with. Eric Garbison of Cherith Brook in Kansas City related his community's tensions between sustainability and hospitality to the poor. From the Catholic workers' perspective, he said, their guests use shower water wastefully, but many of those they serve do not have faucets so the residents do not want to adopt a paternalistic attitude. "It is a gift," he said, "of letting go of control and power." In seeking solidarity with the poor and homeless, residents of Cherith Brook spend several nights a year on the streets because the experience of eating "dumpstered pizza" and experiencing homelessness is transformative.

As we have seen, Catholic worker communities also illustrate integral nonviolence through their discussions and direct action. In fact, in response to the Ferguson, Missouri, riots, Possibility Alliance resident Mark Becker relocated to a St. Louis Catholic worker community to integrate what he learned at the Possibility Alliance about integral nonviolence into larger social movements such as Black Lives Matter.

Many Catholic worker houses are located in urban or suburban regions, and they welcome volunteers and invite the public to their signature roundtable discussions. These conversations expose volunteers and participants to unfamiliar worlds and help them engage with often invisible others on a personal level. For instance, I gained compassion for and insight into the realities of life for homeless people at both Cherith Brook and the Gainesville Catholic Worker House during face-to-face dinners and discussions.

The building and population densities of urban regions encourage grassroots organizations and cooperatives that are less likely to be created in rural and suburban regions. Olivia LaVecchia describes Minneapolis's Northeast Investment Cooperative (NEIC), which helps residents buy and develop real estate. The once rundown neighborhood now boasts numerous small businesses—a brewery, bakery, and co-op grocery store—that are pumping money back into the local economy.[16] This grassroots effort demonstrates one self-help model, but concerns remain about what will happen to existing residents as the community redevelops and whether this collection of breweries and bicycle shops will attract a broad range of customers.

Threatening the System

Intentional communities and movements that advocate practices and technologies that threaten powerful business interests, whether in energy, transportation, or food, face pushback and retaliation from these groups. Some sustainable practices, such as alternative transportation, alternative energy, and local foods, have now entered the mainstream. For example, many municipalities offer incentives or rebates for customers who install solar panels or solar water heaters. The very fact of the mainstream success of these alternatives, however, has provoked resistance. For example, both Dancing Rabbit and Pioneer Valley sell power back to the grid, also called reverse metering. One Pioneer Valley resident told me that the reverse metering from his photovoltaic system and solar water heater has given him a $500 credit with the power company. Nonetheless, in April 2014, both the *New York Times* and the *Washington Post* reported on a well-funded oil and gas industry campaign that attempted to portray solar users as freeloaders on the power grid.[17] Vested interests in status quo energy usage feel increasingly threatened as alternative energies become mainstream.

According to reporter Isaiah Poole, "Making solar energy cost-prohibitive for homeowners and businesses is part of a larger ALEC [American Legislative Exchange Council] objective, affirmed at its recent annual meeting, to continue its effort to eliminate state renewable energy mandates." Despite its innocuous-sounding name, ALEC is a coalition of groups hostile to alternative energy, among other things. ALEC pushed regulations to make homeowners in Flagler, Arizona, "pay an average of about $5 extra a month for the privilege of generating solar energy."[18] This campaign highlighted the large government subsidies received by the solar industry while neglecting to mention the much larger subsidies that the oil and gas industry enjoys.

Many sustainability-focused intentional communities exist, in part, to test and demonstrate alternatives, and their innovations and micro-industries illustrate their successes as well as, occasionally, their failures. They face challenges—some populations are simply indifferent to experimental communities, while others mount a hostile opposition. Baltimore Free Farm, situated in a white, working-class neighborhood, has won over neighbors who might otherwise resent its programs with beer and pizza nights. Residents brew their own beer and donate some to neighborhood gatherings.

Hostility to off-the-grid communities and innovative technologies can comprise serious threats to those who might wish to adopt these technologies. Florida has made living off the grid illegal, requiring residents to be hooked into services whether they use them or not, according to a ruling in Cape Coral by special magistrate Harold S. Eskin.[19] A State of Texas SWAT team raided Garden of Eden, an organic farm, to search for an alleged marijuana farm—and found tomatoes.[20]

Similarly, the growing popularity of bicycling, both for commuting and for recreation, has produced a sometimes incomprehensible anger among critics. Some drivers resent having to "share the road" with bicyclists, especially those wearing spandex shorts or using clipless pedals, or they assume that cyclists think that *everyone* should abandon their cars for bikes. Other critics view infrastructure such as bike racks and bike lanes as a middle-class entitlement, not realizing that bicycles might be the only transportation option for some low-income people.

The Citi Bike program in New York City provoked an uproar across the city that reminded me of an episode of *Seinfeld*. Many people simply loathed the bicycles and the racks, including *Wall Street Journal* editorialist Dorothy Rabinowitz. When George Gurley interviewed her, Rabinowitz recalled the day the bike racks arrived. "On her block, people were panicking, she said. They were saying things like, 'Is this really going to be in front of my apartment?' 'I realized it was like some science-fiction thing,' Ms. Rabinowitz recalled. 'The pods have landed, only they've landed with the racks, and they're coming with allies called bicyclists. The activating force behind all of the fury was the racks, instruments of aesthetic torture.'"[21]

Rabinowitz explained her resentment of the "religious zealotry attached to the riding of bicycles in this city," which she links to a middle-class, environmentalist entitlement. Gurley wrote, "Bicycle messengers and delivery people, though often reckless, don't really bother her. 'I'm talking about the much less recognized world of entitled, middle-class and upper-middle-class riders in the city who think they are serving a noble cause. It's basically their very identity that they are special people, that they're helping the environment, and nobody has ever instilled any notion in them of the necessity of following a traffic rule.'"[22]

Not surprisingly, Rabinowitz's comments, which were mocked on *The Daily Show*, prompted a barrage of comments pro and con, but her distrust of the bike program reveals that debates about sustainability parallel contemporary tensions over class and access to resources or subsidies. In the case of solar subsidies, some critics perceive benefits such as reverse metering going unfairly to those who can afford expensive solar systems, benefits subsidized by those who remain on the grid. Critics of bike lanes argue that cyclists do not pay their fair share, ignoring the reality that cyclists subsidize local roads with their property taxes just as car drivers do. Rabinowitz's criticism seems to epitomize an inchoate anger—disproportionately borne in this case by cyclists—that those testing alternatives to existing systems see themselves as better than others and are getting more than their fair share of resources.

When I give public talks, people sometimes question the economic sustainability of intentional communities, some of which receive donations or grants for farming projects, without considering the massive subsidies that make industrial agriculture possible and profitable. Some Catholic worker communities consciously live below the poverty line so that they do not pay the federal taxes that subsidize war, following an American resistance pattern established by Henry David Thoreau. It's true that some residents of these communities do rely on state and local assistance for healthcare, for example, but critiquing their reliance on outside assistance demands a much broader discussion of who and what else receives subsidies and assistance.

Mainstreaming Sustainability

According to a quotation widely attributed to Mohandas K. Gandhi, "First they ignore you, then they ridicule you, then they fight you, and then you win." Urban cycling programs, solar power energy, and transportation alternatives have engaged the mainstream. Many of the practices I saw in the communities I visited parallel contemporary trends. Towns and school districts have adopted programs based on nonviolent communication to address bullying; urban gardening and eating locally, or at least bioregionally, have regained popularity across a broad spectrum of the United States in recent years. Perhaps the food aspect of voluntary simplicity best resonates with both intentional community residents and the general public. Farmers' markets, CSAs, and farm-to-table meals have proliferated, and a complementary movement, farm-to-table *living*, has also begun to flourish. Writer Kate Murphy describes one such venture, Agritopia, as an "agrihood"—a residential development designed around a working farm.[23]

Transportation alternatives such as bike commuting and bus travel have entered the mainstream. I recall a discussion when I began teaching in 1995 about whether pre-tenure faculty, especially women, should bike to work—a practice that seems unlikely to arouse controversy today. NPR reported that bike commuting has increased 60 percent in the last decade, and cities such as New York and Baltimore now have public bike-sharing or rental programs. And many cities have added bike racks to the fronts of their buses.[24] Lois Arkin and LA Eco-village have focused on public transportation issues, and their efforts have improved bus and train travel as well as bike and pedestrian options in LA. LA Eco-village residents helped start the CicLAvia bike-oriented street festivals (which now draw more than one hundred thousand people several times a year); the self-help Bicycle Kitchen; and the premiere bicycle advocacy organization, Los Angeles County Bicycle Coalition, which also provides bicycle commuting maps (la-bike.org/resources/bike-commuting).

Even more interesting, millennials tend to favor public transportation, and many of them have not purchased cars, which up to now has been seen as an American rite of passage. A Rockefeller Foundation survey of millennials in ten major cities found that they value access to public transportation and desire to be less reliant on cars.[25] Upscale bus companies such as Megabus and Red Coach, which provide Internet service, clean rest rooms, and comfortable seats, appeal especially to millennials, but increasingly to others. Megabus recently added a route from Gainesville to New Orleans, and several of my friends, who are not millennials, have already made the trip. Even overnight bus travel is less aggravating than flying to many these days.

Ditching your car for a bike or the bus offers benefits that might not be obvious at the outset. In both cases, I have enjoyed increased social interactions—stopping for a brief conversation when meeting a friend on a bike or running into an old acquaintance on the bus. Such spontaneous interactions are unlikely to occur when one is encased in two tons of steel. Lois Arkin linked alternative transportation to increased opportunities for discussion and civic engagement. She noted that spontaneous encounters allow people to "strike up specific conversations in concerned ways. This is something we don't do in this society, and it is something that happens frequently on our subways and our buses, one of the things that comes when you're not addicted to your car."

Sowing the Seeds

Researching and writing this book have forced me to think about the community I want to live in—and grow old in. Kevin and I are committed to Gainesville—we love the year-round growing, cycling, sailing, and kayaking. We do not plan to move to an intentional community, but we have had many conversations about creating secure and resilient bonds among like-minded friends and neighbors in the hope that we can create lifeways that can replicate the best features of these communities.

Although Possibility Alliance's abstinence from fossil fuels, chocolate, and coffee mark it as highly divergent from the US mainstream, the community's practice of nonviolence at multiple levels makes it the heart of this book. Even though I drive, eat chocolate, and drink coffee, I filter my choices through the lens of Possibility Alliance—what would they do at Possibility Alliance? My visits there encouraged me to look more clearly at my own practices, including the irony that I traveled around the United States to learn more about sustainable living. Since then, I have reduced my travel, and my future research and writing will focus on the ecoheritage of my own watershed, the St. Johns River.

Ecovillages, Catholic worker communities, cohousing groups, and a variety of other intentional communities across the United States have sought to be the change they wish to see in the world by creating and testing alternative modes of governance, eating, and building. As microcosms of larger social bodies, intentional communities model deliberations, experiments, and challenges, and they exemplify new ways of eating, living, and creating community. Their experiments in nonviolence, self-sufficiency, equity, and voluntary simplicity demonstrate benefits and trade-offs as the communities translate these values within their specific cultures and geographies.

The intentional communities I explored were residential, and indeed most definitions of intentional community presume residence. But what about nonresidential communities? Since most people will not move to an intentional community, perhaps we should explore the potential of nonresidential communities such as religious or civic organizations, affinity groups (for example, Resilience Circles), and informal but committed associations of friends within a city.

In 2014, I spoke with a group of young adults and pastors associated with Eco-Stewards, a Presbyterian youth program described as "where faith and environmental stewardship meet" (http://ecostewardsprogram.wordpress.com/). One pastor asked how churches fit with the concept of intentional community, and her question led to an extended discussion about the importance of residence for intentional community. Several participants were currently living in intentional communities, and their experiences reflected my conversations with community residents: that living in community and resolving conflicts led to enormous personal growth but was indeed more difficult than practices such as voluntary simplicity. But we all agreed that lessons learned in community, such as knowing how to argue and what battles are important, imparted skills necessary to sustaining relationships.

This discussion with the Eco-Stewards paralleled others I have had with friends, family, and colleagues about integrating the fruits of intentional community into our existing lives and neighborhoods. The question of proximity arises again and again—that is, do we really need to be physical neighbors, or could extended networks across cities or regions provide the same benefits? While networks and safety nets across regions would offer distinct benefits, I surmise that the frequent and often spontaneous contact afforded by intentional neighborhoods or perhaps those in smaller cities builds the strongest sense of community and security.

Intentional communities such as Lothlorien Nature Sanctuary (http://www.elvinhome.org/index.php) in southern Indiana and the Rainbow Family (http://www.welcomehome.org/rainbow/), are examples of communities that are proximate in time rather than residence. Both Lothlorien and the Rainbow Family gather during specified festival periods, drawing residents across a broad geographic range. Although residents are proximate in space only for short periods, the community bonds persist over time. These organized gatherings embody the promise of temporary communities that Rebecca Solnit discussed in *A Paradise Built in Hell*, citing the spontaneous and temporary communities that arose and responded to disasters such as 9/11 and Hurricane Katrina. Planned gatherings, or proximity in time, might consolidate social bonds for communities that are spread throughout a city or metropolitan area in the same way that regular potlucks consolidate bonds in the three communities in Missouri. Anthropologist Lucinda Carspecken speculates that the bonds forged between festivalgoers over the course of many years might prove more stable than residential intentional communities.[26] Further, social media and efforts by groups such as the Valhalla Movement to link communities and individuals can maintain bonds established during festivals and meetings. Forms of social media will be especially important to millennials—and increasingly to others—who conduct much of their social lives through these avenues.

For people who would like to consider alternative lifeways, the intentional communities I discussed in this book offer a place to start. Their experiments in nonviolence, interdependence, and voluntary simplicity, enacted in specific contexts and geographies, help us imagine new pathways of living and being together sustainably.

Acknowledgments

Researching and writing this book has been an incredible journey and opened my eyes to a new world of community, sustainability, nonviolence and, most important, kindness. Many people and communities have helped me on my way and graciously opened their homes and hearts to me. I am not able to list everyone, but I would like to give a special shout-out to the following people and communities.

First and foremost, I owe an enormous debt of gratitude to the individuals at communities who hosted me, sat for interviews, and allowed me to "help" them in their work and chores. I fondly recall sitting with Alline Anderson and Kurt Kessner over many cups of coffee in the Milkweed Mercantile as they helped me process my visits and discussions with residents at Dancing Rabbit and other communities. Alline, Kurt, Allyson Ewald of Red Earth Farms, and Victoria Albright read early drafts of this book and provided good feedback and insight on my emerging thoughts. Alice McGary of Mustard Seed Catholic Worker Farm in Ames, Iowa, let me tag along on garden chores twice, and Lois Arkin taught me a great deal about LA transportation and social equity as I conducted an interview with her while we rode several buses across Los Angeles. Ethan Hughes and Sarah Wilcox-Hughes, Mark Becker, Dan Truesdale, Victoria Albright, and residents of the Possibility Alliance shared their vision of nonviolence and joyful productivity as we gardened, picked cherries, and feasted on their garden's abundance and later offered comments on the manuscript. Ruth and Alan Keitt, friends of Gainesville, Florida, friends, opened their home to me in Cobb Hill Cohousing, and Judith Bush organized a tour and round table discussion. Peter Jessop assembled a table of discussants at Pioneer Valley's weekly community dinner where we considered religion, sustainability, and sociocracy. For those individuals and communities not mentioned here, know that you have my gratitude.

Dialogue with colleagues and students at the University of Florida shaped this project from the start. My arrival at UF coincided with an ongoing discussion on translating values into practice with Anna Peterson and Les Thiele, and their Values to Practice symposium helped me crystallize themes that later emerged in this book. Later, I shared drafts of chapters with students in Religion and Food, Religion and Sustainability, Religion and Fieldwork, and Religion, Nature, and Society and received valuable feedback. The College of Liberal Arts and Sciences and the Center for Humanities in the Public Sphere have generously supported my work through grants and fellowships. Finally, at UF, thanks to Vasudha Narayanan, who has supported all of my diverse intellectual interests.

Colleagues and longtime friends—David Aftandilian, Carol Anderson, Corinne Dempsey, and Max Grossman—read drafts of the manuscript and pointed out gaps, strengthening the final book. I also thank my anonymous readers for their careful and constructive criticism. Both saw where I was trying to go and helped me get there. And a special thank-you to Bobbi Patterson of Emory University, who has been a mentor, colleague, and friend and listened to me talk about this project at many American Academy of Religion conferences.

Steve Wrinn and Allison Webster at the University Press of Kentucky have given me nothing but support. Steve and I spent many hours discussing this project, and he nurtured the seed and read early drafts, seeing the potential in the material and my ideas. His thoughtful mentoring has helped me on the path to being the writer I would like to be. Vicky Machado transcribed numerous interviews, read through drafts, and offered comments and insight. I cannot say how much I value my ongoing partnership with my friend, writing coach, and editor Christianna White of Ames. We have worked together on three books now, and she consistently teases out of me what I am really trying to say.

Earlier versions of some material was printed in the *Communal Studies Journal* and the *Journal for the Study of Religion, Nature, and Culture*, and my work has benefited from their feedback.

Finally, and most important, my husband, Kevin Veach, and my parents, Mary and Charles Sanford, have gifted me with their enduring love and support. They have been with me every step of the way, read drafts, and patiently listened to me think out loud. Kevin took on extra cat duty while I traveled. When I visited more remote communities, I had to climb hills to gain cell coverage, and although I loved this fieldwork, I loved nothing better than to hear his voice at the end of the day. My parents recently moved to Gainesville, and now we can focus together on building our own community.

Appendix A
Communities Discussed in This Book

Acorn Community, Louisa, Virginia—Established 1993

Focus: "An egalitarian, income-sharing, secular, anarchist, feminist, consensus-based intentional community. Supporting radical sharing, positive communication, compassion, consent culture, sustainability, and anti-oppression activism. Living free of hierarchy and coercion" (acorn.org).

Description: A farming homestead surrounded by fields and gardens.

Baltimore Free Farm/Horizontal Housing, Baltimore, Maryland—Established 2010

Focus: "An egalitarian collective of gardeners and activists who aim to provide access to healthy food for all" (http://www.baltimorefreefarm.org/).

Description: A "leafy utopia" of reinhabited buildings and urban farms in vacant lots in the Hampden section of Baltimore.

Belfast Cohousing and Ecovillage, Belfast, Maine—Established 2007

Focus: "A model environmentally sustainable, affordable, multi-generational cohousing community that is easily accessible to Belfast, includes land reserved for agricultural use and open space, and is an innovative housing option for rural Maine" (mainecohousing.org).

Description: Duplexes and triplexes built on a well-loved fourth-generation dairy farm on the rolling hills near Penobscot Bay.

Cherith Brook Catholic Worker, Kansas City, Missouri—Established 2007

Focus: A "residential Christian community practicing the works of mercy as found in Jesus' teachings and a 'school' for peacemaking in all its dimensions: political, communal, and personal, working constantly to undo poverty, racism and militarism" (http://cherithbrookcw.blogspot.com/).

Description: Victorian home and storefront with gardens and chickens in an impoverished urban neighborhood.

Cobb Hill Cohousing, Hartland, Vermont— Established 1996

Focus: A cohousing "community of people who want to explore the challenge of living in ways that are materially sufficient, socially and ecologically responsible, and satisfying to the soul" (cobbhill.org).

Description: 260 acres of farm and forest including a common building and multiple homes perched above a working farm, a farm store, and agricultural enterprises.

Dancing Rabbit Ecovillage, Rutledge, Missouri— Established 1993

Focus: "An ecovillage dedicated to radical environmental sustainability, flexible enough to include egalitarian and co-housing communities, and individual households" (www.dancingrabbit.org).

Description: Resident-constructed buildings, including gnome-domes, repurposed grain bins, and straw-bale houses laid out amid rolling prairie.

Daybreak Cohousing, Portland, Oregon— Established 2005

Focus: "Individuals, couples, and families of varied backgrounds and ages—from one-year old to 70 plus—who live in a community where we know each other like extended family, while honoring our personal needs for privacy and independence" (http://www.daybreakcohousing.org/CommunityVision.html).

Description: A dense urban village with individual homes and shared facilities designed to encourage social interaction.

Findhorn Foundation, Findhorn, Scotland— Established 1962

Focus: "The Findhorn Foundation community is an experiment in conscious living, a learning centre and an ecovillage" (findhorn.org).

Description: A large ecovillage in rural northern Scotland.

Gainesville Catholic Worker, Gainesville, Florida— Established 2000; reestablished as Open Table Intentional Community in 2015; now closed

Focus: "We strive to live as an intentional, faith-based community committed to a life of prayer, scripture study and culture critique; to stand in solidarity with those who are impoverished; to live simply and engage in an alternative economy rooted in biblical principles; to resist the violence and injustice of our culture through public witness and protest; to offer space for alternative discipleship formation and deeper theological reflection" (gainesvillecw.org).

Description: A homey bungalow in downtown Gainesville.

Land Co-op, Miccosukee, Florida—Established 1972

Focus: "Living in a rural area where the land and environment are respected and interaction between neighbors is a sought-after experience" (http://www.ic.org/directory/miccosukee-land-co-op/).

Description: One hundred families and individuals who cooperatively own 344 acres east of Tallahassee.

Los Angeles Eco-village or LA Eco-village, Los Angeles, California—Established 1985

Focus: "Reinventing how we live in the city by reducing environmental impacts while raising the quality of neighborhood life and demonstrating sustainable community development" (laecovillage.org).

Description: A two-block, eleven-acre community of apartments and gardens in LA's Koreatown.

Lost Valley Education and Event Center, Dexter, Oregon—Established 1988

Focus: "A center for the practical application of sustainable living skills" (http://lostvalley.org/).

Description: An educational center and ecovillage (Meadowsong) on eighty-eight acres in rural Oregon.

Mustard Seed Community Farm, Ames, Iowa—Established 2008

Focus: "A collective group of farmers and gardeners inspired by the examples of The Catholic worker, Gandhi, Buddhist teachings, Fukuoka and many others. They are committed to service, to their workers, to the land, and to the hungry" (mustardseedfarm.org).

Description: A small Catholic worker farm (eleven acres) in agricultural central Iowa.

New Hope Catholic Worker Farm and Agronomic University, LaMotte, Iowa—Established 2001

Focus: Living the intellectual and agrarian dimensions of the Catholic Worker Movement as a community.

Description: Four families farming and living on twenty-eight acres in a river valley near Dubuque.

Pioneer Valley Cohousing, Amherst, Massachusetts— Established 1989

Focus: "A living environment that encourages a strong sense of community, supports our need for privacy, makes life affordable, and provides a secure and enriched setting for children and adults" (http://www.cohousing.com/).

Description: A common house and individual homes ring a common green, surrounded by gardens and fields.

Possibility Alliance, La Plata, Missouri— Established 2007

Focus: "Living so that all life can thrive with practices valuable to our well-being and to the planet's well-being: radical simplicity, service, social activism, inner work and gratitude" (Possibility Alliance Mission Statement).

Description: Fossil-free, electricity-free community housed in an eighty-acre Mennonite homestead with fields and forest in rural northeast Missouri.

Red Earth Farms, Rutledge, Missouri—Established 2005

Focus: A "homesteading community aiming to creatively explore and evaluate sustainable ways to meet our needs in accordance with our guiding principle: 'Love the land; love your neighbors'" (Redearthfarms.org).

Description: Individual homesteads nestled in seventy-six acres of rolling prairie.

Sandhill Farm, Rutledge, Missouri—Established 1973

Focus: "Income-sharing farming community, striving for simple and healthy lifestyles; creativity, ecological sustainability, nonviolence, personal freedom, honest communication, consensus decision-making and emotional support" (sandhillfarm.org).

Description: Farm buildings, outhouses, and homes on 135 acres of Missouri prairie.

Sirius Community, Shutesbury, Massachusetts—Established 1978

Focus: "A non-profit educational organization offering sustainable living for the public, and spiritual community demonstrating attunement to nature and ecologically based lifestyles" (http://www.siriuscommunity.org/)

Description: Community buildings, gardens, and residences integrated into a woodland landscape; includes retreat building, labyrinth, and meditation rooms.

Twin Oaks Community, Louisa, Virginia—Established 1967

Focus: "A self-supporting income-sharing community based on values of cooperation, sharing, nonviolence, equality, and ecology" (twinoakscommunity.org).

Description: Community buildings, gardens, and streams nestled in the hills of rural Virginia.

Two Echo Cohousing, Brunswick, Maine—Established 1991

Focus: "A safe and friendly neighborhood, surrounded by woods and fields, where residents exchange recipes, children run and play without fear of cars, and friends of all ages stop to chat in the road" (two-echo.org).

Description: A common house and individual homes linked by walking paths surrounded by gardens and fields in rural Maine.

Appendix B
Resources

Catholic Worker Communities Directory (http://www.catholicworker.org/communities/commlistall.cfm)

Database of Catholic worker communities.

Cohousing Association (cohousing.org)

Database of cohousing communities; resources for existing communities and those in the process of formation. Holds a biannual conference whose location switches back and forth between the coasts.

Creative Commons (http://us.creativecommons.org/)

"Creative Commons develops, supports, and stewards legal and technical infrastructure that maximizes digital creativity, sharing, and innovation."

FEC: Federation of Egalitarian Communities (thefec.org/)

Database of egalitarian communities; resources for existing communities and those in the process of formation.

FIC: Federation of Intentional Community (ic.org)

Database of intentional communities; resources for existing communities and those in the process of formation; includes extensive wiki of related topics. Holds annual Art of Community Conference in Twin Oaks, Louisa, Virginia.

The Freecycle Network (freecycle.org)

Database of freecycling groups in the United States

GEN: Global Ecovillage Network (gen.ecovillage.org)

Database of global ecovillages; resources for existing communities and those in the process of formation.

Global Footprint Network (http://www.footprintnetwork.org/en/index.php/GFN/)

Tool for evaluating your global footprint.

Humanure Headquarters (humanurehandbook.com)

Articles, books, and resources on composting human waste.

Local Harvest (localharvest.org)

Database of family farms, CSAs, and local products.

NASCO: North American Students of Cooperation (nasco.coop)

Resources for and database of student co-ops.

National Complete Streets Coalition (http://www.smartgrowthamerica.org/complete-streets)

"A nationwide movement launched by the National Complete Streets Coalition in 2004, Complete Streets integrates people and place in the planning, design, construction, operation, and maintenance of our transportation networks."

New Economy Coalition (http://neweconomy.net/)

Organization that coordinates efforts among different groups working for economic change; lists over one hundred associations; developed from E. F. Schumacher Society.

NVC: Nonviolent Communications (cnvc.org)

Communication process developed by Marshall Rosenberg, based on compassionate listening.

Open Source Ecology (http://opensourceecology.org/)

"We're developing open source industrial machines that can be made for a fraction of commercial costs, and sharing our designs online for free. The goal of Open Source Ecology is to create an open source economy—an efficient economy which increases innovation by open collaboration."

Permaculture Principles (permacultureprinciples.com)

Books, articles, and links regarding the ethics and practices of permaculture, a form of ecological design that integrates biological and ethical principles.

"Piedmont Solidarity Economy Map: Mapping Our Local Values-Based Economy" (Solidaritypiedmont.org)

Maps local projects to build regional capacities.

Pocket Neighborhoods (pocket-neighborhoods.net)

Describes and answers frequently asked questions about pocket neighborhoods.

Restorative Justice (http://www.restorativejustice.org/)

Provides a history of and resources for restorative justice.

Schumacher Center for a New Economics (http://www.centerforneweconomics.org)

"To educate the public about an economics that supports both people and the planet. We believe that a fair and sustainable economy is possible and that citizens working for the common interest can build systems to achieve it. We recognize that the environmental and equity crises we now face have their roots in the current economic system."

Seed Savers Exchange (http://www.seedsavers.org/)

A nonprofit organization dedicated to saving and sharing heirloom seeds.

Smart Growth/National Complete Streets Coalition (smartgrowthamerica.org)

Rethinks neighborhood development based on bicycle and pedestrian access to public spaces.

Sociocracy (http://thesociocracygroup.com/)

Explains the governance system of sociocracy, and how sociocracy offers transparency, inclusiveness, and accountability.
SolidarityNYC (Solidaritynyc.org)
   Maps local projects to build regional capacities.

Transition United States (transitions.org)

Resources for towns and regions considering transition to a fossil-free future.

Valhalla Movement (valhallamovement.com)

Articles and stories about individuals and communities focused on self-reliance, collaboration, and sustainability.

Women for Living in Community, Aging in Community (womenlivingincommunity.com)

Resources focused on women, community, and aging.

Appendix C
How to . . .

Clay Plaster

http://www.dancingrabbit.org/about-dancing-rabbit-ecovillage/eco-living/building/natural-building/earthen-plaster/

Build a Cob Oven

http://buildnaturally.blogspot.com/2013/06/build-clay-cob-oven-in-your-yard.html

Build a Rocket Stove

http://www.motherearthnews.com/diy/how-to-build-a-rocket-stove-zb0z1311zmar.aspx

Notes

Introduction

1. "Intentional Communities—Ecovillages, Communes, Cohousing, Coops."
2. Miller, "A Matter of Definition," 7–8.
3. Ziggy, "Four Missouri Communities Demonstrate Sustainability."
4. "America's Urban Population."
5. Arkin, "Diversity Issues in Los Angeles Eco-village."
6. "Guiding Principles: The Wheel of Integral Nonviolence."
7. Global Ecovillage Network, "What Is an Ecovillage?"
8. "Dancing Rabbit Ecovillage: Building Sustainable Community."
9. Benfield, "LA's Eco-village"; "CRSP: Los Angeles Eco-village."
10. "CRSP: Los Angeles Eco-village."
11. "The Works of Mercy." See McKanan, *The Catholic Worker after Dorothy* for information about the Catholic Worker Movement, past and present.
12. Day, "Peter Maurin."
13. "What Is Cohousing?"
14. "Available Homes."

1. Examining Change

1. Feuer, "The Preppers Next Door."
2. Solnit, *A Paradise Built in Hell*, 196–97.
3. Easterly, *The White Man's Burden*.
4. Feuer, "The Doomsday Preppers Next Door."
5. Abrahms, "Sharing Home Sweet Home," 16–18.
6. Beck, "Glenn Unveils His Most Ambitious and Visionary Dream."
7. "Arun Gandhi"; "Be the Change with Arun Gandhi, Grandson of Mahatma Gandhi"; B'Hahn, "Be the Change You Wish to See."
8. Scheer and Moss, "Bottle Bills."
9. Bellah, *Habits of the Heart*, 244–45, 246, 237.
10. Putnam, *Bowling Alone*.
11. Morton, "Falser Words Were Never Spoken."
12. Shute, "When Older People Walk Now"; Leinberger, "Now Coveted."
13. Murphy, "Farm-to-Table Living."
14. DuPuis and Goodman, "Should We Go 'Home' to Eat?" 360–61.

15. Lockyer, "Intentional Communities and Sustainability," 20.
16. Mawdsley, "Hindu Nationalism"; Nanda, *Prophets Facing Backward*.
17. Berry, "Why I Am Not Going to Buy a Computer."
18. Kennedy, "Vernon Hershberger Trial Verdict."
19. Peterson, *Seeds of the Kingdom*.
20. Leach, "Greening Your 'Hood."
21. Morris, "Local Galleries on the Rise in Gainesville."
22. Cano, "Porters Community Farm."
23. "Blue Oven Kitchens."
24. "Welcome to the Civic Media Center."
25. "About the Farm."
26. "'Right Livelihood Award.'"
27. Shin, "Spotlight."
28. "Cecil Scheib"; Ewald, "Did DR Help NYU Cut Energy Use 30%?"; Shin, "Spotlight"; Tregaskis, "The Green Apple."
29. "Micanopy Community Garden Gets Underway."
30. Byrnes and Collins, "Rocky Times Ahead"; "Resilience Circles."
31. Collins, "Neighbors for a New Economy."
32. "What Is the Tiny House Movement?"
33. Chapin and Susanka, *Pocket Neighborhoods*, 8–13.
34. "Pocket Neighborhoods."
35. Schneider and England, "What Are the Boundaries of an Intentional Community?"

2. Standing on the Shoulders of Giants

1. Miller, *The 60s Communes*, 7.
2. Flagg, "It Takes a Village."
3. http://ww.ic.org/wiki/cults-intentional-communities/.
4. Hollenbach, *Lost and Found*, ix.
5. Christian, *Finding Community*, 14–15.
6. http://www.ic.org/wiki/cults-intentional-communities/.
7. Paulson, *An Unconventional Journey*; Kashia, "Pioneers for the Planet."
8. Stock, "The Perennial Nature of Catholic Worker Farms," 163.
9. Drew, "The Commune as Badlands," 52.
10. Doyle, "Conviviality and Perspicacity," 24; Drew, "The Commune as Badlands," 52.
11. Bates, "From Intentional Community to Ecovillage."
12. Fike, *Voices from the Farm*, 54.
13. Bates, "From Intentional Community to Ecovillage."
14. Gould, *At Home in Nature*, 198–99.
15. Letter to Possibility Alliance from White Rose Catholic Worker House in Chicago, 2014.

16. Mortimer-Sandilands, *The Good-Natured Feminist*, 202.

3. Choosing a Life

1. Melnick, "Generation Now!"
2. Aguilar, "Food Choices and Voluntary Simplicity," 85.
3. Arkin, "Diversity Issues in Los Angeles Eco-village."
4. http://curs.unc.edu/2015/03/19/friday-march-27th-perspectives-on-cohousing-and-ecovillages-building-diversity-in-intentional-communities/.
5. Eaves, "Ecotopia"; Lerner, "Home but Not Alone"; "Communities by Country."
6. Christian, *Finding Community*, 109–12.
7. Ibid., 193.
8. Ibid., 155–57.
9. "How to Become a Resident and Member of Dancing Rabbit."
10. Ibid.
11. Flagg, "It Takes a Village."
12. Mason, *The View from #410*, 177.
13. Day, "Room for Christ."
14. Abrahms, "Sharing Home Sweet Home."
15. Ibid.
16. Golant, *Aging in the Right Place*.
17. Mason, *The View from #410*, 173–74.
18. "Frequently Asked Questions about Cohousing."
19. Rovner, "Boomer Housemates Have More Fun."
20. Bhakta, "Accessibility in Sustainable Communities."
21. "Twin Oaks Intentional Community—Visitor Program."
22. Schaub, "The Intergenerational Challenge."
23. Korkki, "In Retiree Housing."
24. "Generations of Hope."

4. Creating Cultures

1. "The Valhalla Mission."
2. Ibid.
3. "Possibility Alliance Mission Statement and Guiding Principles."
4. Wink and Fellowship of Reconciliation, *Peace Is the Way*, 79.
5. Sanford, "Gandhi's Agrarian Legacy," 70.
6. Gandhi, *Village Swaraj*, 43.
7. Day, "The Long Loneliness."
8. Anglada, "Growing Roots."
9. Day, "'Peter's Program.'"
10. Killinger, *The Good Life of Helen K. Nearing*, 49.

11. Alexis-Baker, "Jesus Radicals."
12. USDA, "Agricultural Marketing Service."
13. Moss, "The Extraordinary Science of Addictive Junk Food."
14. Nestle, *Food Politics*.
15. Rampell, "Outsource Your Way to Success."
16. Sollisch, "I Want to Be a Millennial When I Retire."
17. Gould, *At Home in Nature*, 217.
18. Anglada, "Growing Roots."
19. Ibid.
20. McKanan, *The Catholic Worker after Dorothy*.

5. Asking What's for Dinner

1. The National Chicken Council deems eight-tenths of a square foot an appropriate size enclosure for an adult chicken. Factory-farmed chickens raised as broilers live in these crates until slaughtered. Writer Jonathan Safran Foer describes factory farming and asks if we should even eat animals, examining the question in the context of both contemporary American culture and his own Jewish heritage. *Eating Animals*, 129–30.

2. Daniel Jaffee's *Brewing Justice* describes the fair trade process and argues that fair trade, as currently constructed, is not really fair to farmers and growers.

3. Peterson, *Seeds of the Kingdom*, 119.
4. "Guiding Principles: The Wheel of Integral Nonviolence."
5. Jaffee, *Brewing Justice*, 11, 19.
6. McGinnis, *Bioregionalism*; Parajuli, "Revisiting Gandhi and Zapata."
7. "Cherith Brook Catholic Worker."
8. Tammeus, "Presbyterian-Run Catholic Worker House."
9. Day, "Peter Maurin."
10. "Food Theology."
11. Bose, *Studies in Gandhism*, 15, 27.
12. Taylor, *Green Sisters*, 210–30.
13. In *The Death of Ramón González*, Angus Wright uses a peasant's death to illustrate the link between pesticides and unfair labor practices.
14. "Cherith Brook Catholic Worker."
15. Anderson, "Livin' the Good Life."
16. Ibid.
17. "Critter Internships."
18. Mason, *The View from #410*, 106, 109, 107.

6. Sustainability in Community

1. Gandhi, *Village Swaraj*, 3.

2. Chernus, *American Nonviolence*, 3, 6.
3. Weber, "Gandhi."
4. Guha, *How Much Should a Person Consume?*; Guha and Martínez-Alier, *Varieties of Environmentalism*.
5. Kothari, Parajuli, and Sachs, *No Nature without Social Justice*.
6. Sanford, *Growing Stories*, 218–19.
7. United Nations, *Our Common Future*.
8. Lotherington, "The Lure of Benign Dictatorship."
9. "[Announce] Fw: Gandhi and Integral Nonviolence."
10. Moore-Backman, "Walking with Gandhi," 3.
11. Ibid., 95–96.
12. *Urban Dictionary*, s.v. "Slacktivism."
13. The 1997 documentary *Doing Time, Doing Vipassana* explains the practice and is available on YouTube (https://www.youtube.com/watch?v=WkxSyv5R1sg).
14. Gottlieb, *A Greener Faith*, 238–39.
15. Fox, *Gandhian Utopia*, 6.
16. Ewald, "Hugelkultur on the Prairie."
17. Albright, "And I Listen."
18. Putnam, *Bowling Alone*.
19. Turkle, *Alone Together*.
20. Oppenheimer, "The Not So-Lonely City."
21. Ibid.
22. Sandilands, "Lesbian Separatist Communities," 138–39.
23. "Queer in Community."
24. "Feminism, Empowerment and Justice."
25. Dalton, *Gandhi's Power*, 198.
26. Calta, "Who Decides?"
27. Mortimer-Sandilands, *The Good-Natured Feminist*, 202.
28. "Governance."
29. Rosenberg, *Nonviolent Communication*.
30. Juergensmeyer, *Gandhi's Way*, 4.
31. Calta, "Who Decides?"
32. Christian, "Busting the Myth"; Christian, "Why Earthaven Ecovillage, U.S.A, Changed Its Decision-Making Method."
33. Kashia, "Pioneers for the Planet."
34. O'Connell, "Living the Questions."
35. Litfin, *Ecovillages*, 189–90.

7. Rethinking Abundance

1. "What Is the Tiny House Movement?"
2. Day, "On Pilgrimage."

3. "The Freecycle Network."
4. Byrnes, "The Problem with the Simple Living Movement."
5. Cohen, *A Consumer's Republic*.
6. Shrader-Frechette, "Ethics and the Environment," 316.
7. Fox, *Gandhian Utopia*, 6.
8. Gould, *At Home in Nature*.
9. See Savage, *The Plain Reader*.
10. "Passive Solar Home Design"; "Reducing Energy Use."
11. Altieri, *Agroecology*. See also Altieri, "Agroecology, Small Farms, and Food Sovereignty."
12. Badgley et al., "Organic Agriculture and the Global Food Supply."
13. Bittman, "How to Feed the World."
14. Haspel, "Farm Bill." Daniel Imhoff's *Food Fight* explains where the farm bill subsidies actually go.
15. "Humanure Composting Basics."
16. Lyson's *Civic Agriculture* describes the transition from regional to globalized food economies.
17. Off, *Bitter Chocolate*.
18. "Straw Bale House Construction."
19. Kirschenmann, "Anticipating the Future." See also Neff et al., "Peak Oil."
20. Kirschenmann, "Leopold's Ongoing Dilemma."
21. Newton and Freyfogle, "Sustainability."
22. Gottlieb and Joshi, *Food Justice*, 184–85.
23. Friedman, *Hot, Flat, and Crowded*.

8. Extreme DIY for Interdependence

1. The Cohousing website lists a number of books and resources. See http://www.cohousing.org/store.
2. "New Economy Coalition."
3. "SolidarityNYC"; "Piedmont Solidarity Economy Map."
4. "Open Source Ecology."
5. Charles, "Plant Breeders Release First 'Open Source Seeds.'"
6. Schumacher, *Small Is Beautiful*.
7. Gandhi, *Village Swaraj*, 26–27.
8. "Clay Plaster How To" on Dancing Rabbit's website describes how to use earth plaster.
9. See "Local Currencies" for legal and other resources about local currencies and time banks as well as a directory of local currencies in the United States.
10. Collins, "Neighbors for a New Economy."
11. Byrnes and Collins, "Rocky Times Ahead"; "Resilience Circles."
12. "Bicycle Kitchen"; LA Eco-village Food Coop Wiki Page."
13. "Sandhill Farm: Sorghum Season."

14. Raver, "Farm Equipment That Runs on Oats."
15. Leslie, *The New Horse-Powered Farm,* xvi.
16. Raver, "Farm Equipment That Runs on Oats."
17. Rabbit, "10 Reasons Why EarthShips Are F!#%ing Awesome."
18. "Pete McAvoy Replaces Fossil Fuels with Cooking Oil."
19. Hardin, "The Tragedy of the Commons."
20. "Natural Building Materials."
21. Kennedy, "An Overview of Natural Building Techniques."
22. Eberlein, "10 Ideas for Building Community Resilience"; Liloia, *The Year of Mud.*
23. Solomon, "Interview."
24. Griswold, "Strawtron Archives."
25. "Wex Position."
26. Jones, "Toward Sustainable Community."
27. Nik, "A Traveler Returns." See also Sirna, "Cutting Our Carbon Footprint."
28. Anderson, "Ten Year Snapshot."
29. Franey, "Composting Toilets," 7.
30. *Regulatory Provisions.*
31. Peterson, "Recycling Greywater."
32. "Bella Ciao."
33. Pickerill, "Who Builds the Houses?"
34. Makita, "Sexism at Dancing Rabbit."
35. Pickerill, "Who Builds the Houses?"
36. Makita, "Sexism at Dancing Rabbit."
37. Brown, "At This Workshop, They Teach 'Skills of Resilience.'"
38. Warren, "Aspiring to the Working Class."

9. Bringing It Home

1. Miller, *The 60's Communes,* xiv, citing Goodman and Goodman, *Communitas,* 109.
2. Nordahl, *Public Produce.*
3. "National Complete Streets Coalition."
4. Leach, "Greening Your 'Hood."
5. Abrahms, "Share Common Ground."
6. Durrett, "Achieving Affordability with Cohousing."
7. "Safe Routes to School."
8. Guthman, "Bringing Good Food to Others."
9. Younge, "The Unbearable Whiteness of the American Left."
10. Roman-Alcala, "In Search of Good Food."
11. Danielle, "A Place for Us."
12. Bowens, "CSA Is Rooted in Black History."

13. Penniman, "Radical Farmers Use Fresh Food"; "Soul Fire Farm."
14. Winne, "The Color of Food Leadership."
15. "Modern Intentional Organic Hipster Activist Farmer Homesteader."
16. LaVecchia, "These Neighbors Got Together."
17. Brunwasser, "*NY Times* Editorial: The Koch Attack on Solar Energy"; Eskew, "The Koch Brothers' Extra Baggage."
18. Poole, "Solar Panel Users as Freeloaders."
19. Solis, "Cape Woman Living 'off the Grid' Challenged by City."
20. Ortiz, "Pot Bust Turns Up Empty"; St. Amant, "Months After Failed Drug Raid."
21. Gurley, "Dorothy Rabinowitz Lets Loose."
22. Ibid.
23. Murphy, "Farm-to-Table Living Takes Root."
24. Corley, "Across the U.S., Bicycle Commuting Picks Up Speed."
25. http://www.rockefellerfoundation.org/newsroom/access-public-transportation-top.
26. Carspecken, *An Unreal Estate,* 215, 218.

Bibliography

"About the Farm." *Thefarmcommunity.com.* Accessed April 7, 2015. http://www.thefarmcommunity.com/.

Abrahms, Sally. "Share Common Ground." *AARP Bulletin,* May 2012. http://www.aarp.org/home-family/livable-communities/info-05-2012/pocket-neighborhoods-common-ground.html.

———. "Sharing Home Sweet Home." *AARP Bulletin/Real Possibilities,* June 2013. http://pubs.aarp.org/aarpbulletin/201306_DC?folio=16#article_id=301022.

"Access to Public Transportation a Top Criterion for Millennials When Deciding Where to Live, New Survey Shows." *Rockefellerfoundation.org,* 2015. http://www.rockefellerfoundation.org/about-us/news-media/access-public-transportation-top/.

Aguilar, Jade. "Food Choices and Voluntary Simplicity in Intentional Communities: What's Race and Class Got to Do with It?" *Utopian Studies* 26, no. 1 (2015): 79–100.

Albright, Victoria. "And I Listen." *Communities Magazine* 149 (Winter 2010). http://www.ic.org/and-i-listen/.

Alexis-Baker, Nekeisha. "Jesus Radicals, Reflections from a Co-founder." *Geez,* November 12, 2015. http://www.geezmagazine.org/magazine/article/jesus-radicals-reflection-from-a-co-founder/.

Altieri, M. A. "Agroecology, Small Farms, and Food Sovereignty." *Monthly Review* 61, no. 3 (2009): 102–13.

———. *Agroecology: The Science of Sustainable Agriculture.* Boulder: Westview, 1995.

"America's Urban Population." *Proximityone.com.* Accessed March 19, 2015. http://proximityone.com/urbanpopulation.htm.

Anderson, Alline. "Livin' the Good Life at Dancing Rabbit Ecovillage—Food Coops." *Ecovillagemusings.Blogspot.It,* November 8, 2013. http://ecovillagemusings.blogspot.it/2013/11/livin-good-life-at-dancing-rabbit.html.

———. "Ten Year Snapshot: A Visitor's Eye View of Dancing Rabbit Ecovillage." *Marchhareblog.com,* October 16 2012. http://www.marchhareblog.com/2012/10/16/ten-year-snapshot-a-visitors-eye-view-of-dancing-rabbit-ecovillage/.

Anglada, Eric. "Growing Roots: Peter Maurin and the Agronomic University." *Cjd.org,* April 1, 2011. http://cjd.org/2011/04/01/growing-roots-peter-maurin-and-the-agronomic-university/.

"[Announce] Fw: Gandhi and Integral Nonviolence—March 15–17th @ New

Hope CW Farm." *Shire.Symonds.Net.* Accessed June 15, 2014. http://shire.symonds.net/pipermail/announce/2011-February/000619.html.

Arkin, Lois. "Diversity Issues in Los Angeles Eco-village." *Communities Magazine*, June 7, 2012. http://www.ic.org/diversity-issues-in-los-angeles-eco-village/.

"Arun Gandhi." *Arungandhi.org.* Accessed March 20, 2013. http://arungandhi.org/.

"Available Homes." *Mainecohousing.org.* Accessed March 19, 2015. http://www.mainecohousing.org/homes/homes.html.

Badgley, Catherine, Jeremy Moghtader, Eileen Quintero, Emily Zakem, M. Jahi Chappell, Katia Aviles-Vazquez, Andrea Samulon, and Ivette Perfecto. "Organic Agriculture and the Global Food Supply." *Renewable Agriculture and Food Systems* 22, no. 2 (2007): 86–108. doi:10.1017/S1742170507001640.

Bates, Albert. "From Intentional Community to Ecovillage: The Farm in the Nineties." Paper presented at the International Communal Studies Association Annual Meeting, Yad Tabenkin, Ramat Efal, Israel, June 1, 1995. http://www.thefarm.org/lifestyle/albertbates/akbp4.html.

Beck, Glenn. "Glenn Unveils His Most Ambitious and Visionary Dream: Independence," January 10, 2013. http://www.glennbeck.com/2013/01/10/take-a-tour-of-glenns-visionary-plans-for-independence/.

"Bella Ciao." *Dancingrabbit.org.* Accessed April 7, 2015. http://www.dancingrabbit.org/about-dancing-rabbit-ecovillage/eco-living/building/natural-building/bella-ciao/.

Bellah, Robert Neelly. *Habits of the Heart: Individualism and Commitment in American Life.* Berkeley: University of California Press, 2008.

Benfield, Kaid. "LA's Eco-village: A Venture in Intentional Community and Sustainability." *Switchboard.Nrdc.org*, April 27, 2010. http://switchboard.nrdc.org/blogs/kbenfield/las_ecovillage_a_venture_in_in.html.

Berry, Wendell. "Why I Am Not Going to Buy a Computer." In *What Are People For?* 170–78. Berkeley, CA: Counterpoint, 1990.

"Be the Change with Arun Gandhi, Grandson of Mahatma Gandhi." *Ww2.Blogtalkradio.com*, November 23, 2010. http://ww2.blogtalkradio.com/mondaynightradio/2010/11/23/how-to-be-the-change-and-promote-nonviolence-with.

B'Hahn, Carmella. "Be the Change You Wish to See: an Interview with Arun Gandhi." *Reclaiming Children and Youth* 10, no. 1 (2001): 6–9.

Bhakta, Amita. "Accessibility in Sustainable Communities: Inclusive Eco-Living for Disabled People?" *Naturalbuild.Wordpress.com*, March 14, 2014. http://naturalbuild.wordpress.com/.

"Bicycle Kitchen • Los Angeles." *Bicyclekitchen.com.* Accessed March 19, 2015. http://www.bicyclekitchen.com/index.php?/about-this-site/;%20%20http://urbansoil.net/wiki.cgi/LA Eco-Village_Food_Coop.

Bittman, Mark. "How to Feed the World." *New York Times*, October 14, 2013. http://www.nytimes.com/2013/10/15/opinion/how-to-feed-the-world.html.

"Blue Oven Kitchens: Cultivating Food Entrepreneurs, Growing the Local Food Economy." *Blueovenkitchens.org.* Accessed April 7, 2015. http://www.blueovenkitchens.org/.

Bose, N. K. *Studies in Gandhism.* Ahmedabad: Navajivan, 1972.

Bowens, Natasha. "CSA Is Rooted in Black History." *Mother Earth News,* February 13, 2015. http://www.motherearthnews.com/organic-gardening/csas-rooted-in-black-history-zbcz1502.aspx.

Brown, Hannah O. "At This Workshop, They Teach 'Skills of Resilience.'" *Gainesville Sun,* December 11, 2014. http://www.gainesville.com/article/20141211/ARTICLES/141219905?fb_action_ids=10152993360919744&fb_action_types=og.comment.

Brunwasser, Jan. "NY Times Editorial: The Koch Attack on Solar Energy." *Opednews.com,* April 27, 2014. http://www.opednews.com/Quicklink/NY-TImes-Editorial-The-Ko-in-Best_Web_OpEds-Energy_Energy-Biomass_Energy-Coal_Energy-Alternative-Non-Fossil-Fuel-140427–402.html.

Bush, Karen M., Louise S. Machinist, and Jean McQuillin. *My House, Our House: Living Far Better for Far Less in a Cooperative Household.* Pittsburgh: St. Lynn's, 2013.

Byrnes, Ron. "The Problem with the Simple Living Movement." *Pressingpause.com,* March 11, 2013. http://pressingpause.com/2013/03/11/the-problem-with-the-simple-living-movement/.

Byrnes, Sarah, and Chuck Collins. "Rocky Times Ahead: Are You Ready?" *Yes! Magazine,* January 20, 2011. http://www.yesmagazine.org/people-power/rocky-times-ahead-are-you-ready.

Calta, Paxus. "Who Decides? Three Communes Models." *Funologist.org,* January 27, 2014. http://funologist.org/2014/01/.

Cano, Chris. "Porters Community Farm: Help Fund an Inspiring Urban Farm in Downtown Gainesville." *Gainesvillecompost.com,* September 14, 2012. http://gainesvillecompost.com/news/porters-community-farm/.

Carspecken, Lucinda. *An Unreal Estate: Sustainability and Freedom in an Evolving Community.* Bloomington: Indiana University Press, 2012.

"Cecil Scheib: Dancing Rabbit Member Bio." *Dancingrabbit.org.* Accessed February 4, 2015. http://www.dancingrabbit.org/about-dancing-rabbit-ecovillage/member-bios/cecil-scheib/#sthash.6PUsnGxd.dpuf.

Chapin, Ross, and Sarah Susanka. *Pocket Neighborhoods: Creating Small-Scale Community in a Large-Scale World.* Newton, CT: Taunton, 2011.

Charles, Dan. "Plant Breeders Release First 'Open Source Seeds.'" *Npr.org,* April 17, 2014. http://www.npr.org/blogs/thesalt/2014/04/17/303772556/plant-breeders-release-first-open-source-seeds?sc=17&f=1001.

"Cherith Brook Catholic Worker." *Cherithbrookcw.Blogspot.com.* Accessed March 21, 2015. http://cherithbrookcw.blogspot.com/.

Chernus, Ira. *American Nonviolence: The History of an Idea.* Maryknoll, NY: Orbis Books, 2004.

Christian, Diana Leafe. "Busting the Myth That Consensus-with-Unanimity Is Good for Communities, Part I—Ecovillages." *Ecovillagenewsletter.org*, December 2012. http://www.ecovillagenewsletter.org/wiki/index.php/Busting_the_Myth_that_Consensus-with-Unanimity_is_Good_for_Communities,_Part_I.

———. *Creating Life Together: Practical Tools to Grow Ecovillages and Intentional Communities.* Gabriola Island, BC: New Society, 2003.

———. *Finding Community: How to Join an Ecovillage or Intentional Community.* Gabriola Island, BC: New Society, 2007.

———. "Why Earthaven Ecovillage, U.S.A, Changed Its Decision-Making Method." *Gen.Ecovillage.org*, April 30, 2013. http://gen-europe.org/activities/news/news-detail/artikel/why-earthaven-ecovillage-usa-changed-its-decision-making-method/index.htm.

"Clay Plaster How To." *Dancingrabbit.org*. Accessed March 31, 2015. http://www.dancingrabbit.org/about-dancing-rabbit-ecovillage/eco-living/building/natural-building/earthen-plaster/.

Cohen, Lizabeth. *A Consumer's Republic: The Politics of Mass Consumption in Postwar America.* New York: Vintage Books, 2013.

Collins, Chuck. "Neighbors for a New Economy." *Yes! Magazine,* May 5, 2010. http://www.yesmagazine.org/blogs/common-security-clubs/neighbors-for-a-new-economy.

"Communities by Country." *Ic.org*. Accessed August 17, 2013. http://www.ic.org/directory/intentional-communities-by-country/.

Corley, Cheryl. "Across the U.S., Bicycle Commuting Picks Up Speed." *Npr.org*, April 15, 2014. http://www.npr.org/2014/05/15/312486947/across-the-u-s-bicycle-commuting-picks-up-speed.

"Critter Internships." *Dancingrabbit.org.* Accessed March 31, 2015. http://www.dancingrabbit.org/visit-dancing-rabbit-ecovillage/work-exchange/critter-internships/.

"CRSP: Los Angeles Eco-village." *Laecovillage.org*. Accessed March 20, 2013. http://laecovillage.org/crsp/.

"Cults" and Intentional Communities. *Ic.org*. Accessed November 14, 2016. http://www.ic.org/wiki/cults-intentional-communities/.

Dalton, Dennis. *Gandhi's Power: Nonviolence in Action.* New York: Oxford University Press, 1998.

"Dancing Rabbit Ecovillage: Building Sustainable Community." *Dancingrabbit.org.* Accessed April 7, 2015. http://www.dancingrabbit.org/.

Danielle, Melissa. "A Place for Us: The Black Farmers and Urban Gardeners Conference." *Civileats.com,* December 2, 2010. http://civileats.com/2010/12/02/a-place-for-us-the-black-farmers-and-urban-gardeners-conference/.

Dawson, Jonathan. *Ecovillages: New Frontiers for Sustainability.* White River Junction, VT: Chelsea Green, 2006.

Day, Dorothy. "The Long Loneliness." *Catholic Worker,* February 1952, 3. http://www.catholicworker.org/dorothyday/daytext.cfm?TextID=628.

———. "On Pilgrimage—February 1959." *Catholic Worker,* February 1959, 2, 6. http://www.catholicworker.org/dorothyday/daytext.cfm?TextID=749.

———. "Peter Maurin, 1877–1977." *Catholic Worker,* May 1977, 1, 9. http://www.catholicworker.org/dorothyday/daytext.cfm?TextID=256.

———. "'Peter's Program.'" *Catholic Worker,* May 1955, 2. http://www.catholicworker.org/dorothyday/daytext.cfm?TextID=176.

———. "Room for Christ." *Catholic Worker,* December 1945, 2. http://www.catholicworker.org/dorothyday/daytext.cfm?TextID=416.

Doyle, Michael William. "Conviviality and Perspicacity: Evaluating 1960s Communitarianism." In *West of Eden,* edited by Iain Boal and Janferie Stone, 13–26, Oakland, CA: PM, 2012.

Drew, Jesse. "The Commune as Badlands and Utopia as Autonomous Zone." In *West of Eden,* edited by Iain Boal and Janferie Stone, 41–56, Oakland, CA: PM, 2012.

DuPuis, E. Melanie, and David Goodman. "Should We Go 'Home' to Eat? Toward a Reflexive Politics of Localism." *Journal of Rural Studies* 21, no. 3 (2005): 359–71.

Durrett, Chuck. "Achieving Affordability with Cohousing." *Ic.org,* March 7, 2013. http://www.ic.org/achieving-affordability-with-cohousing/.

———. *Senior Cohousing: A Community Approach to Independent Living—The Handbook.* Berkeley, CA: Habitat, 2005.

Easterly, William. *The White Man's Burden: Why the West's Efforts to Aid the Rest Have Done So Much Ill and So Little Good.* New York: Penguin Books, 2006.

Eaves, Elizabeth. "Ecotopia." *Forbes,* April 10, 2008. http://www.forbes.com/2008/04/10/enviromental-utopias-communities-oped-utopia08-cx_ee_0410ecotopia.html.

Eberlein, Sven. "10 Ideas for Building Community Resilience: A Hand-Built Home." *Yes! Magazine,* July 1, 2010. http://www.yesmagazine.org/issues/a-resilient-community/a-hand-built-home

Eskew, Carter. "The Koch Brothers' Extra Baggage." *Washington Post,* April 23, 2014. http://www.washingtonpost.com/blogs/post-partisan/wp/2014/04/23/the-koch-brothers-extra-baggage/.

Estill, Lyle. *Small Is Possible: Life in a Local Economy.* Gabriola Island, BC: New Society, 2008.

Ewald, Alyson. "Did DR Help NYU Cut Energy Use 30%?" *Dancingrabbit.org,* December 16, 2014. http://www.dancingrabbit.org/nyu/.

———. "Hugelkultur on the Prairie; or, Learning From Our Mistakes." *Communities Magazine,* December 7, 2011, 30–31.

"Feminism, Empowerment and Justice." *Dancingrabbit.org.* Accessed September 2, 2015. http://www.dancingrabbit.org/about-dancing-rabbit-ecovillage/social-change/dr-culture/feminism-empowerment-and-justice/.

Feuer, Alan. "The Preppers Next Door." *New York Times Magazine,* January 27, 2013. http://www.nytimes.com/2013/01/27/nyregion/the-doomsday-preppers-of-new-york.html?pagewanted=all&_r=0.

Fike, Rupert. *Voices from the Farm: Adventures in Community Living.* 2nd ed. Summertown, TN: Book Publishing Company, 2012.

Flagg, Katherine. "It Takes a Village." *Seven Days 7dvt.com,* September 19, 2012. http://www.7dvt.com/2012vermont-intentional-communities.

Foer, Jonathan Safran. *Eating Animals.* New York: Little, Brown, 2009.

"Food Theology." *Gainesvillecw.org.* Accessed March 21, 2015. http://gainesvillecw.org/food-theology/.

Fox, Richard Gabriel. *Gandhian Utopia: Experiments with Culture.* Boston: Beacon, 1989.

Franey, Tara. "Composting Toilets: Alleviating Regulatory Barriers to an Integrated Green Solution." Accessed February 14, 2014. vermontlaw.edu.

"Freecycle Network." *freecycle.org.* Accessed August 29, 2015. https://www.freecycle.org/.

"Frequently Asked Questions about Cohousing." *Harbourside.Ca.* Accessed March 20, 2015. http://www.harbourside.ca/pdf/Frequently%20Asked%20Questions.pdf.

Friedman, Thomas L. *Hot, Flat, and Crowded 2.0: Why We Need a Green Revolution—and How It Can Renew America.* New York: Macmillan, 2009.

Gandhi, Mohandas K. *Village Swaraj.* Edited by H. M. Vyas. Ahmedabad: Navajivan, 1962.

"Generations of Hope." *Generationsofhope.org.* Accessed January 1, 2015. http://www.generationsofhope.org/.

Global Ecovillage Network (GEN). "About Ecovillages." *Gen.Ecovillage.org,* 2014. http://gen.ecovillage.org/en/projects.

———, ed. "What Is an Ecovillage?" *Sites.Ecovillage.org.* Accessed March 30, 2015. http://sites.ecovillage.org/article/what-ecovillage.

Golant, Stephen M. *Aging in the Right Place.* Baltimore: Health Professions, 2015.

Goodman, Percival, and Paul Goodman. *Communitas: Means of Livelihood and Ways of Life.* New York: Columbia University Press, 1990.

Gottlieb, Robert, and Anupama Joshi. *Food Justice.* Cambridge, MA: MIT Press, 2010.

Gottlieb, Roger S. *A Greener Faith: Religious Environmentalism and Our Planet's Future.* Oxford: Oxford University Press, 2006.

Gould, Rebecca Kneale. *At Home in Nature: Modern Homesteading and Spiritual Practice in America.* Berkeley: University of California Press, 2005.

"Governance." *Dancingrabbit.org.* Accessed April 24, 2014. http://www.dancingrabbit.org/about-dancing-rabbit-ecovillage/social-change/function/governance/.

Green Survivalist. "Preparing to Survive: Dancing Rabbit Ecovillage." *Greensur-*

vivalist.Blogspot.com, August 19, 2012. http://greensurvivalist.blogspot.com/2012/08/dancing-rabbit-ecovillage.html.

Griswold, Kent. "Strawtron Archives." *Tinyhouseblog.com,* March 13, 2012. http://tinyhouseblog.com/tag/strawtron/.

Guha, Ramachandra. *How Much Should a Person Consume? Environmentalism in India and the United States.* Berkeley: University of California Press, 2006.

Guha, Ramachandra, and Juan Martínez-Alier. *Varieties of Environmentalism: Essays North and South.* New York: Routledge, 1998.

"Guiding Principles: The Wheel of Integral Nonviolence." *Chico-Peace.org.* Accessed March 31, 2015. http://chico-peace.org/whoweare.

Gurley, George. "Dorothy Rabinowitz Lets Loose." *Nymag.com,* June 27, 2013. http://nymag.com/daily/intelligencer/2013/06/dorothy-rabinowitz-lets-loose.html.

Guthman, Julie. "Bringing Good Food to Others: Investigating the Subjects of Alternative Food Practice." *Cultural Geographies* 15, no. 4 (2008): 431–47. doi:10.1177/1474474008094315.

Hardiman, David. *Gandhi in His Time and Ours: The Global Legacy of His Ideas.* New York: Columbia University Press, 2003.

Hardin, Garrett. "The Tragedy of the Commons." *Science* 162, no. 3859 (1968): 1243–48.

Haspel, Tamara. "Farm Bill: Why Don't Taxpayers Subsidize the Foods That Are Better for Us?" *Washington Post,* February 18, 2014. http://www.washingtonpost.com/lifestyle/food/farm-bill-why-dont-taxpayers-subsidize-the-foods-that-are-better-for-us/2014/02/14/d7642a3c-9434-11e3-84e1-27626c5ef5fb_story.html.

Hollenbach, Margaret. *Lost and Found: My Life in a Group Marriage Commune.* Albuquerque: University of New Mexico Press, 2004.

"How to Become a Resident and Member of Dancing Rabbit." *Dancingrabbit.org.* Accessed March 20, 2015. http://www.dancingrabbit.org/about-dancing-rabbit-ecovillage/residency-membership/.

"Humanure Composting Basics." *Humanurehandbook.com.* Accessed August 29, 2015. http://humanurehandbook.com/instructions.html.

Hyde, Lewis. *The Gift: Creativity and the Artist in the Modern World,* New York: Vintage, 2009.

Imhoff, Daniel. *Food Fight: The Citizen's Guide to the Next Food and Farm Bill.* Healdsburg, CA: Watershed Media, 2012.

"Intentional Communities—Ecovillages, Communes, Cohousing, Coops." *Ic.org.* Accessed March 18, 2013. http://www.ic.org/.

Jaffee, Daniel. *Brewing Justice: Fair Trade Coffee, Sustainability, and Survival.* Berkeley: University of California Press, 2007.

Jones, Kayla Brooke. "Toward Sustainable Community: Assessing Progress at Dancing Rabbit Ecovillage." ProQuest Dissertations, 2014.

Juergensmeyer, Mark. *Gandhi's Way: A Handbook of Conflict Resolution*. Berkeley: University of California Press, 2005.

Kashia, Miriam. "Pioneers for the Planet: The High Wind Story." *Blueplanetgreenliving.com*, September 16, 2011. http://www.blueplanetgreenliving.com/2011/09/16/high-wind/.

Kennedy, Joseph F. "An Overview of Natural Building Techniques." *Networkearth.org*. Accessed March 25, 2015. http://www.networkearth.org/naturalbuilding/overview.html.

Kennedy, Pete. "Vernon Hershberger Trial Verdict: Acquitted on Three of Four Charges." *Farmtoconsumer.org*, May 25, 2013. http://www.farmtoconsumer.org/news_wp/?p=9236.

Killinger, Margaret O. *The Good Life of Helen K. Nearing*. Burlington: University of Vermont Press, 2007.

Kinkade, Kat. *Is It Utopia Yet? An Insider's View of Twin Oaks Community in Its Twenty-Sixth Year*. Louisa, VA: Twin Oaks, 1994.

Kirschenmann, Frederick. "Anticipating the Future." *leopold.iastate.edu*, Fall 2012. http://lib.dr.iastate.edu/leopold_letter/60./

———. "Leopold's Ongoing Dilemma." *leopold.iastate.edu*, Summer 2013. http://lib.dr.iastate.edu/leopold_letter/57/.

Kirschenmann, Frederick L., and Constance Falk. *Cultivating an Ecological Conscience: Essays from a Farmer Philosopher*. Lexington: University Press of Kentucky, 2010.

Korkki, Phyllis. "In Retiree Housing, Talking about Multigenerations." *New York Times*, March 12, 2013. http://www.nytimes.com/2013/03/13/business/retirementspecial/retirees-choose-intergenerational-cohousing.html.

Kothari, Smitu, Pramod Parajuli, and Wolfgang Sachs. *No Nature without Social Justice: A Plea for Cultural and Ecological Pluralism in India*. London: Zed Books, 1993.

"LA Eco-village Food Coop Wiki Page." *Urbansoil.Net*. Accessed March 20, 2013. http://urbansoil.net/wiki.cgi/LA Eco-Village_Food_Coop.

LaVecchia, Olivia. "These Neighbors Got Together to Buy Vacant Buildings: Now They're Renting to Bakers and Brewers." *Yes! Magazine*, February 23, 2015. http://www.yesmagazine.org/new-economy/neighbors-got-together-buy-vacant-buildings-renting-bike-shop-brewer.

Leach, David. "Greening Your 'Hood." *Communities Magazine*, December 7, 2012. http://communities.ic.org/articles/1619/Greening_Your_Hood.

Leinberger, Christopher B. "Now Coveted—A Walkable, Convenient Place." *New York Times*, May 27, 2012. http://www.nytimes.com/2012/05/27/opinion/sunday/now-coveted-a-walkable-convenient-place.html?_r=0.

Lerner, Sharon. "Home but Not Alone." *More.com*, May 7, 2012. http://www.more.com/home-not-alone.

Leslie, Stephen. *The New Horse-Powered Farm: Tools and Systems for the Small-Scale, Sustainable Market Grower*. White River Junction, VT: Chelsea Green, 2013.

Liloia, Brian Ziggy. *The Year of Mud: Building a Cob House*. Blurb, 2011.
Litfin, Karen T. *Ecovillages: Lessons for Sustainable Community*. Cambridge, MA: Polity, 2014.
"Local Currencies." *Schumacher Center for a New Economics*. Accessed September 7, 2015. http://www.centerforneweconomics.org/content/local-currencies.
"Local Currency." *Dancingrabbit.org*. Accessed April 7, 2015. http://www.dancingrabbit.org/about-dancing-rabbit-ecovillage/social-change/economy/local-currency/.
"Local Harvest." *Localharvest.org*. Accessed March 19, 2015. http://www.localharvest.org/.
Lockyer, Joshua P. "Intentional Communities and Sustainability." *Communal Societies* 30, no. 1 (2010): 14–33.
Lockyer, Joshua, and James R. Veteto. *Environmental Anthropology Engaging Ecotopia: Bioregionalism, Permaculture, and Ecovillages*. New York: Berghahn Books, 2013. http://public.eblib.com/choice/publicfullrecord.aspx?p=1337727.
Lotherington, John. "The False Lure of Benign Dictatorship." *Fdsd.org*, February 2, 2010. http://www.fdsd.org/2010/02/the-lure-of-benign-dictatorship/.
Ludwig, Ma'ikwe Schaub. *Passion as Big as a Planet: Evolving Eco-Activism in America*. Lulu.com, 2007.
Lyson, Thomas A. *Civic Agriculture: Reconnecting Farm, Food, and Community*. Medford, MA: Tufts University Press, 2004.
Makita, Sam. "Sexism at Dancing Rabbit—Fellowship for Intentional Community." *Ic.org*, April 17, 2014. http://www.ic.org/sexism-dancing-rabbit/.
Mason, Jean K. *The View from #410: When Home Is Cohousing*. Bloomington, IN: iUniverse, 2010.
Mawdsley, Emma. "Hindu Nationalism, Neo-Traditionalism and Environmental Discourses in India." *Geoforum* 37, no. 3 (2006): 380–90. doi:10.1016/j.geoforum.2005.06.004.
McCamant, Kathryn, and Charles Durrett. *Creating Cohousing: Building Sustainable Communities*. Gabriola, BC: New Society, 2011. http://www.deslibris.ca/ID/436563.
McDonough, William, and Michael Braungart. *Cradle to Cradle: Remaking the Way We Make Things*. New York: Macmillan, 2010.
McGinnis, Michael Vincent. *Bioregionalism*. New York: Routledge, 1998.
McKanan, Dan. *The Catholic Worker After Dorothy: Practicing the Works of Mercy in a New Generation*. Collegeville, MN: Liturgical, 2008.
Meadows, Donella, Jorgen Randers, and Dennis Meadows. *Limits to Growth: The 30 Year Update*. White River Junction, VT: Chelsea Green, 2004.
Melnick, Jordan. "Generation Now!" *Www2.Qsrmagazine.com*, 2015. https://www.qsrmagazine.com/promotions/generation-now.
Meltzer, Graham Stuart. *Sustainable Community: Learning from the Cohousing Model*. Victoria, BC: Trafford, 2005.

"Micanopy Community Garden Gets Underway." *Transitionmicanopy.Wordpress.com*, April 9, 2011. https://transitionmicanopy.wordpress.com/.

Miller, Timothy. "A Matter of Definition: Just What Is an Intentional Community?" *Communal Societies* 30, no. 1 (2010): 1–15.

———. *The 60's Communes: Hippies and Beyond*. Syracuse: Syracuse University Press, 1999.

———. *Spiritual and Visionary Communities: Out to Save the World*. Burlington: Ashgate, 2013.

"Modern Intentional Organic Hipster Activist Farmer Homesteader: Truth vs Caricature." *Homegrown.org*, August 12, 2012. http://homegrown.org/blog/2010/08/homegrown-life-modern-intentional-organic-hipster-activist-farmer-homesteader-truth-vs-caricature/.

Moore-Backman, Chris. "Walking with Gandhi." *Geez Holy Mischief in an Age of Fast Faith*, Fall/Winter 2008, 5–18.

Morris, Ashira. "Local Art Galleries on the Rise in Gainesville." *Wuft.org*, July 5, 2013. http://www.wuft.org/news/2013/07/05/local-art-galleries/.

Mortimer-Sandilands, Catriona. *The Good-Natured Feminist: Ecofeminism and the Quest for Democracy*. Minneapolis: University of Minnesota Press, 1999.

Morton, Brian. "Falser Words Were Never Spoken." *New York Times*, August 30, 2011. http://www.nytimes.com/2011/08/30/opinion/falser-words-were-never-spoken.html?_r=0.

Moss, Michael. "The Extraordinary Science of Addictive Junk Food." *New York Times*, February 24, 2013. http://www.nytimes.com/2013/02/24/magazine/the-extraordinary-science-of-junk-food.html?pagewanted=all&_r=0.

Murphy, Kate. "Farm-to-Table Living Takes Root." *New York Times*, March 11, 2014. http://www.nytimes.com/2014/03/12/dining/farm-to-table-living-takes-root.html?emc=eta1&_r=0.

"My Intentional Life." *Grist.org*. Accessed April 7, 2015. http://grist.org/my-intentional-life/.

Nanda, Meera. *Prophets Facing Backward: Postmodern Critiques of Science and Hindu Nationalism in India*. New Brunswick, NJ: Rutgers University Press, 2003.

"National Complete Streets Coalition." *Smartgrowthamerica.org*. Accessed April 7, 2015. http://www.smartgrowthamerica.org/complete-streets.

"Natural Building Materials, Techniques & Technologies at Dancing Rabbit." *Dancingrabbit.org*. Accessed April 7, 2015. http://www.dancingrabbit.org/about-dancing-rabbit-ecovillage/eco-living/building/natural-building/.

Nearing, Helen, and Scott Nearing. *Living the Good Life: How to Live Sanely and Simply in a Troubled World*. New York: Schocken Books, 1974.

Neff, Roni A., et al. "Peak Oil, Food Systems, and Public Health." *American Journal of Public Health* 101, no. 9 (2011): 1587–97.

Nestle, Marion. *Food Politics: How the Food Industry Influences Health and Nutrition*. Berkeley: University of California Press, 2013.

"New Economy Coalition." *Neweconomy.Net.* Accessed April 6, 2015. http://new-economy.net/.

Newton, Julianne, and Eric Freyfogle. "Sustainability: A Dissent." *Conservation Biology* 19, no. 1 (2005): 23–32.

Nik. "A Traveler Returns, Insightful: A Dancing Rabbit Update." *Marchhareblog.com,* April 8, 2014. http://www.marchhareblog.com/2014/04/08/a-traveler-returns/.

Nordahl, Darrin. *Public Produce: The New Urban Agriculture.* Washington, DC: Island, 2009.

O'Connell, Coleen. "Living the Questions." *Ic.org,* September 7, 2012. http://www.ic.org/living-the-questions/.

Off, Carol. *Bitter Chocolate: Investigating the Dark Side of the World's Most Seductive Sweet.* Toronto: Random House Canada, 2006.

"Open Source Ecology." *Opensourceecology.org.* Accessed March 1, 2015. http://opensourceecology.org/.

Oppenheimer, Mark. "The Not-So-Lonely City." *New York Times,* January 17, 2014. http://www.nytimes.com/2014/01/19/magazine/technology-is-not-driving-us-apart-after-all.html?_r=0.

Ortiz, Erik. "Pot Bust Turns Up Empty at Texas Farm, Angering Residents." *New York Daily News,* August 15, 2013. http://www.nydailynews.com/news/national/pot-bust-turns-empty-texas-farm-angering-residents-article-1.1428294.

Parajuli, Pramod. "Revisiting Gandhi and Zapata: Motion of Global Capital, Geographies of Difference and the Formation of Ecological Ethnicities." In *In the Way of Development: Indigenous Peoples, Life Projects and Globalization,* edited by Mario Blaser, Harvey A. Feit, and Glenn McRae, 235–55. London: Zed Books, 2004.

"Passive Solar Home Design." *Epa.gov.* Accessed September 1, 2015. http://energy.gov/energysaver/articles/passive-solar-home-design.

Paulson, Lisa. *An Unconventional Journey: The Story of High Wind from Vision to Community to Eco-Neighborhood.* Plymouth, WI: Thistlefield Books, 2010.

Penniman, Leah. "Radical Farmers Use Fresh Food to Fight Racial Injustice and the New Jim Crow." *Yes! Magazine,* January 28, 2015. http://www.yesmagazine.org/peace-justice/radical-farmers-use-fresh-food-fight-racial-injustice-black-lives-matter.

"Perspectives on Cohousing and Ecovillages: Diversity in Intentional Communities." *Center for Urban and Regional Studies, University of North Carolina at Chapel Hill.* Accessed Septeember 3, 2015. http://curs.unc.edu/2015/03/19/friday-march-27th-perspectives-on-cohousing-and-ecovillages-building-diversity-in-intentional-communities/.

"Pete McAvoy Replaces Fossil Fuels with Cooking Oil." *Baxandobrien.Rock102.com,* April 2012. http://baxandobrien.rock102.com/podcast/2012/04/pete-mcavoy-recycles-cooking-oil-for-food/.

Peterson, Anna L. *Seeds of the Kingdom: Utopian Communities in the Americas.* New York: Oxford University Press, 2005.

Peterson, Molly. "Recycling Greywater as California Drought Persists." *Hereandnow.Wbur.org,* April 18, 2014. http://hereandnow.wbur.org/2014/04/18/recycling-gray-water.

Pickerill, Jenny. "Who Builds the Houses? Gender in Eco-Communities." *Ic.org,* March 17, 2014. http://www.ic.org/builds-houses-gender-eco-communities/.

"Piedmont Solidarity Economy Map: Mapping Our Local Values-Based Economy." *Solidaritypiedmont.org.* Accessed January 1, 2015. http://solidaritypiedmont.org/map/mapintro.html.

Pluhar, Annamarie. *Sharing Housing: A Guidebook for Finding and Keeping Good Housemates.* Homemade, 2011.

"Pocket Neighborhoods: Creating Small Scale Community in a Large Scale World." *Pocket-Neighborhoods.Net.* Accessed March 20, 2013. http://www.pocket-neighborhoods.net/whatisaPN.html.

Poole, Isaiah J. "Solar Panel Users as Freeloaders: ALEC Network's State Lobbyists Attack Homeowner and Business Subsidies." *Flaglerlive.com,* December 28, 2014. http://flaglerlive.com/62523/solar-panel-subsidies/.

"Possibility Alliance Mission Statement and Guiding Principles," January 28, 2007. Unpublished document.

Putnam, Robert D. *Bowling Alone: The Collapse and Revival of American Community.* New York: Simon and Schuster, 2001.

"Queer in Community." *Ic.org.* Accessed September 8, 2015. http://www.ic.org/wiki/queer-community/.

Rabbit. "10 Reasons Why EarthShips Are F!#%Ing Awesome." *Valhallamovement.com.* Accessed April 30, 2014. http://valhallamovement.com/blog/2012/10/08/10-reasons-why-earthships-are-fing-awesome/.

Rampell, Catherine. "Outsource Your Way to Success." *New York Times,* November 10, 2013. http://www.nytimes.com/2013/11/10/magazine/outsource-your-way-to-success.html?hpw.

Raver, Anne. "Farm Equipment That Runs on Oats." *New York Times,* May 15, 2013. http://www.nytimes.com/2013/05/16/garden/farm-equipment-that-runs-on-oats.html?_r=1&.

"Reducing Energy Use." *Epa.gov.* Accessed September 1, 2015. http://www.epa.gov/greenhomes/ReduceEnergy.htm.

Regulatory Provisions: Composting Toilets, Greywater Systems. Mass.Gov. Accessed November 10, 2015. http://www.mass.gov/eea/agencies/massdep/water/wastewater/regulatory- provisions-for-compost-toilets-and-greywater.html.

"Resilience Circles." *Localcircles.org,* 2014. http://localcircles.org/.

"Right Livelihood Award: The 'Alternative Nobel Prize.'" *rightlivelihood.org.* Accessed April 7, 2015. http://www.rightlivelihood.org/inamay_gaskin.html.

Roman-Alcala, Antonio. "In Search of Good Food: Concerning the Unbearable Whiteness of Urban Farming." *Insearchofgoodfood.Blogspot.com*, June 29, 2010. http://insearchofgoodfood.blogspot.com/2010/06/concerning-unbearable-whiteness-of.html.

Rosenberg, Marshall. *Nonviolent Communication: A Language of Life*. Encinitas, CA: PuddleDancer, 2003.

Rovner, Julie. "Boomer Housemates Have More Fun." *Npr.org*, May 22, 2013. http://www.npr.org/blogs/health/2013/05/22/183903991/Boomer-Housemates-Have-More-Fun.

"Safe Routes to School." *Fhwa.Dot.Gov*. Accessed April 2, 2015. http://www.fhwa.dot.gov/environment/safe_routes_to_school/.

St. Amant, Claire. "Months After Failed Drug Raid, Arlington Farmers Still Seek Answers." *Dallas.Culturemap.com*, September 27, 2013. http://dallas.culturemap.com/news/city-life/09-27-13-drug-raid-garden-of-eden-arlington-police-investigation/.

"Sandhill Farm: Sorghum Season." *Sandhillfarm.org*. Accessed March 31, 2015. http://www.sandhillfarm.org/sorghum_season.php.

Sandilands, Catriona. "Lesbian Separatist Communities and the Experience of Nature: Toward a Queer Ecology." *Organization & Environment* 15, no. 131 (2002): 131–63. doi:10.1177/10826602015002002.

Sanford, A. Whitney. "Gandhi's Agrarian Legacy: Practicing Food, Justice, and Sustainability in India." *Journal of the Society of Religion, Nature, and Culture* 7, no. 1 (2013): 65–87. doi:10.1558/jsrnc.v7i1.65.

———. *Growing Stories from India: Religion and the Fate of Agriculture*. Lexington: University Press of Kentucky, 2011.

Savage, Scott. *The Plain Reader: Essays on Making a Simple Life*. New York: Ballantine Books, 1998.

Schaub, Laird. "The Intergenerational Challenge." *Communityandconsensus.Blogspot.com*, December 27, 2013. http://communityandconsensus.blogspot.com/2013/12/the-intergenerational-challenge.html.

Scheer, Roddy, and Doug Moss. "Bottle Bills." *E-Magazine*, October 30, 2011. http://www.emagazine.com/earth-talk/bottle-bills.

Schneider, Don, and Elin England. "What Are the Boundaries of an Intentional Community?" *Communities Magazine*, July 1, 2009, 60–62.

Schumacher, Ernst Friedrich. *Small Is Beautiful: A Study of Economics as if People Mattered*. New York: Random House, 1993.

Shepard, Mark. *The Community of the Ark: A Visit with Lanza del Vasto, His Fellow Disciples of Mahatma Gandhi, and Their Utopian Community in France*. Santa Fe: Ocean Tree Books, 1992.

Shin, Laura. "Spotlight: Cecil Scheib, '92." *Alumni.Stanford.Edu*, February 4, 2011. https://alumni.stanford.edu/get/page/magazine/article/?article_id=28606.

Shrader-Frechette, Kristin. "Ethics and the Environment." *World Health Forum* 12 (1991): 311–21.

Shute, Nancy. "When Older People Walk Now, They Stay Independent Later." *Npr.org*, May 27, 2014. http://www.npr.org/blogs/health/2014/05/27/316325223/when-older-people-walk-now-they-stay-independent-later.

Sirna, Tony. "Cutting Our Carbon Footprint." *dancingrabbit.org*. Accessed December 13, 2014. http://www.dancingrabbit.org/about-dancing-rabbit-ecovillage/eco-living/cutting-our-carbon-footprint/.

"SolidarityNYC." *Solidaritynyc.org*. Accessed April 2, 2015. http://solidaritynyc.org/.

Solis, George. "Cape Woman Living 'off the Grid' Challenged by City." *Nbc-2.com*, February 21, 2014. http://www.nbc-2.com/story/24790572/cape-woman-living-of-the-grid-challenged-by-city#.VIylXYeop7V.

Sollisch, Jim. "I Want to Be a Millennial When I Retire." *New York Times*, November 5, 2013. http://www.nytimes.com/2013/11/05/booming/i-want-to-be-a-millennial-when-i-retire.html.

Solnit, Rebecca. *A Paradise Built in Hell: The Extraordinary Communities That Arise in Disaster*. New York: Penguin Books, 2010.

Solomon, Avi. "Interview: Brian 'Ziggy' Liloia on How to Build Your Own Hobbit House." *Boingboing.Net*, May 11, 2011. http://boingboing.net/2011/05/11/hobbithouse.html.

"Soul Fire Farm." *Soulfirefarm.com*. Accessed March 30, 2015. http://www.soulfirefarm.com/.

Stock, Paul V. "The Perennial Nature of the Catholic Worker Farms: A Reconsideration of Failure." *Rural Sociology* 79, no. 2 (2013): 143–73.

"Straw Bale House Construction." *Dancingrabbit.org*. Accessed August 30, 2015. http://www.dancingrabbit.org/about-dancing-rabbit-ecovillage/eco-living/building/natural-building/straw-bale-house-construction/.

Susanka, Sarah, with Kira Obolensky. *The Not So Big House: A Blueprint for the Way We Really Live*. Newton, CT: Taunton, 2008.

Tammeus, Bill. "Presbyterian-Run Catholic Worker House Does Things Backward—Like Jesus." *Ncronline.org*, February 20, 2013. http://ncronline.org/blogs/small-c-catholic/presbyterian-run-catholic-worker-house-does-things-backward-jesus.

Taylor, Sarah McFarland. *Green Sisters: A Spiritual Ecology*. Cambridge, MA: Harvard University Press, 2007.

Tendulkar, Dinesh G. *Mahatma*. 2nd ed. Vol. 4. Ahmedabad: Navajivan, 1960.

Tregaskis, Sharon. "The Green Apple." *Nyu.Edu*, February 4, 2007. https://www.nyu.edu/alumni.magazine/issue09/feature_heat_apple.html.

Turkle, Sherry. *Alone Together: Why We Expect More from Technology and Less from Each Other*. New York: Basic Books, 2011.

"Twin Oaks Intentional Community—Visitor Program." *Twinoakscommunity.org*. Accessed April 7, 2015. http://www.twinoakscommunity.org/twinoaks-visits-60/visit-tour/visitor-program.

United Nations. *Our Common Future: Report of the World Commission on Envi-*

ronment and Development. *Un-Documents.Net,* 1987. http://www.un-documents.net/our-common-future.pdf.
Urban Dictionary, s.v. "Slacktivism." *Urbandictionary.com.* Accessed April 7, 2015. http://www.urbandictionary.com/define.php?term=slacktivism.
USDA. "Agricultural Marketing Service—Creating Access to Healthy, Affordable Food." *Apps.Ams.Usda.Gov.* Accessed November 4, 2013. http://apps.ams.usda.gov/fooddeserts/foodDeserts.aspx.
"The Valhalla Mission." *Valhallamovement.com.* Accessed April 7, 2015. http://valhallamovement.com/mission/.
Walker, Liz. *EcoVillage at Ithaca: Pioneering a Sustainable Culture.* Gabriola Island, BC: New Society, 2005.
Warren, Lee Walker. "Aspiring to the Working Class." *Ic.org,* September 7, 2012. http://www.ic.org/aspiring-to-the-working-class/.
Weber, Thomas. "Gandhi, Deep Ecology, Peace Research and Buddhist Economics." *Journal of Peace Research* 36, no. 3 (1999): 349–61. doi:10.1177/0022343 399036003007.
"Welcome to the Civic Media Center." *Civicmediacenter.org.* Accessed April 7, 2015. http://www.civicmediacenter.org/welcome-civic-media-center.
"Welcome to Women for Living in Community, Aging in Community." *Womenlivingincommunity.com.* Accessed April 7, 2015. http://www.womenlivingincommunity.com/.
"Wex Position: Dennis and Sharon." *Dancingrabbit.org.* Accessed January 1, 2015. http://www.dancingrabbit.org/visit-dancing-rabbit-ecovillage/workexchange/wex-position-dennis-and-sharon/.
"What Is Cohousing?" *Cohousing.org.* Accessed March 19, 2015. http://www.cohousing.org/what_is_cohousing.
"What Is the Tiny House Movement?" *Thetinylife.com.* Accessed March 27, 2015. http://thetinylife.com/what-is-the-tiny-house-movement/.
Wink, Walter, and Fellowship of Reconciliation (US). *Peace Is the Way: Writings on Nonviolence from the Fellowship of Reconciliation.* Maryknoll, NY: Orbis Books, 2000.
Winne, Mark. "The Color of Food Leadership." *Markwinne.com,* January 12, 2015. http://www.markwinne.com/the-color-of-food-leadership/.
Wirzba, Norman. *The Essential Agrarian Reader: The Future of Culture, Community, and the Land.* Lexington: University Press of Kentucky, 2003.
"The Works of Mercy." *Catholic Worker.* Accessed March 19, 2015. http://www.catholicworker.org/aimsandmeanstext.cfm?number=28.
Wright, Angus L. *The Death of Ramón González: The Modern Agricultural Dilemma.* Austin: University of Texas Press, 1990.
Younge, Gary. "The Unbearable Whiteness of the American Left." *Nation,* April 23, 2014. http://www.thenation.com/article/179507/unbearable-whiteness-american-left.

Ziggy. "Four Missouri Communities Demonstrate Sustainability." *Sustainablog*, February 24, 2010. http://sustainablog.org/2010/02/four-missouri-communities-demonstrate-sustainability/.

Index

Abrahms, Sally, 80
Acorn Community Farm, 53, 54, 65, 204–6, 245
African Americans, 8, 233. *See also* Black Lives Matter
aging, 43, 57, 84–88; baby boomers and, 25, 59, 79–80, 81, 83; cohousing communities and, 81, 82–86; housing and, 84–85; multigenerational communities and, 81–82, 88
agriculture: appropriate technology and, 191, 200–201; businesses and, 198–206; community-supported agriculture (CSAs), 23, 31, 233, 239; experimentation and, 145–46; nonviolence and, 8, 108, 122; productivity and, 173; small farms, 23, 55, 173, 201, 205; sustainability and, 7, 11, 32, 39, 66, 180. *See also* food production; industrial agriculture; organic farming
Agritopia, 31, 239
agroecology, 173
agronomic university, 11, 14, 28, 96, 104, 193, 248
Aguilar, Jade, 60
ahimsa, 108
Albright, Victoria, 148–49, 161

ALEC (American Legislative Exchange Council), 236
Allen, Laura, 219
alternative currencies, 189, 194–96
Altieri, Miguel, 173
Amish, 7, 9, 10, 54, 55, 97, 191
Anabaptists, 134. *See also* Amish; Hutterites; Old Order Mennonites
Anderson, Alline, 91, 93, 124, 125, 145, 176–79, 188, 219
Anglada, Eric, 61, 104–6, 163, 169–70
Aplin, Mary, 40
Arkin, Lois, 13–14, 60, 156, 171, 179–80, 183, 185, 195–96, 197, 218, 239–40
Arroyo Seco Network of Time Banks, 195–96
ashrams, 58, 96, 151
Ash Street Community Garden, 102
At Home in Nature (Gould), 103

baby boomers, 25, 59, 79–80, 81, 83, 88, 93, 94
Bagetell, Sharon, 214
Baltimore Free Farm, 101, 102, 186, 197, 233, 237, 245
banking, 194–96
Bates, Albert, 51
Beck, Glenn, 26

Index

Becker, Mark, 1, 21, 94, 95, 97–99, 100–101, 104, 141, 142–43, 144, 225–26, 235
Being the Change urban homestead project, 234
Belfast Cohousing and Ecovillage, 16–18, 25–26, 40, 52–53, 82, 160, 187, 228–29, 245
Bellah, Robert, 30
Berry, Wendell, 28, 35
"be the change," 2–3, 27, 34, 240
Bhakta, Amita, 86–87
Bhave, Vinobha, 151
Bicycle Kitchen, 185–86, 197, 239
bicycles, 5, 13, 168, 169, 179, 181–82, 197, 206–7, 239; class diversity and, 237–38
biofuels, 51, 201, 207
Bittman, Mark, 173
Black Acres Farm, 119
Black Lives Matter, 138–39, 226, 233, 235
Blue Moon Cooperative, 45
Bonaref, T. M., 96
Boston, Sandra, 196
Bowens, Natasha, 233
Bowling Alone: The Collapse and Revival of American Community (Putnam), 30
Braungart, Michael, 173
bread labor, 19, 66–67, 84, 87, 94–97, 98–99, 103, 104; Gandhi and, 96–97, 106, 165
bug-out bags, 25
building codes, 6, 183, 216–19
building materials, 12, 192, 211–17, 255; cobs and, 213–14; gender equity and, 219–22; "repurposed" materials and, 211–12, 215; roofs and, 215; spirituality and, 212; straw-bale buildings, 178, 206, 211, 212, 214, 217, 219
Brundtland Report, 135
Bush, Judith, 85, 86, 155, 199–200, 201–2

Bush, Karen, 79, 80, 87
Butterfly Hill Farm, 53
Byrnes, Ron, 164

Calta, Paxus, 151, 158
Cambridge Cohousing, 75
Cambridge Housekeeping Cooperative, 130
Campbell, Adam, 105, 165
canning, 35–36, 37, 185
carbon footprint, 93, 173, 214, 227, 230, 232
Carspecken, Lucinda, 241–42
Catholic worker communities, 7, 8, 45, 49; bread labor and, 96, 97, 104, 106; class diversity and, 60; community engagement and, 74, 77; DIY skills and, 190; food practices and, 6, 15, 107, 117–19, 120–21, 172; food production and, 104, 106; sharing resources and, 74, 162; values and, 14–16, 28, 61, 104, 105–6, 235, 238; visitors and, 64, 77, 114–20; website listings and, 63, 251. *See also* Cherith Brook Catholic Worker community; Gainesville Catholic Worker House; New Hope Catholic Worker Farm
Catholic Worker Farmer (community newsletter), 106
Catholic Worker Movement, 14, 15, 28
Cedar Mountain Farm, 199, 200
Center for Nonviolent Communication, 155
Chapin, Ross, 42
cheese, 201, 203
Cherith Brook Catholic Worker community, 15, 246; community engagement and, 9, 77; food practices and, 107, 121, 172, 186; housing and, 73, 77; nonviolence and, 110, 235; sharing resources and, 162; visitors and, 114–19, 122, 191, 235
Chernoff, Bruce, 85
Chicago, 15, 53, 227

Chico Peace and Justice Center, 136
children, 16, 25–26, 81–82
chocolate, 112, 122, 126, 174, 240
Christian, Diana Leafe, 47, 63–64, 67, 68, 158
Christian Works of Mercy, 14–15, 61, 62, 115, 162
Circle, The (Eggar), 139
class diversity, 60–61, 164, 232–36; bicycles and, 237–38; cohousing communities and, 229–30
climate change, 22–23, 180
clothing, 55, 116, 162–63, 172, 182, 190
Cobb Hill Cohousing, 45, 189, 246; aging and, 84–86; community engagement and, 74, 75; composting toilets and, 217–18; food businesses and, 198–202; governance and, 155; heating and, 186
coffee, 112, 113, 122, 174–75, 240
Cohousing Association of the United States, 63, 65, 251
cohousing communities, 9, 45; aging and, 81, 82–86; community engagement and, 25–26, 74–76, 129–30; governance and, 17–18, 68, 74, 160, 202, 216–17; housing options and, 16, 71; sharing resources and, 172, 228–30; sharing spaces and, 76, 227–28; sustainability and, 7–8, 187, 230–32; values and, 6, 16–18, 228–29. *See also* Belfast Cohousing and Ecovillage; Cobb Hill Cohousing; Pioneer Valley Cohousing; Two Echo Cohousing
Columbia University, 24
Common Security Clubs. *See* Resilience Circles
Communities Conference, 4, 8, 9, 51, 64–65, 159, 204; aging and, 78–79, 80, 82–83, 87; joining communities and, 67–68; New Economy and, 189; racial diversity and, 233; sharing resources and, 78–79, 80, 181
community engagement, 29–31, 47–48, 74–78, 84, 89–90; cohousing communities and, 25–26, 74–76, 129–30; public transportation and, 239–40. *See also* particular communities
Community of the Ark, 95, 136
Community of the Ark, The (Shepard), 136
community-supported agriculture (CSAs), 23, 31, 233, 239
composting toilets, 18, 69, 84, 173–74, 175, 217–18
conflict resolution, 12, 129–30, 133, 148–49, 150, 154–58, 159–60, 224, 226
consensus, 6, 12–13, 134, 149, 151, 153, 155, 156–58
consumerism, 26, 161, 164, 167–69, 178
Cooperative Resources and Services Project (CRSP), 14, 195–96
Cottage Food Act of 2011 (FL), 36
covenants, 18, 30, 147, 154
Cradle to Cradle: Remaking the Way We Make Things (McDonough and Braungart), 173
Crazy Woman Farm, 222
Creating Life Together: Practical Tools to Grow Ecovillages and Intentional Communities (Christian), 64
Creative Commons, 189–90, 251
Critchlow, Margaret, 83, 84
"cult of busy," 163
cults, 46–47
culture creation, 70, 91–94

Dancing Rabbit Ecovillage, 9, 23, 45, 246; aging and, 59, 84, 87, 88; building materials and, 6, 12, 192, 211–17, 219; community engagement and, 53, 54–56; composting toilets and, 18, 84, 174, 175; conflict resolution and, 155, 158, 226; costs and, 60; culture creation and, 70, 91; ELM (exchange local money system), 194–95; energy production and, 35,

Dancing Rabbit Ecovillage (cont'd) 127, 209–11, 236; establishment and, 6, 11, 152–53; food businesses and, 126, 202–3; food practices and, 70, 114, 123, 124–29, 187; food production and, 124–25, 128–29; gender equity and, 150–51, 220–21; governance and, 5, 12–13, 145, 151, 153–54; heating and, 166–67, 210; housing and, 73, 192, 213–15, 219; regulations and, 93, 147, 154; residency process and, 12, 68, 69–71, 176–77; sharing resources and, 165–66, 182–83; sustainability and, 40–41, 153, 154, 188; values and, 5, 11–13, 43, 127, 128–29, 153, 175–79; visitors and, 49, 64, 127–28, 158–59, 176, 178–79

Day, Dorothy, 14, 15, 28, 45, 77, 96, 105–6, 116, 162, 165

Daybreak Cohousing, 76, 246–47

del Vasto, Lanza, 95–96, 136

disability, 25, 84, 86–87

disasters, 23, 24–25, 234, 241

DIY skills, 185–86, 190, 192–94, 222–23, 255

Drew, Jesse, 49

DuPuis, Melanie, 33, 34

Durica, Dan, 203

Durrett, Chuck, 229

Earth Deeds, 186–87

Earthhaven Ecovillage, 8, 158, 222

Easterly, William, 25

eco-auditing, 146–48

Eco-Stewards, 241

Ecovillage at Ithaca (EVI), 8, 45, 60

Ecovillage at Ithaca: Pioneering a Sustainable Culture (Walker), 45

ecovillages, 160, 211, 240; defined, 11. *See also* Dancing Rabbit Ecovillage; LA Eco-village

Ecovillage Training Center (The Farm), 3–4, 51

Edwards, Anton, 25

E. F. Schumacher Society, 189

Eggar, Dave, 139

Elderspirit Community, 82–83

electricity, 4–5, 11. *See also* solar power

Ellis, Joni, 222

environmentalism, 28, 134–35. *See also* sustainability

Eskin, Harold S., 237

Estill, Lyle, 51

"Ethics and the Environment" (Shrader-Frechette), 165–66

Ewald, Alyson, 69, 144–47, 173–74, 188, 191, 193, 203

fair trade, 107, 113, 122, 126

Farm, The (Summertown, TN), 3–4, 34, 40, 50–51

Farm Ecovillage Training Center, 3–4, 51

farmers' markets, 23, 36, 203–4, 233, 239

Farm-to-Consumer Legal Defense Fund, 36

Federation of Egalitarian Communities (FEC), 63, 87, 181, 251

Fellowship for Intentional Community (FIC), 32, 48, 59, 251; community visitors and, 64, 65; cults and, 46–47; gender equity/diversity and, 151, 220–21; listings and, 3, 4, 5, 45, 56–57, 62–63

Feuer, Alan, 24

FIC. *See* Fellowship for Intentional Community (FIC)

Fike, Rupert, 50

Fillie, Chris, 39

Findhorn Foundation community, 9, 48, 83, 247

Finding Community: How to Join an Ecovillage or Intentional Community (Christian), 47, 64, 68

First Magnitude Brewing Company, 39

Flagg, Katherine, 45, 73

Florida, 7, 23, 26, 31–32, 41. *See also* Gainesville, FLFlorida Organic Growers, 39

food deserts, 100, 102
food practices, 103, 109–10, 232–33; conflict resolution and, 129–30; donated food and, 117–18; food businesses and, 126, 198–203; food choices and, 11, 112, 113–14, 120–21, 128, 146–47, 160, 174–75, 240; food co-ops and, 19, 70, 124–25, 127–28, 183–84; local food and, 11, 23, 108, 122, 136, 161–62, 166–67, 173, 174, 175, 187, 198; nonviolence and, 19, 33, 100–101, 107–14, 136; organic food and, 108, 126; sharing meals and, 108, 123–25, 130; sustainability and, 40, 66, 118, 199; voluntary simplicity and, 118, 120, 128, 161–62, 174–75, 183–84, 239
food production, 6, 15, 98–102, 104, 106, 124–25, 128–29; gardening and, 98–99, 102, 141, 191; greenhouses and, 207–9; nonviolence and, 107–9. *See also* agriculture; seed sharing
food rescue, 102, 118, 186
food safety, 18, 36–38
food sovereignty, 134
Food Sovereignty Solidarity Working Group of Gainesville, 39
fossil fuels, 7, 41, 214; alternative fuels and, 51, 201, 207; appropriate technology and, 191; cohousing communities and, 82; zero-fossil fuel communities, 11, 54, 65, 112–13, 167, 169, 240
Foundation for Democracy and Sustainable Development, 135
Fox, Richard, 144, 167
Fredericks, Sarah, 214
Freecycle Network, 251
freedom, 92, 93, 99, 100, 102–3
Freyfogle, Eric, 180
Friedman, Thomas, 184

Gainesville, FL, 21, 27, 39–40, 72, 99, 110, 222, 240

Gainesville Catholic Worker House, 7, 15, 60, 119–21, 235, 247
Gainesville Cohousing, 40
Gandhi, Arun, 27
Gandhi, Mohandas K., 30, 144, 170, 238; appropriate technology and, 35, 187, 190–91, 205; bread labor and, 96–97, 106, 165; environmentalism and, 28, 134; governance and, 133–34, 151, 156; integral nonviolence and, 10–11, 110, 133–34, 136, 137, 138, 139; interdependence and, 187, 203; nonviolence and, 28, 44, 61–62, 100–101, 113, 140, 143, 151; personal transformation and, 111–12, 137, 138, 139–40, 141; values and, 14, 21, 27–28, 40, 67, 132
Garbison, Eric, 77, 107, 116, 121, 235
Garbison, Jodi, 77
gardening, 98–99, 102, 141, 191
Gaskin, Ina May, 40
Gaskin, Stephen, 40, 50
Gawalt, Kerry, 200
gender diversity, 9, 57, 151
gender equity, 56, 103, 133, 150–51, 195, 219–22
Giangrande, Naresh, 41
Gift, The (Hyde), 194
Global Ecovillage Network (GEN), 11, 252
Global Footprint Network, 168, 252
Global Village Construction Set (GVCS), 190
GMOs (genetically modified organisms), 205
Golant, Stephen, 80
Goodman, David, 33, 34
Gottlieb, Roger, 143
Gould, Rebecca Kneale, 103, 167
governance, 33–34, 47; cohousing communities and, 17–18, 68, 74, 155, 160, 202, 216–17; conflict resolution and, 12, 156–58, 159–60; consensus and, 6, 12–13, 134, 149, 151, 153, 155, 156–58; covenants and, 18, 30,

governance (cont'd) 147, 154; experimentation and, 151–52, 158; nonviolence and, 133–34, 151–52; participatory democracy and, 1, 5, 8, 12–13, 38; radical democracy and, 33, 135, 148–51, 153, 184; sustainability and, 131–33, 135, 153–54, 160; voluntary simplicity and, 172–73. *See also* particular communities
Great Depression, 14, 28
Greenberg, Dan, 186–87
Greener Faith, A (Gottlieb), 143
Green House. See Gainesville Catholic Worker House
Green Revolution, 96–97, 187
Greywater Action, 219
Grow Gainesville, 23, 37
Growing Stories from India: Religion and the Fate of Agriculture (Sanford), 32, 66
Gudmand-Hoyer, Jan, 187
Guha, Ramachandra, 134
Gurley, George, 237–38
Guthman, Julie, 232–33

Hamblen, Stephanie, 37
hammocks, 195, 198
Hampton, Keith, 150
Harbourside, 83–84
Hardin, Garret, 209
health care, 59, 85, 87–88, 92, 93, 181, 238
Hearthstone Village, 78, 186
heating, 82, 166–67, 170–72, 186, 207–9, 210
Hershberger, Vernon, 36
High Wind community, 48–49, 159
Hofarth, Dennis, 214
Hollenbach, Margaret, 47
homeowners' associations (HOA), 68, 74, 216, 217, 229
home sharing. *See* shared housing
honey, 146, 198
Hooton, Reagan, 197
Hope Meadows, 88
Hopkins, Rob, 41
horses, 200–201
hugelkultur, 145, 190
Hughes, Ethan, 7, 10–11, 91, 95, 97, 144, 154, 177, 193–94, 234–35; nonviolence and, 44, 110, 112, 113, 114, 133, 136–37, 138, 139
Humanure Headquarters, 252
humanure systems, 69, 84, 173–74, 217–18. *See also* composting toilets
hunting, 108, 125–26
Hutterites, 53
Hyde, Lewis, 194

Illegal Jam Company, 37
income-sharing, 3, 5, 51, 63, 68, 77–78, 87, 124, 129, 145, 162, 181
Independence, USA, 26
India, 58, 65–66, 67, 96, 108, 114, 161
industrial agriculture, 8, 32, 37, 97, 100, 108, 122, 173, 238
intentional communities: 1970s and, 3, 40, 45–48, 50, 52, 56–57; costs and, 60, 229; defined, 1, 3, 32; joining communities and, 19, 62–65, 66, 67–71, 89, 176. *See also* particular communities; sustainability
interdependence, 4, 6, 7, 186–87, 203
International Communal Studies Association, 9, 51
International Preparedness Network, 25
Iowa, 15, 26, 61, 106, 169, 170. *See also* Mustard Seed Community Farm; New Hope Catholic Worker Farm
Iowa State University, 180
Is It Utopia Yet? An Insider's View of Twin Oaks Community in Its Twenty-Sixth Year (Kinkade), 45
ISKCON (International Society for Krishna Consciousness), 46
isolation, 7, 89, 224, 227

Jessop, Peter, 85, 86, 131, 216–17, 227, 229–30, 231–32

Jesus Radicals, 97, 105
Jones, Kayla Brooke, 214
"joyful productivity," 98, 142
Juergensmeyer, Mark, 155–56

Kaplan, Temma, 25
Keitt, Alan, 45, 199, 202
Keitt, Ruth, 199
Kessner, Kurt, 84, 126, 176–79, 187, 192, 215–16
Kilkenny, Marianne, 80
Kinkade, Kat, 45
Kirschenmann, Fred, 180
Korkki, Phyllis, 88

LA Eco-village, 11, 234, 248; community engagement and, 8–9, 74; costs and, 60; establishment and, 13–14; food practices and, 102; governance and, 149, 156–57; heating and, 170–71; housing and, 71, 73; micro-industries and, 185–86, 196–97; money systems and, 195–96; transportation and, 197, 206–7, 239–40; values and, 7, 14; visitors and, 64, 72; voluntary simplicity and, 179–80, 183; water systems and, 218–19
Laishley Park Marina, 31–32
land health, 180
LaVecchia, Olivia, 236
La Via Campesina, 134
Leach, David, 38–39, 227–28
Leete, Nicholas, 179
Leinberger, Christopher, 31
Leopold, Aldo, 180
Leslie, Stephen, 200–201
LGBTQ. *See* gender diversity
Liloia, April, 213–14
Liloia, Brian "Ziggy," 213–14
Limits to Growth (Meadows et al), 201
Litfin, Karen, 160
Living Energy Farm, 53–54, 65
Living Machine, 218
Living Routes, 186
Living the Good Life: How to Live Simply and Sanely in a Troubled World (Nearing and Nearing), 52
Local Harvest, 23, 252
Lockyer, Joshua, 33, 214
Los Angeles County Bicycle Coalition, 239
Lost and Found: My Life in a Group Marriage Commune (Hollenbach), 47
Lost Valley Education and Event Center, 60, 64, 148–49, 168, 169, 186, 248
Lotherington, John, 135
Lothlorien Nature Sanctuary, 241
Ludwig, Ma'ikwe Schaub, 45

Maine, 16, 25–26, 52, 81–82, 232. *See also* Belfast Cohousing and Ecovillage
Maine Organic Farmers and Gardeners Association (MOGFA), 53
Makita, Sam, 220–21
Mandela, Nelson, 30
marina residents, 31–32
Marx, Karl, 173
Mason, Jean, 75, 81, 129–30
Massachusetts, 75, 130, 194, 196, 207, 216–17, 218, 227. *See also* Pioneer Valley Cohousing; Sirius Community
Maurin, Peter, 15, 45, 105, 119, 133, 187, 203, 205; agronomic universities and, 11, 14, 28, 96–97, 104, 193
Mawdsley, Emma, 34
McAvoy, Pete, 207
McDonough, William, 173
McGary, Alice, 61, 67, 99, 106, 170, 191
McKanan, Dan, 105
Meadows, Donella "Dana," 45, 201
meat-eating, 109, 113–14, 118, 120–21, 124, 125–26, 128, 222
Mennonites. *See* Old Order Mennonites
Merbitz, Betsy, 215
Miccosukee Land Co-op, 87–88, 226, 247

micro-industries, 185–86, 196–98, 202–6
Midden, the, 233–34
Milkweed Mercantile B&B, 49, 64, 126, 177–78, 195, 203, 206, 209–10, 217. *See also* Dancing Rabbit Ecovillage
millennials, 59–60, 88, 93, 94, 165, 239
Miller, Timothy, 3, 44, 47
Missouri, 4–5, 6–7, 15, 54–55, 59. *See also* Cherith Brook Catholic Worker community; Dancing Rabbit Ecovillage; Possibility Alliance; Red Earth Farms; Sandhill Farm
money. *See* alternative currencies
Moon, Sun Myung, 46
Moore-Backman, Chris, 10, 136, 137, 138, 139
Morrison, Lara, 149
Mortimer-Sandiland, Catriona, 57, 152
Morton, Brian, 30
Moss, Michael, 101
multigenerational communities, 81–82
Murphy, Kate, 239
Mustard Seed Community Farm, 15, 61, 67, 106, 170, 179, 191, 248
My House, Our House: Living Far Better for Far Less in a Cooperative Household (Bush, Machinist, and McQuillin), 79
My Intentional Life (comic), 233

Naess, Arne, 134
Nakamura, Emi, 102
Nanda, Meera, 34
NASCO (North American Students of Cooperation), 63, 252
National Complete Streets Coalition, 227, 252
Natural Buildings, 211–17
Nearing, Helen, 52, 96, 97, 103, 167
Nearing, Scott, 52, 96, 97, 103, 167
Neighbors, the, 196
Nestle, Marion, 101
New Economy, 188–90, 196
New Economy Coalition, 189, 252
New Eden, 64

New Hope Catholic Worker Farm, 61, 104–6, 137, 163, 165, 169–70, 248
New Horse-Powered Farm: Tools and Systems for the Small-Scale, Sustainable Market Grower, The (Leslie), 201
New New Economy, 59–60, 188–89, 190
new religious movements (NRM), 46, 47
Newton, Julianne, 180
New Urbanism, 227
New York City, 24, 40–41; bicycles and, 237–38, 239
New York Times, 102, 164, 173, 236
New York University (NYU), 41
9/11, 24–25, 241
nonresidential communities, 240–42
nonviolence, 1, 4, 61–62, 114, 240; agriculture and, 8, 108, 122; experimentation and, 44, 144–45; food practices and, 19, 33, 100–101, 107–14, 136; fossil fuels and, 113; governance and, 133–34, 151–52; integral nonviolence, 10–11, 110–11, 113, 133–34, 136–40, 144, 234–35; personal transformation and, 111–12, 132, 137, 139–40, 141–43. *See also* Gandhi, Mohandas K.
nonviolent communications (NVC), 40, 56, 238–39, 252; conflict resolution and, 12, 133, 148, 155–56, 224; food practices and, 108; personal transformation and, 111–12
Nordahl, Darrin, 227
Northeast Investment Cooperative (NEIC, Minneapolis), 236
Not So Big House, The (Susanka and Obolensky), 42
Nuri, Rashid, 233

Oak Hammock, 27, 88
Obolensky, Kira, 42
Occupy Wall Street, 155
O'Connell, Coleen, 25–26, 52, 53, 82, 160, 187, 228–29

Old Order Mennonites, 7, 9, 10, 54–56, 127, 203
Open Source Ecology, 190, 253
Oppenheimer, Mark, 150
organic farming, 12, 31, 39, 53, 61, 108, 128, 173, 183, 192, 205–6. *See also* small farms
Our Common Future (UN World Commission on Environment and Development), 135

Paradise Built in Hell: The Extraordinary Communities That Arise in Disaster, A (Solnit), 24, 241
participatory democracy, 1, 5, 8, 12–13, 38
Passion as Big as a Planet: Evolving Eco-Activism in America (Ludwig), 45
Paulson, Belden, 48
Paulson, Lisa, 48, 159
Peace and Permaculture Center, 11, 98, 185, 193–94
Penniman, Leah, 233
permaculture, 105, 185, 192, 209, 253
personal transformation, 111–12, 132, 137, 138, 139–40, 141–43, 154
Peterson, Anna, 33
Pickerill, Jenny, 220, 221
Piedmont Biofuels, 51
Pioneer Valley Cohousing, 131, 249; aging and, 84–86; costs and, 229; governance and, 216–17; sharing resources and, 172; sharing spaces and, 227; sustainability and, 230–32, 236
Pluhar, Annamarie, 80
Plymouth Institute, 48
pocket neighborhoods, 42–43, 228, 253
Pocket Neighborhoods (Chapin and Susanka), 42
polyamory, 56
Poole, Isaiah, 236
Porters Community Farm, 39
Possibility Alliance, 1, 6, 35, 58, 97, 105, 217, 249; bread labor and, 66–67, 94–95, 98–99, 104, 106, 165; community engagement and, 7, 10, 11, 55, 95, 234–35; culture creation and, 91, 94; electricity and, 4–5, 11; food practices and, 11, 109–14, 122, 128, 175, 240; food production and, 98–99, 101–2, 186; fossil fuels and, 11, 112–13, 167, 169, 240; governance and, 148–49, 154; nonviolence and, 44, 56, 61–62, 133, 135, 136–37, 139–40, 144; Peace and Permaculture Center, 11, 98, 185, 193–94; personal transformation and, 139–40, 141–43; values and, 10–11, 21, 53, 94, 122, 135–36; visitors and, 10, 159, 177, 224, 225–26; voluntary simplicity and, 128, 161, 165, 167–69, 177
poverty, 184, 203–4, 224, 234
prepper movements, 23, 24
Prophets Facing Backward (Nanda), 34
public spaces, 150, 227
public transportation, 13, 197, 206–7, 239–40
Putnam, Robert, 30, 149, 150

Quakers, 10, 61–62, 134, 152

Rabinowitz, Dorothy, 237–38
racial diversity, 8, 9, 60, 232–33
radical democracy, 33, 135, 148–51, 153, 184
Rainbow Family, 241
Rand, Ayn, 26
raw milk, 36, 202
ReCycle, 197
Red Clover Collective, 67–68
Red Earth Farms, 5, 11, 53, 249; appropriate technology and, 191; community engagement and, 54, 145, 187–88; composting toilets and, 173–74; experimentation and, 144–45, 146; food practices and, 123, 146–47, 175; food production and, 145, 146, 174, 202, 203; governance

Red Earth Farms (*cont'd*)
    and, 146, 147; housing and, 145, 174; residency process and, 69; visitors and, 193
Redlener, Irwin, 24
religious communities, 4, 44, 46, 47, 58, 121, 151, 241
Resilience Circles, 41–42, 196
restorative justice, 12, 133, 253
Rich, Elizabeth, 36
River Phoenix Center for Peacemaking, 39, 40
Rockefeller Foundation, 97, 239
Roman-Alcala, Antonio, 233
Rosenberg, Marshall, 155

Safe Routes to School, 232
Safe Seed Pledge, 205
Sandhill Farm, 5, 11, 53, 249–50; community engagement and, 54, 129, 145; food businesses and, 146, 198, 202; food practices and, 123, 126; food production and, 174; governance and, 78, 129
Sanford, A. Whitney, 32, 66
SCAN Foundation, 85
Schaub, Laird, 68, 87, 88, 129, 181, 182
Scheib, Cecil, 40–41, 154
Schumacher, E. F., 190
Schumacher Center for a New Economics, 253
sects, 30
seed banks, 121–22, 205–6
Seed Savers Exchange, 190, 253
seed sharing, 23, 190, 204, 205–6
self-sufficiency, 7, 23, 35, 94; interdependence and, 4, 186–87, 203
service, 106, 114, 116
shared housing, 25, 79, 80–81, 87, 89, 183
Sharing Housing: A Guidebook for Finding and Keeping Good Housemates (Pluhar), 80
sharing spaces, 71–74, 76, 84–85, 89, 160, 172, 206, 226–28

Shepard, Mark, 136
Shiva, Vandana, 134
Shrader-Frechette, Kristin, 165–66
Sirius community, 28, 93, 98, 191, 227, 250; building materials and, 206, 211, 212, 213; community engagement and, 78, 94; composting toilets and, 218; conflict resolution and, 148; food production and, 186, 192, 208–9; heating and, 186, 207–9; interdependence and, 187; personal transformation and, 143, 154; transportation and, 207; visitors and, 64, 192–93, 206; voluntary simplicity and, 163–64
Sirna, Tony, 70, 128, 152–53, 154, 158, 175–76, 182, 211, 216
small farms, 23, 55, 173, 201, 205
Small Is Possible: Life in a Local Economy (Estill), 51
Smart Growth Principles, 26, 254
social capital, 51–52, 177
social equity, 135–36, 183, 184
social media, 163–64
sociocracy, 158, 254
solar power, 170–71, 207, 208, 209, 212, 236–37, 238
SolidarityNYC, 189
Solidarity Piedmont, 189, 253
Sollisch, Jim, 102–3
Solnit, Rebecca, 24, 25, 241
Solomon, Avi, 213
sorghum syrup, 198
Soul Fire Farm, 233
Southern Exposure Seed Exchange, 204, 205, 206
Steinsson, Jon, 102
Stewart, Jon, 26
Stock, Paul, 49
straw-bale buildings, 178, 206, 211, 212, 214, 217, 219
survivalism, 23–24
Susanka, Sarah, 42
sustainability, 2, 4, 6, 11–12, 45, 188; agriculture and, 7, 11, 32, 39, 66,

180; class diversity and, 61, 164, 232–36; cohousing communities and, 7–8, 187, 230–32; eco-auditing and, 146–48; experimentation and, 144–46; food practices and, 40, 66, 118, 199; freedom culture and, 93–94; governance and, 131–33, 135, 153–54, 160; nonviolence and, 133–34, 135; social equity and, 135–36, 184; three legs of, 5, 135, 153; urban communities and, 7, 38–41, 114, 234–36
Sustainable Food Laboratory, 199
Swallowtail Farm, 110

technology, 255; appropriate technology, 35, 187, 188, 190–92, 205; canning and, 35–36, 37, 185; communications and, 59, 94, 95, 150, 163–64; traditional practices and, 35, 62, 67, 99, 109, 191
Thiele, Les, 33
Thoreau, Henry David, 28, 30, 238
time banks, 195–96
Tiny House Movement, 42, 162, 214
Tolstoy, Leo, 96, 97
Transition Network, 41, 254
transportation, 113, 237–38, 239; alternative fuels and, 201, 207; public transportation and, 13, 197, 206–7, 239–40; sharing resources and, 181–82, 183, 207; voluntary simplicity and, 185–86; walking and, 31, 82, 175, 231–32. *See also* bicycles; fossil fuels
triple bottom line, 183
Truesdale, Dan, 58, 143, 159, 167
Truly Living Well Farm, 233
Turkle, Sherry, 149–50
Twin Oaks Community, 8, 9, 34, 45, 53, 189, 250; community engagement and, 54, 78, 87, 89, 92–93; gender equity and, 150–51, 219, 221–22; governance and, 151–52, 158, 159–60; health care and, 59, 87, 92–93;

181; housing and, 71; labor system and, 92, 159–60, 179, 195, 204, 221–22; micro-industries and, 179, 197–98; sharing resources and, 180–82; transportation and, 181–82; visitors and, 64–65, 158–59. *See also* Communities Conference
Two Echo Cohousing, 81–82, 84, 232, 250

Unconventional Journey: The Story of High Wind from Vision to Community to Eco-Neighborhood, An (Paulson), 48
U.S. Public Interest Research Group (U.S. PIRG), 29
University of Florida, 21, 36, 39, 65, 80
University of Michigan, 173
University of North Texas, 214
UN World Commission on Environment and Development, 135
urban communities, 7, 15, 67–68, 114–19, 184, 206–7, 232–36. *See also* Baltimore Free Farm; LA Eco-village
Urban Green Council, 41
utopian communities, 26, 34

Valhalla Movement, 93–94, 106, 150, 189, 242, 254
Vallianatos, Mark, 219
values, 1, 2, 5–6, 19–20, 21–22, 50, 103, 107, 224; Catholic worker communities and, 14–16, 28, 61, 104, 105–6, 235, 238; cohousing communities and, 6, 16–18, 228–29; Dancing Rabbit Ecovillage and, 5, 11–13, 43, 127, 128–29, 153, 175–79; Gandhi and, 14, 21, 27–28, 40, 67, 132; individualism vs. society and, 29–31; LA Eco-village and, 7, 14; Possibility Alliance and, 10–11, 21, 53, 94, 122, 135–36. *See also* nonviolence; participatory democracy; voluntary simplicity
vegetarianism, 121, 124, 126

Vermont, 45, 52, 74, 84–86, 186, 198–99, 201, 217–18. *See also* Cobb Hill Cohousing
Veteto, James, 214
View from #410: When Home Is Cohousing, The (Mason), 75, 129–30
Virginia, 82–83. *See also* Acorn Community Farm; Twin Oaks Community
Voices from the Farm: Adventures in Community Living (Fike), 50
voluntary poverty, 60, 61, 118, 162, 164–65, 170, 238
voluntary simplicity, 1, 2, 18, 104; class diversity and, 60, 164; communications technology and, 58–59, 163–64; DIY skills and, 19, 185–86; experimentation and, 161, 167–72; food practices and, 118, 120, 128, 161–62, 174–75, 183–84, 239; governance and, 172–73; housing and, 32, 162; sharing resources and, 153, 161–63, 164–68, 175–80, 225; as spiritual value and, 164–65

Vote with Your Fork, 136, 160

Walker, Liz, 45
Warren, Lee Walker, 222
water systems, 209, 218–19
Whatley, Booker T., 233
White Rose Catholic Workers House, 15, 53
Wilcox, Dave, 61
Wilcox-Hughes, Sarah, 10–11, 61, 62, 91, 97, 110, 113, 136, 139, 148, 224
wind power, 208, 209
Winne, Mark, 233
Women for Living in Community, 80, 254
women-only communities, 150
Works of Mercy. *See* Christian Works of Mercy

Younge, Gary, 233

Zimmerman's Store, 55, 126–27, 146
ZipCar, 181
zoning, 183

Culture of the Land
A Series in the New Agrarianism

This series is devoted to the exploration and articulation of a new agrarianism that considers the health of habitats and human communities together. It demonstrates how agrarian insights and responsibilities can be worked out in diverse fields of learning and living: history, science, art, politics, economics, literature, philosophy, religion, urban planning, education, and public policy. Agrarianism is a comprehensive worldview that appreciates the intimate and practical connections that exist between humans and the earth. It stands as our most promising alternative to the unsustainable and destructive ways of current global, industrial, and consumer culture.

Series Editor

Norman Wirzba, Duke University, North Carolina

Advisory Board

Wendell Berry, Port Royal, Kentucky
Ellen Davis, Duke University, North Carolina
Patrick Holden, Soil Association, United Kingdom
Wes Jackson, Land Institute, Kansas
Gene Logsdon, Upper Sandusky, Ohio
Bill McKibben, Middlebury College, Vermont
David Orr, Oberlin College, Ohio
Michael Pollan, University of California at Berkeley, California
Jennifer Sahn, *Orion* Magazine, Massachusetts
Vandana Shiva, Research Foundation for Science, Technology and Ecology, India
Bill Vitek, Clarkson University, New York

www.ingramcontent.com/pod-product-compliance
Lightning Source LLC
Chambersburg PA
CBHW021959220426
43663CB00007B/883